LAON AND CYTHNA

broadview editions
series editor: Martin R. Boyne

LAON AND CYTHNA; OR, THE REVOLUTION OF THE GOLDEN CITY

Percy Bysshe Shelley

edited by Anahid Nersessian

broadview editions

BROADVIEW PRESS – www.broadviewpress.com
Peterborough, Ontario, Canada

Founded in 1985, Broadview Press remains a wholly independent publishing house. Broadview's focus is on academic publishing; our titles are accessible to university and college students as well as scholars and general readers. With over 600 titles in print, Broadview has become a leading international publisher in the humanities, with world-wide distribution. Broadview is committed to environmentally responsible publishing and fair business practices.

The interior of this book is printed on 100% recycled paper.

Library and Archives Canada Cataloguing in Publication

Shelley, Percy Bysshe, 1792-1822
[Revolt of Islam]
Laon and Cythna; or, The revolution of the golden city / Percy Bysshe Shelley ; edited by Anahid Nersessian.

(Broadview editions)
Includes bibliographical references.
ISBN 978-1-55481-194-6 (paperback)

I. Nersessian, Anahid, 1982-, editor II. Title. III. Title: Revolt of Islam IV. Series: Broadview editions

PR5418.A2N47 2016 821'.7 C2016-900825-8

Broadview Editions
The Broadview Editions series is an effort to represent the ever-evolving canon of texts in the disciplines of literary studies, history, philosophy, and political theory. A distinguishing feature of the series is the inclusion of primary source documents contemporaneous with the work.

Advisory editor for this volume: Denis Johnston

Broadview Press handles its own distribution in North America
PO Box 1243, Peterborough, Ontario K9J 7H5, Canada
555 Riverwalk Parkway, Tonawanda, NY 14150, USA
Tel: (705) 743-8990; Fax: (705) 743-8353
email: customerservice@broadviewpress.com

Distribution is handled by Eurospan Group in the UK, Europe, Central Asia, Middle East, Africa, India, Southeast Asia, Central America, South America, and the Caribbean. Distribution is handled by Footprint Books in Australia and New Zealand.

Broadview Press acknowledges the financial support of the Government of Canada through the Canada Book Fund for our publishing activities.

Typesetting and assembly: True to Type Inc., Claremont, Canada
Cover Design: Lisa Brawn

PRINTED IN CANADA

Contents

Acknowledgements

I would like to extend special thanks to the staffs of the Rare Book and Manuscript Library at Columbia University, of the William Andrews Clark Memorial Library at the University of California, Los Angeles, and of the Carl H. Pforzheimer Collection of Shelley and His Circle at the New York Public Library. Thanks in particular to Elizabeth Denlinger at the NYPL, and to Barbara Fuchs for helping me access the materials I needed even after the Clark closed for its seismic retrofit. Broadview Press has been astonishingly supportive of this sometimes unwieldy enterprise; I am grateful to Don LePan for seeking me out as a potential editor for *Laon and Cythna*, to Don and to Marjorie Mather for their faith in the project, and to Martin Boyne and Denis Johnston for their scrupulous attention to the manuscript in all its forms. Kevis Goodman, Theresa Kelley, and Karla Nielsen offered advice and encouragement, while my anonymous readers gave generously of their time and insight. My students at the University of Chicago, Columbia University, and UCLA inspired me to produce this edition, which is, finally, for them.

Introduction

Laon and Cythna; or, The Revolution of the Golden City is one of three great epic poems of the Romantic period. Like William Wordsworth's *The Prelude* (pub. 1850), it is an intensely personal exploration of the relationship between the individual and his community, and between human beings and the natural world. Like Lord Byron's *Don Juan* (1819–24), it displays a sophisticated awareness of the geopolitical climate of the early 1800s, and of the imperial expansion that would shape the remainder of the nineteenth century. It is also a profoundly original work of literature. At once philosophical treatise and love story, *Laon and Cythna* is about a pair of siblings who lead a political uprising predicated on socialist, feminist, and ecological ideals, only to be executed for treason. It is also an allegory of the French Revolution that began in 1789: of what it might have achieved had it remained non-violent, and of its defeat by a confederacy of European states, including Great Britain, anxious to protect themselves from the threat of popular insurrection. Finally, it is a meditation upon poetry, and upon the uses of art in a troubled, increasingly fragile world. In its own time, Shelley's poem was either reviled for promoting sedition, atheism, promiscuity, and incest, or praised hedgingly for being well intentioned but mostly incomprehensible. Today, *Laon and Cythna* is hardly read except by scholars. This edition seeks to correct that oversight, and to introduce new audiences to this important and powerful text.

The Poet

Percy Bysshe Shelley was born near Horsham, West Sussex, on 4 August 1792, the same year France declared itself a republic. He was the eldest child in an aristocratic family, with four younger sisters (a fifth died in infancy) and one brother. Adventurous but high-strung, he was miserable at school—first Syon House Academy and then Eton College—and would later describe being bullied as one of the formative experiences of his life, an early goad to his hatred of arbitrary power. Ill at ease among his peers, the adolescent Shelley was nonetheless confident in his own abilities. In 1810 he anonymously published two Gothic novels, *Zastrozzi* and *St. Irvyne* (dated 1811), along with two volumes of poetry: *Original Poetry by Victor and Cazire*, written with his sister Elizabeth, and *Posthumous Fragments of Margaret Nicholson*, a collaboration with his friend Thomas Jefferson Hogg. Shelley entered Oxford University in the fall of the same year, only to be expelled early in 1811 following the publication of *The Necessity of Atheism*, a provocative essay (and also a Hogg-Shelley production) on the intellectual and moral folly of organized religion; already far from his father's good graces, he was effectively disowned when, in August 1811, he eloped with sixteen-year-old Harriet Westbrook, who came from a social class well beneath that of the Shelley family. He and Harriet lived briefly in Wales and Ireland while Shelley wrote a number of political treatises before returning to London in April 1813. Shelley's first significant literary achievement came with *Queen Mab* (1813), a philosophical poem that argues, in both its text and its long footnotes, for radical democracy, vegetarianism, and free love. Born in June 1813, Shelley and Harriet's daughter Ianthe was named after the poem's heroine.

The year 1814 marks a turning point in Shelley's life. That summer he left Harriet for Mary Wollstonecraft Godwin (hereafter Mary Shelley; 1797–1851), the daughter of two of his personal heroes, William Godwin (1756–1836) and Mary Wollstonecraft (1759–97), and together with her stepsister Claire Claremont the couple embarked on a tour of France and Switzerland. As the dedicatory verses of *Laon and Cythna* reveal, Shelley considered the relationship to be exemplary of his radical ideals; here and throughout his writings he represents Mary Shelley as his sister or twin, a figurative description literalized in the incestuous pairing of the siblings Laon and Cythna. Where Laon and Cythna collaborate on a revolution, the Shelleys collaborated on their work, including (most famously) the novel *Frankenstein* (1816). As any reader of *Frankenstein* will know, that text is haunted by Mary Shelley's experience of the death of her first child; if the author's Dedication to *Laon and Cythna* lovingly acknowledges William ("Wilmouse") and Clara Everina, the "two gentle babes" (p. 55, line 77) born in 1816 and 1817, Cythna's account in Canto Seventh of losing her infant daughter surely draws on this ordeal.

In 1815, Napoleon's defeat at Waterloo and the restoration of the Bourbon monarchy put the last nails in the coffin of the French Revolution. For radicals like Shelley, the return of the Bourbons was a catastrophe, one that would inspire the tragic dénouement of *Laon and Cythna*: it seemed to confirm the impossibility of creating and maintaining a democratic state and thus to renege on the optimism of the Enlightenment, when philosophers such as John Locke (1632–1704), Jean-Jacques Rousseau (1712–78), and later Thomas Paine (1737–1809) and Godwin had insisted on the legitimacy and superiority of non-autocratic forms of governance. In the midst of his political despair, Shelley produced some of the most interesting work of his career, including *Alastor; or, The Spirit of Solitude* (1816), *Laon and Cythna* (begun in the summer of 1817), the well-known sonnet "Ozymandias" (1818), and a translation of Plato's *Symposium* (written in 1818). That said, 1819 is Shelley's watershed year, and it coincides with the date of another political disaster: the so-called Peterloo Massacre of 16 August, during which unarmed protesters assembled in the name of parliamentary reform were attacked by government troops on St. Peter's Field, Manchester. The yield of Shelley's "annus mirabilis," as Stuart Curran calls it, includes *Prometheus Unbound*, *Julian and Maddalo* (a window into his friendship with Byron), *The Cenci*, *Peter Bell the Third*, "The Mask of Anarchy," "Ode to the West Wind," and fittingly, the sonnet "England in 1819," as well as a political essay titled *A*

Philosophical View of Reform. This was also the year of the birth of Percy Florence, the only one of the Shelleys' children to survive to adulthood. The output of the next few years was also prodigious: in 1820, Shelley produced, among other compositions, "The Sensitive-Plant," "To a Sky-Lark," and *Swellfoot the Tyrant*, and in 1821 *Epipsychidion*, *Adonais* (an elegy for John Keats), *Hellas*, and the celebrated essay *A Defence of Poetry*.

Despite these artistic accomplishments, Shelley struggled with a severe bout of depression that had begun sometime in late 1817 and continued, with brief periods of respite, until his death. From the spring of 1818 onward, the Shelleys were effectively permanent residents of Italy, and Mary Shelley writes of their time in Naples that "many hours were passed when [Shelley's] thoughts, shadowed by illness, became gloomy, and then he escaped to solitude, and in verses, which he hid from fear of wounding me, poured forth morbid but too natural bursts of discontent and sadness."[1] The Shelleys' life together was a difficult one, and the deaths of Clara Everina (in 1818) and Wilmouse (in 1819) as well as of their first child are only part of the story. After being abandoned by Shelley, Harriet Westbrook gave birth to a son, Charles, in late 1814; two years later her body, heavily pregnant, was found in the Serpentine River, and her death was deemed a suicide. Shelley tried but failed to obtain custody of their children, who were raised by foster parents and then by Harriet's father (Ianthe) and Shelley's father (Charles). Around that same time, Mary Shelley's half-sister Fanny Imlay also committed suicide. Allegra Byron, child of Claire Claremont and Shelley's good friend Lord Byron, had been put into a convent following Byron's refusal to let the Shelleys raise her (he cited the deaths of their children as proof that they were unfit parents). She died at the age of five, perhaps from typhus or a malaria-like illness, in April 1822. Finally, there is the matter of Elena Adelaide Shelley, whose birth Shelley registered under his own name in Naples, in December 1818. Whatever Elena's parentage, which remains uncertain, she was put immediately into foster care and died in June 1820. There were also other difficulties. Mary Shelley was uneasy about her husband's devotion to the principle of free love and his relationships with other women, including Teresa Viviani, who inspired the poem *Epipsychidion*. Meanwhile Shelley, who suffered from chronic ill health, tended to overuse habit-forming sedatives, including laudanum.

The dark cast of Shelley's mind in the last few years of his life has led to vague speculation that his drowning in 1822 was the product of some suicidal impulse. This seems unlikely. When Shelley set out in his boat, the *Don Juan*, accompanied by his friend Edward Williams and eighteen-year-old Charles Vivian, he had just been visiting Leigh Hunt, editor of the progressive journal *The Examiner*, who was newly arrived in Italy. Together, Hunt, Shelley, and Byron were planning a new journal, to be

---

1 Mary Shelley, "Note on the Poems of 1818," in *The Poetical Works of Percy Bysshe Shelley*, 4 vols. (London: Edward Moxon, 1839), 3.162.

called *The Liberal*, and Shelley was at work on a number of new projects, including a dazzling poem called *The Triumph of Life*. In other words, his mood may not have been optimistic, but it was not obviously bent on self-annihilation. After having sailed from Lerici to Livorno without incident, on 8 July the *Don Juan* was caught in a storm on its return trip. All three passengers drowned; within ten days, their bodies had washed ashore. In keeping with health regulations, Shelley's body was later cremated on the beach.

To borrow a phrase from *Laon and Cythna*, Shelley's biography is "a strange tale of strange endurance," formed of the "broken memories of many a heart / Woven into one" (p. 155, VII.iii.19–20). This tale, and these memories, are all part of *Laon and Cythna*, from the explicitly autobiographical musings of the Dedication to Cythna's account of her exile to the events that bring Laon and Cythna's revolution to its unfortunate conclusion. It is also worth considering that the lives led by Shelley and his circle illustrate a principle that lies at the poem's own heart: no philosophy can make life perfect, and no revolution is without its collateral damages.

The Poem

If an antagonism between abstract ideals and the hard reality of life on earth is a principal trope of Shelley's own life, *Laon and Cythna* attempts to use this tension as its own starting point. Shelley famously described the poem as a *beau idéal* (literally, ideal beauty) of the French Revolution, a phrase often taken to mean that *Laon and Cythna* cleans up the Revolution's messy, occasionally blood-curdling details. However, by "beau idéal" Shelley meant something more like "allegory": a symbolic narrative that both makes abstract concepts concrete, say by embodying them in human figures, and subjects concrete things, like historical events, to processes of abstraction. Allegory is, after all, the mode of Edmund Spenser's *The Faerie Queene* (1590–96) and the genre of romance more broadly, and Shelley's poem is a romance written in Spenserian stanzas (on which more below). Like Spenser, Shelley freely collates fictive, historical, and conceptual associations for each of his poem's characters. The sultan Othman, for example, could be any ruler of the Ottoman Empire ("Othman" is a common variant of "Ottoman"), but he is also a figure for tyranny in general; the Golden City, which Shelley also calls "Islam" and which he claims to have based on Constantinople, stands in for Paris during the Revolution, but Paris is merely one example of a city in a "European nation" where the sort of events that transpire in the poem "might be supposed to take place" (Appendix B1, p. 237). Even this last description is somewhat limiting, and Shelley would probably agree that his setting, whether we call it the Golden City or Constantinople or Paris or Manchester, exemplifies a perpetual and universal situation of political injustice, one that knows no fixed time or geographic location.

It is as such a "tale illustrative" that Shelley pitched the poem in October 1817, by way of explaining to a prospective publisher why its first canto functions as "in some measure a distinct poem, though very necessary to the wholeness of the work" (p. 237). It is this canto that lays out the metaphysical as well as political stakes of the poem, through a series of "extreme contrasts or adjustments in scale" that, for Theresa Kelley, "mark the presence of an allegorical, rather than realist, narrative" (146). Following Shelley's dedicatory stanzas to Mary, we find ourselves standing with an unidentified speaker, who looks out over the sea from his position on a rocky cliff. As he is mulling over the failure of the Revolution, he suddenly sees an eagle and a serpent battling each other in the sky; the serpent falls into the water, and the speaker hurries down to the beach to investigate. There he finds a woman sitting on the shore, a small boat beside her, and sees the serpent glide out of the sea and into her arms. As she, the serpent, and the speaker sail off in her boat, the woman tells two stories, the first mythic and the second autobiographical. Drawing on a heady mix of religious and literary traditions, the woman explains that the serpent is the Spirit of Good, cursed to take reptilian shape by his enemy, the Spirit of Evil, who is represented by the eagle, not coincidentally the symbol of the god Jove and, for that matter, of the Roman Empire. For Shelley, the Spirit of Evil connotes not merely wickedness but absolutism: aligned with the Judeo-Christian God, he is said to have caused all the suffering in the world by introducing it to religion, war, money, and, above all, monarchy. The Spirit of Good, meanwhile, is identified with Satan, enemy of God but, like the rebellious Greek god Prometheus, friend to man. The two are locked, the woman explains, in perpetual combat for the fate of the world, and the outcome is uncertain. Shelley is heavily indebted for the content and the structure of this section to his friend Thomas Love Peacock's (1785–1866) unfinished poem *Ahrimanes* (c. 1815), a Zoroastrian epic that begins in nearly identical fashion.[1] As for the second part of the woman's narrative, this seems based on the life of Mary Wollstonecraft. Here the woman describes her profound sense of social alienation, her love affair with the Spirit of Good, her joy at the eruption of the Revolution and her sorrow at its fall into violence, and her current position as the Spirit's disciple. By the end of her tale, the trio has arrived at an island temple, where they meet Laon and Cythna. Laon's version of their story then begins the main narrative of the poem.

Before going forward, it's important to notice how Canto First gives the lie to overly hasty, undernuanced descriptions of Shelley as an "atheist" in our contemporary sense of the word. As Colin Jager has persuasively argued, atheism in the Romantic period meant first and foremost a rejection of orthodoxy and an alignment of oneself with an

1 See Appendix F6. In Peacock's poem, Ahrimanes, also known as Angra Mainyu, represents the destructive spirit of Zoroastrian mythology. He also makes an appearance (as Arimanes) in Byron's verse drama *Manfred* (1817).

Enlightenment tradition of "freethinking radicalism" embodied in philosophers such as Baruch Spinoza (1632–77), Locke, David Hume (1711–76), and the Baron d'Holbach (1723–89); for those in sympathy with such a tradition, "the narrative of atheism" functioned doubly as an allegory of "intellectual heroism" (231). For those on the other side of the philosophical and political divide, however, to characterize someone as an atheist in early nineteenth-century England was not unlike calling someone a communist in the 1950s in the United States: the word was intended as a slur, not a description, and served to identify a person as, in one capacity or another, dangerous to conventional society. When Shelley refers to Laon and Cythna as atheists, as he does throughout the poem, he suggests that the real danger lies with a passive acceptance of the way things are. Moreover, for all its allegorical richness, this first canto seems to take seriously the prospect that supernatural agents have a real and consequential existence. The nature of such an existence, and its effects on human history, will be raised in the poem's second half with invocations of an entity called "Necessity," who often seems to be (in Cian Duffy's words) "synonymous with Shelley's conception of God" (27)—again, the influence of Peacock's *Ahrimanes* shows itself here. Keeping these ideas in mind will help readers make sense of, or at least bear with, the many supernatural elements of the poem, as well as its overall tendency toward unapologetic mysticism.

As action-packed as its first canto is, the rest of the poem has a stop-start momentum that mirrors the view of progress later laid out in "Ode to the West Wind."[1] There, an essentially optimistic perspective on the evolutionary movement of history is yoked to, but also undercut by, the cyclic temporality of the seasons. Even if the poem ends on a hopeful note—asking, "if Winter comes, can Spring be far behind?" (*Shelley's Poetry and Prose* 70)—Shelley is well aware that if spring follows winter, and summer spring, we will inevitably return to the bleaker months of fall and winter once their light and warmth have passed away. *Laon and Cythna* shares in the ode's attempt to reconcile linear and circular models of time, and it registers this investment both in its own narration, whose tranquil scenes are periodically interrupted by dizzying commotion, and in its use of the Spenserian stanza, which Shelley claims to have chosen for its "just and harmonious arrangement of ... pauses" (Preface, p. 46). The second canto, set in a Greece occupied by the Ottomans, begins by lingering over Laon's unhappy childhood, giving special attention to the collapse of his relationship with a close male friend, and on his more stable relationship with his sister Cythna. It also spends quite a bit of time explaining Cythna's feminism, which Laon comes to share through his love for her. This is the poem's first nod to the contagious character of political belief, and its first allusion to the idea, borrowed from Plato's

1 Indeed, Curran describes *Laon and Cythna* as the long first draft of the later, shorter poem (27).

Symposium, that erotic love for another person gradually coaxes us toward a more expansive, philosophical love of justice. Accordingly, Canto Second ends with Cythna's vow to help liberate the female "half of humankind" from their social and sexual slavery, an ambition she has acquired since her exposure to Laon's poetry (p. 89, II.xxxvi.320).

Cythna's mission begins in the next canto, when she is kidnapped by Ottoman soldiers and taken to the Sultan's harem in the Golden City. Laon, who kills three of the soldiers before being knocked unconscious, is imprisoned; dying of hunger and thirst, he is prey to fever dreams in which he tries to eat the dead bodies of the soldiers and Cythna. Finally he is rescued by a saintly hermit who is based, so Mary Shelley suggests, on Dr. James Lind, who looked after Shelley at Eton.[1] Laon spends seven years, in delirium, under the Hermit's care. When Laon finds himself at last in his right mind, the Hermit explains that Laon's poems have radicalized people all over the Ottoman Empire, including the Hermit himself; he also tells Laon of a mysterious young woman who, having suffered at Othman's hands, has convinced the women of the Golden City to revolt. Raising but quickly dismissing the possibility that this might be Cythna, Laon heads off to join the struggle.

Even the least attentive or most credulous of readers will not fail to guess that the leader of the poem's feminist revolution is indeed Cythna, but Shelley will delay this revelation until halfway through Canto Sixth, approximately the poem's midpoint. The very long fifth canto concerns the triumph of the revolutionary army—which includes Laon's long-lost friend from Canto Second—over Othman's soldiers. After murdering some members of the insurrection in their sleep, the soldiers are persuaded to drop their weapons when Laon bravely intercepts a blow intended for one of their comrades. Moved by Laon's plea for nonviolence, the two armies unite in a peaceful takeover of the Golden City. Eventually they find Othman hiding in his palace, a little girl by his side; barricaded in the palace since the revolt began, both Othman and the child are starving. The revolutionaries—or as Shelley calls them, "patriots"—give them food and place Othman under a kind of house arrest, and the canto concludes with a victory celebration based on the revolutionary *fêtes* held in France during the 1790s, except that this particular celebration features a vegetarian feast and no alcohol.[2] Now identified as "Laone"—the feminine version of the name "Laon"—the mysterious woman performs a hymn to "divine Equality," and the revolutionaries lie down for the night.

The remainder of the poem is a vivid account of what happens when, to paraphrase "Ode to the West Wind," winter has come but spring remains

1 Mary Shelley, "Note on *The Revolt of Islam*" (Appendix G1, p. 290). Nigel Leask suggests that the Hermit is a composite of Lind and William Godwin (132).

2 For an extended discussion of the vegetarian "poetics" of *Laon and Cythna*, see Morton, *Shelley and the Revolution in Taste* 110–16.

far behind. No sooner has the revolution seen its first success than Othman rallies more troops to have it put down. A terrible battle ensues, in which both Laon's old friend and the Hermit, who has also joined the rebellion, are killed along with most of the other patriots. Laon is rescued by Cythna, whom he has recognized since the previous night but not yet sought out. Taking shelter in a ruin outside the city, the reunited siblings make love. Eventually, Laon goes looking for food only to find the ruins of a village destroyed in the battle. At this point, Shelley begins to show his debt to Thucydides' *History of the Peloponnesian War* (late fifth century BCE) for many of the more horrifying images in this and subsequent cantos. Among the ruins Laon encounters a woman who calls herself Pestilence: she has arranged the dead bodies of her children, killed by Othman's soldiers, around a makeshift hearth and encourages Laon to eat with them. Taking the bread Pestilence offers, Laon returns to Cythna, whose own story makes up the bulk of the seventh, eighth, and ninth cantos.

Cythna's story—that "strange tale of strange endurance"—contains both the most realistic and the most fanciful elements of the poem. It begins with her rape by Othman, a traumatic event that nonetheless turns her into a kind of prophet or mystic, whose words have a strange power over the other women in the harem. Terrified, Othman has Cythna rowed out by two of his slaves onto the Bosphorus (a waterway that connects the Black Sea to the Mediterranean) and chained in an underwater prison. There, she gives birth to a baby girl, or so she thinks; when the child one day vanishes, Cythna assumes the child was a hallucination brought on by her dire circumstances. Left alone with her thoughts, she begins to see the deep truth of reality: namely, that it is underwritten by an impersonal force called Necessity, a "moveless wave" that directs the course of everything in the universe but cannot itself be altered or disturbed, and by a not-unrelated power called love (p. 164, VII.xxxi.275). One day an earthquake destroys her prison and leaves her stranded on a rock, from which she is rescued by a ship bearing women to be sold into slavery. She persuades the sailors to free the women, and also offers them a sermon based on the teachings of the Greek philosopher Epicurus (341–270 BCE), who claimed (among other things) that if God exists He certainly would not take an interest in human affairs. The ship docks, and Cythna begins a political ministry in the Golden City, drawing passionate support and equally passionate hatred with her feminist and egalitarian teachings. At the end of Canto Ninth, Cythna revisits the topic of Necessity in language that will resurface, at times verbatim, in "Ode to the West Wind." Here, she maintains that, although "this is the winter of the world," humanity is nonetheless moving gradually toward its own liberation (p. 186, IX.xxv.218). She also adds that while she and Laon will not be alive to see this enterprise concluded, their wisdom will continue to guide future generations.

Though it is one of the least discussed sections of the poem, Canto Tenth contains some of Shelley's most sophisticated political thinking as well as his most compelling verse. Clearly inspired by European responses to the French Revolution and the rise of Napoleon, Shelley shows an alliance of world leaders who might otherwise be enemies forming a united front against the political unrest in the Golden City. Eastern Europe, France, Russia, India, and Idumea (present-day Israel and Jordan) all send their armies to join Othman's, and the result is yet more slaughter and devastation. This time, however, the unburied bodies of the dead also unleash the plague. Shelley adds famine to the mix, offering scene after scene of extreme suffering as both human and animal populations are wiped out and the people of the Golden City turn to cannibalism. Othman and his cronies are hoarding food in the palace, but they cannot keep out the plague, and members of the court also fall ill. Enter one of the broadest depictions of villainy in all of Shelley's work, the Christian Priest. To him, the threat represented by the revolution is aimed not primarily at religious belief but at social hierarchy; nonetheless, he stirs his fellow clergymen, of all faiths, to demand the execution of Laon and Cythna as the only thing that will appease each man's god. A pyre is built and heaped with poisonous snakes and scorpions. In the meantime, some of the sick and starved throw themselves and their children willingly on the pyre, as do an unidentified man and a group of maidens in an act of protest.

The two cantos that conclude the poem continue in this vein, as Laon goes in disguise to the court of Othman and pretends to be someone willing to turn in Laon in exchange for Cythna's safe passage to America, which Shelley, referencing the American Revolution (which preceded the French one by roughly a decade), styles as a haven for republican ideals. As soon as the bargain is made, he reveals his true identity and is taken to the pyre. Just as it is about to be lit, Cythna arrives to join Laon. As they near death, Laon sees Othman's child collapse. Suddenly, the whole horrible scene vanishes, and Laon and Cythna find themselves on a beach. A boat approaches, its sail the wings of a cherubic child—Othman's child, who is also (as we might have guessed) Cythna's lost baby. The child tells Laon and Cythna how, as they went willingly to their deaths, an unnamed man excoriated the people for their betrayal of their leaders before stabbing himself in the heart; at this, the child says, she felt her "brain gr[o]w dark in death" (p. 223, XII.xxx.268), only to snap back to consciousness in the island temple that we first saw in Shelley's second canto. Laon and Cythna climb into the boat, and the trio sails for three days and nights to the sacred island; the poem ends just as land comes into view.

The Publication

In his preface to the poem, Shelley claims to have written *Laon and Cythna* in about six months, although the "thoughts" behind the poem were, he notes, "slowly gathered in as many years" (Preface, p. 48). Even though the poem was Shelley's longest, arguably his most challenging, and loaded with provocative material, and even though his father-in-law Godwin discouraged its publication, Shelley seemed sanguine about his capacity to find an audience. Writing to a potential publisher in October 1817, he suggested that the poem might be sent to Thomas Moore (1779–1852), a prolific poet and a good friend of Byron's whose own poetic romance *Lalla Rookh* (also set in the Muslim world) had been published earlier that year (see Appendix B1). The firm that actually published *Laon and Cythna*—under the full title of *Laon and Cythna; or, The Revolution of the Golden City: A Vision of the Nineteenth Century*, with a second subtitle reading "In the Stanza of Spenser"—was that of Charles and James Ollier, who co-published the poem with another firm by the name of Sherwood, Neely, and Jones. Problems arose in early December when Buchanan McMillan, the man hired to print the poem, took umbrage at its content. The Olliers panicked and pulled the poem, whose printing Shelley himself had financed, sending the poet into a fit of righteous indignation: "Assume the high and the secure ground of courage," he exhorted Charles Ollier, urging him to keep in mind that while there had been some recent, high-profile cases of publishers getting into legal trouble for disseminating controversial material, erring on the side of safety and censorship had not won the publishing community any tolerance from an oppressive political establishment (Appendix B4, p. 241; see Appendix B for key sections of the correspondence between Shelley and Ollier, as well as Shelley's letters to Godwin and Moore). Meanwhile John Keats (1795–1821), whose feelings toward Shelley were a mixture of suspicion, envy, and occasional grudging admiration, informed his brothers George and Tom with not a little smugness, "Shelley's poem is out & there are words about its being objected to as much as Queen Mab was." "Poor Shelley," Keats added, "I think he has his Quota of good qualities, in sooth la!"[1]

Over the course of the next few weeks, Shelley was persuaded by Ollier, Mary Shelley, and Peacock to rewrite the offending sections of *Laon and Cythna*—or perhaps to allow them to be rewritten.[2] A total of 49 changes were made, the most salient of which are these: in the new version of the poem, Cythna is Laon's adoptive rather than biological sister, the name of

1 Letter dated 21, 27 (?) December 1817, in *The Letters of John Keats* 1.191–94. Rollins suggests that Keats had heard about Shelley's troubles from Godwin, whom he apparently met on 25 December.

2 The idea that it might have been Peacock who rewrote most if not all of the offending parts of *Laon and Cythna* stems from Peacock's own account of the revision process in his *Memoirs of Shelley* (1858–62), which describes the poet "contest[ing] the proposed alterations step by step: in the end, sometimes adopting, more frequently modifying, never originating, and always insisting that his poem was spoiled" (2.365). Although Shelley's correspondence presents the circumstances in a less dramatic light, Nora Crook and Stephen Allen have recently reopened the case to insist on Peacock's authorship of the modified passages (14).

God is here and there replaced by circumlocutions, references to atheism have been exchanged for more general remarks on Laon and Cythna's moral courage, and the Christian Priest is identified specifically as an "Iberian," which is to say a Spanish Catholic whose malevolence reads as an indictment less of Christianity than of its distortion by the Spanish Inquisition. The new poem was published by the Olliers in January 1818 as *The Revolt of Islam; A Poem, in Twelve Cantos.*[1]

As contemporary reviews of *The Revolt of Islam* show, the poem had a hard time shaking off the scandal of its earlier abortive publication, and some readers—most notably John Taylor Coleridge of *The Quarterly Review*—insisted on discussing Shelley's treatment of incest even after its erasure from the revised text (Appendix C4). More to the point, Shelley's softening of his remarks against Christianity had fooled no one, and conservative periodicals such as the *Quarterly* and *Blackwood's Edinburgh Magazine* (Appendix C3) did not hesitate to draw attention to the poem's anti-clerical content. The poem's greatest hurdle for readers, however, remained its sheer difficulty, and even Leigh Hunt's positive series of reviews of *The Revolt* admit that it has "defects" of "obscurity, inartificial and yet not natural economy," anachronism, "and too great a sameness and gratuitousness of image and metaphor." "The work," Hunt concludes sadly, "cannot possibly become popular" (Appendix C2, p. 246). Byron, for his part, suggested that, if anything, the withdrawal of *Laon and Cythna* "*sold* an edition of *The Revolt of Islam*, which, otherwise, nobody would have thought of reading, and few who read can understand—I for one."[2]

Literary and Historical Contexts

It is no slight against his contemporaries to suggest that Shelley was the best read of all the Romantic poets; he was certainly the most versed in the Western philosophical tradition. Attempts to show that Shelley was a full-fledged member of this or that philosophical school will inevitably run aground on his ecumenical sensibility, which predisposed him to draw on a wide variety of sometimes incompatible ideas. On one hand, Shelley was embedded in the idealist tradition and particularly in Platonism, even translating Plato's *Symposium* and *Ion* into English (though he struggled with Plato's endorsement of sexual relationships between men). What appealed to Shelley about Plato was his account of the division between the known world and the higher reality that determines it, as well as his suggestion that love—of other people, but more importantly of wisdom itself—might help us apprehend the true nature of things, as Laon and

---

1 A few rare copies of *The Revolt of Islam* (one of which is housed at the William Andrews Clark Memorial Library at UCLA) bear a publication date of 1817.

2 Letter to John Murray dated 24 November 1818, in *Byron's Letters and Journals* 6.83.

Cythna's love helps them know the true nature of justice. On the other hand, Shelley was equally attracted to the materialism of Epicurus, and to its articulation in the work of Lucretius, Roman poet of the first century BCE and author of the Epicurean epic *De Rerum Natura* ("On the Nature of Things"). Cythna's speeches in Cantos Eighth and Ninth, for example, notably rehearse some of Lucretius' criticisms of narrow-minded ideas about the gods and his arguments against the fear of death.[1] In short, Shelley has no unified theory or system; he rather layers multiple philosophical perspectives, rarely if ever committing to one view to the exclusion of others.

The debt to moral and natural philosophy so evident in *Laon and Cythna* can overshadow its equally impassioned and, in some ways, more interesting engagement with popular traditions, from the chivalric revival of the later eighteenth century to the so-called oriental tale. These traditions sometimes support and sometimes resist what Saree Makdisi has called Romanticism's "hegemonic liberal-radical position," whose best exemplars are none other than Wollstonecraft and Godwin (*William Blake* 60). Marrying into the Wollstonecraft-Godwin family helped Shelley see himself as the legitimate heir to such a position, but while he shared its enthusiasm for political liberty and sexual equality he rejected the aspects that made it so "hegemonic" or mainstream: its emphases on bourgeois values of self-control, emotional detachment, rational deliberation, and incremental rather than sudden and comprehensive sociopolitical change. In the sort of overwrought and erotically charged novels he had tried to write as a teenager, and in the fantastical dreamscapes of fairy-tale worlds or of the imagined "East," Shelley found the aesthetic and affective resources he would need for this story about "a nation / Made free by love" (p. 120, V.xiv.120–21), where revolutionary fervor is spread by emotional contagion, not well-reasoned arguments. In short, Shelley, like most of us, expresses his beliefs in the cultural vernacular of his own time. For all their self-conscious grounding in the wisdom of the ages, his political commitments are not just democratic; they are genuinely popular.

Reviving the Romance

Spenserian stanzas—the verse-form of *Laon and Cythna*—are named after Edmund Spenser (c. 1552–99), whose epic poem *The Faerie Queene* brought them into the world at the end of the sixteenth century. Consisting of eight lines of iambic pentameter followed by a final twelve-syllable alexandrine, with a rhyme scheme of ababbcbcc, the Spenserian stanza is also notable, as Shelley has already told us, for its pauses. To this we might add William Empson's characterization of the form as forcing the reader "to yield ... to it very completely [in order] to take in the variety of its movement" without having to make a clear-cut "judgment" about what

1 See *De Rerum Natura*, especially 3.417–831, 6.50–79, and 6.1138–1246.

the poetry relates (34)—a quality that would come in handy in *Laon and Cythna* which is, after all, a poem about the physiological irresistibility of revolution.

Both Spenser and his stanza form experienced tremendous popularity during the Romantic period, which coincided—as its name suggests—with a revival of interest in the literary romances of the Middle Ages and the Renaissance. Samuel Johnson's *Dictionary* defines romance as "a tale of wild adventures in war and love," and many romances, *The Faerie Queene* included, derived their wildness from the sheer improbability of their plots, with their evil wizards, heroic knights or "chevaliers"—from which is derived our word chivalry—and captive maidens. By the middle of the eighteenth century it was commonplace to view romance as a cultural endorsement of autocratic government and militarized society, though the scholar Richard Hurd (1720–1808) was keen to point out that romances often portray women in an unusually positive if not wholly equitable light (see Appendix D1). To be sure, such portrayals are often idealized, but to a middle-class reading audience that knew women of its rank to have only two occupations—to be attractive and to reproduce—female warriors such as Spenser's Britomart or Torquato Tasso's Clorinda, from the sixteenth-century romance *Gerusalemme Liberata*, an epic poem set during the Crusades, were points of fascination and excitement. Hurd also notes, however, that the genesis of chivalric attitudes about women was probably grounded in what he describes as the ever-present threat of sexual violence in the medieval era. For him, then, the romance's stress on gentility is inextricable from its mania for martial aggression and for the pursuit of enemies (often enemies from other cultures) who must be destroyed at any cost.[1]

When Shelley sat down to write his poem in 1817, these associations were still in place, but their application had been somewhat enlarged and, occasionally, ironized. *Childe Harold's Pilgrimage* (1812–18), takes Spenserian stanzas to be appropriate for the romantic tale of Harold's escapades, but Byron's poem also contains biting indictments of the British Empire.[2] In the same vein is Wordsworth's "The Female Vagrant" (1798), another poem in Spenserian stanzas, this one about an English woman who, having lost everything in the rural devastation caused by the Industrial Revolution, takes her family on an ill-fated journey to America during the War of Independence (Appendix D4). Romance could thus be used, as it is in *Laon and Cythna*, not only to celebrate the glory of a nation but also to tally its high cost; to recount enchanting travels to foreign lands

1 On the threat of sexual violence in the eighteenth century, Hurd is silent.

2 See Appendix D5. In an early draft of *Laon and Cythna*, Shelley wrote a note to himself expressing concern that he was merely retreading the same ground as *Childe Harold*: "Is this an imitation of L[ord] Byron's poem? It is certainly written in the same metre" *(Bodleian Shelley Manuscripts, Vol. XIII. Drafts for "Laon and Cythna,"* MSS. Shelley adds. e. 14 and adds. e. 19, 10–11).

as well as the harms of imperial incursion; to luxuriate in emotionally affecting tales of virtuous heroes and heroines, and to detail the miseries of the poor.

But how did such a seemingly conservative genre become available to these unorthodox uses? The answer lies in the Revolution debates of the 1790s, which saw a fascinating reliance on and retooling of romance's tropes. As David Duff has shown, the vocabulary of romance was used "to depict some aspect of the new political culture in France or at home" by writers both hostile and sympathetic to the cause (8). Take, for example, Edmund Burke's *Reflections on the Revolution in France* (1790), a reckless masterpiece composed shortly after Louis XVI and Marie Antoinette had been arrested following the Women's March on Versailles (Appendix D2). The march began as a bread riot, led by Parisian women enraged and exhausted by chronic food shortages; it is one model for the uprising Cythna inspires among the women of Othman's city (p. 181, IX.x.82–90). For Burke, however, the most significant thing about the march and the raid on Versailles that followed was their simultaneous inversion of gender norms and class hierarchy. When women take to the streets and a queen is arrested in her own bedroom, "the age of chivalry is gone," the "generous loyalty to rank and sex" that characterized it lost forever (Appendix D2, p. 255). As Burke soon learned, however, the rhetoric of chivalry and romance could cut both ways. In her multi-volume series of *Letters from France*, Helen Maria Williams (c. 1761–1827), an English expatriate living in Paris, painted Burke as a magician straight out of Spenser, "waving [his] evil wand" to conjure misleadingly dire pictures of the new regime.[1] Burke, Williams argued, had it backwards. "Living in France at present" was "like living in a region of romance," and the age of chivalry, "instead of being past for ever, is just returned" (Appendix D3, p. 256). Through its own potent alchemy, the Revolution had done away with all the superficial elements of romance but kept its essential tenets, most obviously a willingness to sacrifice one's life for others.

By inserting his self-described "vision of the nineteenth century" into the romance tradition, Shelley, like Wordsworth and Byron, implies that we can see the present more clearly when we estrange ourselves from it, in this case by surrounding it with the archaic frame of romance and its quintessential verse-form. He also follows Williams in linking romance's association with narrative improbability to the conviction that what seems hopelessly unattainable—say, a better world—is in fact within our reach, and that what we need to grasp it is not a magic spell, but the power of collective action. And, like Williams, Shelley is conscious that making romance amenable to radicalism means enlarging the scope of what kinds of things make appropriate objects for a tale of wild adventures: instead of slaying dragons, Laon and Cythna pursue equality between the sexes, the

1 Helen Maria Williams, *Letters Written in France*, ed. Neil Fraistat and Susan S. Lanser (Peterborough, ON: Broadview P, 2001), 147.

nonviolent overthrow of despots, the end of private wealth, and the elimination of meat from the human diet. Meanwhile, it is worth noting how Shelley's treatment of Cythna's rape as a shared trauma that sparks a feminist uprising, which in turn opens the door to a full-scale insurgency, counters Burke's version of the attack on Marie-Antoinette. Rather than saddle rebellion with the threat of sexual violence, Shelley aligns rape with patriarchy, patriarchy with monarchy, and monarchy with a global world order predicated on the uneven distribution of power and wealth. This is a tactical maneuver that places Shelley squarely in the tradition of utopian feminism, but it is also a daring appropriation of romance for ideological aims more or less foreign to those original to the genre.

The Rights of Women

Laon and Cythna could plausibly be called the first feminist epic. In the Romantic period, a belief in women's rights had survived the political tumult of the 1790s in a way a commitment to revolution had not. As France's government became increasingly punitive, and as it became clear that the country's female citizens were not going to be included in its reforms, the rights of women in particular became, in many ways, a less controversial cause than the rights of men in general. Trying to improve what Godwin, in his *Enquiry Concerning Political Justice*, calls "the intercourse" or relationship between "the sexes" (Appendix E2, p. 265) was a way to hold onto the democratic advancements made and then seemingly abandoned by the Revolution. That said, and as *Laon and Cythna* vividly demonstrates, Shelley went much further than most of his contemporaries in advocating for the complete social and political equality of women, whose freedom would only be secured (so he argued) when both marriage and monogamy no longer constrained their access to multiple forms of intimacy and attachment.

France's apparent betrayal of its female population was the occasion for Wollstonecraft's landmark *Vindication of the Rights of Woman* (1792; see Appendix E1), which followed upon her first riposte to Burke in *A Vindication of the Rights of Men* (1790). Wollstonecraft casts a long shadow on *Laon and Cythna*, even appearing in thinly veiled guise as the mysterious woman of Canto First. Although Shelley's dedicatory verses to Mary incline us to consider Cythna as a portrayal of his wife, Cythna's rhetoric is liberally imported from the second *Vindication*, and it would be fair to call her one of the poem's two Wollstonecraftian figures. While her brother's primary focus is, at first, the evils of tyranny, Cythna persuades him that the patriarchal oppression of women is an essential feature of political despotism, that man cannot "be free if woman be a slave" (p. 91, II.xliii.379) and that, as Shelley will put it in his essay *A Defence of Poetry*, "the abolition of personal slavery is the basis of the highest political hope that it can enter into the mind of man to conceive" (*Shelley's Poetry and Prose* 525). These ideas lie at the core of Wollstonecraft's feminism, which began to make sense of the early disappointments of the French Revolution by suggesting that its refusal to extend the franchise to all France's citizens had compromised its success from the start. Indeed, the *Vindication*'s sustained attack on Rousseau may be explained in terms of his significance to the Revolution's own self-mythology. By taking for its spiritual progenitor someone who believed that women were not fit to be educated beyond basic literacy, the Revolution, like Rousseau himself, had beaten "a ferocious flight back to the night of sensual ignorance" (*The Vindications* 125), leaving its female citizens to languish in their age-old condition of being idealized and desired without being taken at all seriously.

Wollstonecraft was nonetheless the first to point out that nothing in the education and experience of the average European or British woman has prepared her to be an active, productive participant in civil society. Cannily turning the rhetoric of female subjection inside out, she makes the surprising argument that women are not only "abject slaves" but also "capricious tyrants" (Appendix E1, p. 264), taught from an early age to extract from men a limited but no less pathetic obedience in lieu of actual respect. At once wielders of "the arbitrary power of beauty" and its victims, women are also utterly alienated from the role Wollstonecraft considers their most important: being a mother (*The Vindications* 129). Here the contemporary reader may find herself pushing back against Wollstonecraft, but it is important to understand that Wollstonecraft's model for both motherhood and citizenship reflects a symbolic conflation, popular in the eighteenth century, between the British and Roman Empires. The image of the Roman matron loomed large for Rousseau, too, and both he and Wollstonecraft evolve an "ideology of republican motherhood" that celebrates the sort of stoic, self-sacrificing maternal virtue vital to the flourishing of a just state; as promised, Wollstonecraft picks up where Rousseau did not go far enough, laying out a plan for female education that would prepare this neglected half of humanity to find in "the home and women's role within it ... a civic purpose" (Landes 129) that might eventually extend beyond the domestic and into the public sphere.

As this emphasis on maternity might reveal, Wollstonecraft was actually quite conservative when it came to imagining women as sexual beings with interests outside the scope of family life. Her husband, William Godwin, was more daring—as a man, he could afford to be—and the appendix on "Cooperation, Cohabitation and Marriage" in his magnum opus *An Enquiry Concerning Political Justice* (first published, without the appendix, in 1793; see Appendix E2) proffers an idea that was shocking in its time: that two people should be able to conduct intimate relationships without being married to each other, and that these relationships, and indeed legal marriages as well, should be able to be dissolved once one or both parties no longer finds the arrangement satisfying. Although Laon and Cythna have eyes only for each other, Shelley's poem hews closely to Godwin's text by insisting that marriage, as a form of exclusivity, does not sanctify love but rather violates its generous spirit. *Laon and Cythna*'s criticism of female bondage, although it argues most directly against Othman's enslavement of women in his harem, is essentially an argument against what Godwin characterized as the "despotic and artificial" ratification of love through the "positive institution" of marriage. Free love, in Shelley's poem, becomes the condition of a free world, not merely the inevitable result of progress.

Over the course of the 1790s, these sorts of ideas about marriage and fidelity were slowly working their way into the public imagination. When Shelley was 20, and recently married to Harriet Westbrook, he read James Lawrence's *Empire of the Nairs* (1811; see Appendix E3), a self-described "utopian romance" about a gynocratic society set on the southwest coast of India. The Nair system—in which there is no such thing as marriage, and women take as many lovers as they wish, whenever they choose—impressed Shelley so much that he wrote to Lawrence in August 1812 to say that the novel had made him "a perfect convert to its doctrines" (*Letters* 1.322–23). As Walter Graham first pointed out in 1925, Cythna's role as prophetess and leader of a women's revolt seems modeled on the story of Samora, the founder of the Nair kingdom.[1] But one of Lawrence's other concerns seems yet more pressing to *Laon and Cythna*: the question, which his book raises, as to whether a society in which extramarital sex is the norm is also a society that still leaves women vulnerable to exploitation. Shelley himself told Lawrence that his only reason for putting "love ... in the prison" of his own marriage was his "knowledge that, in the present state of society, if love is not thus villainously treated," then women "will be treated worse by a misjudging world" (*Letters* 1.323). Lawrence, like Godwin and Thomas Holcroft (1745–1809), is careful to insist that, on the contrary, free love would foster women's rights rather than compromise them. Nonetheless, *Laon and Cythna* subjects its feminist heroine (whose relationship with Laon is not only extramarital but also incestuous) to a rape that—to make matters even more complicated—turns out to be the almost-mystical source of her political power (see p. 157, VII.vii.55–63). Any serious engagement with *Laon and Cythna* therefore requires us to think deeply about how Shelley seems to balance the horror of Cythna's assault with the suggestion that, had it not taken place, she would not have been able to lead the revolution, and about how this suggestion might cut against his insistent denunciation of violence as a tool of popular resistance.

There is something more to be said about *Empire of the Nairs*, namely that its many negative references to Islamic culture, in Graham's words, "emphasize over and over again the idea that the followers of Mohammed were by far the greatest offenders against female liberty or the equality of the sexes" (889). So, for example, we are told that although the Nair

---

1 See also Cameron.

empire "is generally at peace with the Mahometans ... an order of knights have sworn to wage perpetual war with the polygamists, as long as a woman is confined in a harem" (Lawrence 1.95). With this observation we arrive at the most thorny aspects of *Laon and Cythna*, namely its insistence on using consensual sex and sexual violence as metonyms for, respectively, secular revolution and Islamic society. If Shelley's figure for religious bigotry is the Christian Priest, the sultan Othman certainly embodies the kind of oppressive sexual politics that writers from Wollstonecraft to Lawrence openly characterized as slavery. In short, although Shelley himself nearly shrugged off his own poem's setting in the Muslim world—*Laon and Cythna* is, he admits, "without much attempt at minute delineation of Mahometan manners," because the Golden City is an allegorical placeholder for any "European nation"—readers will have to consider how its progressive politics are often accompanied by a negative stereotyping of Muslim culture.

Romantic Orientalism

Orientalism, according to Edward Said's classic definition, "is a style of thought based upon an ontological and epistemological distinction made between 'the Orient' and (most of the time) 'the Occident'" (2). By the Occident or "West," we should understand the self-representation of Western European countries, especially France and Britain; by the Orient or "East," we should understand a set of fantasies concerning the land and the people of Asia, Africa, and some of Eastern Europe, along with the indigenous people of the Americas. The Orient, as Said explains, "is not only adjacent to Europe; it is also the place of Europe's greatest and richest and oldest colonies, the source of its civilizations and languages, its cultural contestant, and one of its deepest and most recurring images of the Other" (1). This business of manufacturing and representing otherness is the primary object of orientalist discourse, which, whether it is offering up images of non-Western people as savage, gentle, credulous and kind, lazy, greedy, unusually beautiful or exceptionally brave, is always insisting that such people are differently intelligible from those in the proverbial West. The point is not whether such difference is construed in negative or complimentary terms, but rather that it makes it possible to imagine some human beings to be so unlike others that their very humanness might be thought to vary in kind or even degree.

Laon and Cythna has a handful of figures like this—Othman, his "green and wrinkled eunuch," the Ethiopian diver, some of the soldiers who are brought in to help Othman defeat the revolt—and Laon and Cythna are not among them, remaining largely unmarked by the language of race or ethnicity (p. 157, VII.viii.66). The fact that they are atheists, while Othman is at least nominally Muslim, allows religion too to be visible as a sign of racialized difference. Because Britain had a vested and ongoing interest in expanding its empire into Ottoman territory, Nigel Leask, among others, has helpfully suggested that *Laon and Cythna* is "a poem in which the liberation of ... women is premised, albeit at a subliminal level, on imperial domination" (122)—that the poem hopes, in other words, for an enlightened British imperium to take its civilizing mission into places and cultures where women live in ways Shelley finds distasteful and oppressive. There is truth in this claim, but the story is also more complicated. On the one hand, what makes *Laon and Cythna* so important a text for contemporary readers is its ability to imagine women's rights as a transnational concern, in a manner that anticipates the development of the language of human rights in the twentieth century. The fact that the revolt of the Golden City is finally crushed by a league of foreign armies modeled on the coalitions that fought against the French Revolution, and that included Britain in their number, means that Shelley has very little faith in any nation to act in anything but its own interests: Britain is not going to bring feminism (or socialism, or vegetarianism) to the world, it is simply going to protect its political and economic status quo both at home and abroad. On the other hand, it is absolutely true that Shelley shares in and promulgates a familiar rhetorical and conceptual habit of Enlightenment thinkers, namely setting so-called universal values against the cultural norms and religious practices of non-Europeans.[1] To put it bluntly, Shelley is unable to view the claim to universality as itself undergirded by a sense of his own national and racial supremacy. We can interpret this failure in many ways—as a defensive disavowal, as intellectual laziness, as genuine naïveté, as a shortsighted insistence that people must believe the same things in order to work together for political purposes—but we should certainly not dismiss or ignore it.

Shelley's way of arguing for feminism against the Orient has an important precursor in Montesquieu's *Persian Letters* (1730; see Appendix F1), which, as Humberto Garcia notes, is itself part of an eighteenth-century vogue for "imaginary letters by Muslim characters" (63). *Persian Letters* is purportedly comprised of the letters two Persian noblemen send home to Iran as they travel the Continent. Although the overt purpose of the *Letters* is to satirize French society, which our correspondents, Usbek and Rica, find hopelessly backward and bizarre, the text also contains an important subplot that gains more and more traction as the narrative unfolds. This subplot concerns Roxana, one of Usbek's wives, who leads a rebellion in the harem before committing suicide at the novel's end. The parallels to Cythna's tales are obvious—although Othman remains more of an inscrutable caricature of despotism than Usbek, whose epistolary perspective we share for most of the *Letters*—and the Enlightenment logic that joins women's rights to anti-Muslim prejudice emerges here in its foundational form. That said, one would be hard pressed to argue that Montesquieu believes in the equality, or even the advancement, of women; the harem plot of his *Letters* is entertaining, often moving, but in

1 For recent and extensive discussions of this tendency, see Aravamudan; Garcia.

contrast to *Laon and Cythna* it does not really have a political agenda. The same cannot be said for Volney's *The Ruins* (1791; see Appendix F2), a hugely influential text seldom read today but a true touchstone for the Romantic period. There we find the critical, even dismissive attitude toward religion equally evident in Shelley's poem, which seems to borrow its framing device—an unidentified, presumptively European speaker in dialogue with a mysterious spirit somewhere in the East—from Volney as well. At the end of the 60-year interval between *Persian Letters* and *The Ruins* lie the origins of what Gerard Cohen-Vrignaud calls "radical orientalism," an overtly politicized deployment of orientalist tropes in service of parsing the ongoing event of the French Revolution. As Cohen-Vrignaud rightly suggests, Shelley must be seen as both inheritor and producer of this specific strand of Romantic orientalism, which treated the East not as a far-off wonderland but as a set of ready-to-hand conceptual tools for defining the purpose and the limits of political action in the early nineteenth century (1–23).

Two later Romantic works, Robert Southey's poem *Thalaba the Destroyer* (1801; Appendix F3) and Sydney Owenson's novel *The Missionary* (1811; Appendix F4) dramatize this split between apolitical treatments of orientalist themes and their more subversive applications. Both idealize non-Western societies—*Thalaba* takes place in the Middle East, *The Missionary* in India—but whereas Southey's poem is set in a very distant, mythical past, Owenson's story unfolds in the seventeenth century. By having the novel's action, including the love plot at its center, "converge," as Gauri Viswanathan puts it, around "the inquisitorial persecution of Portuguese Franciscans by Spanish Jesuits and Dominicans," Owenson allows her Eastern setting to provide "the occasion for a devastating critique of the sectarian savagery at the heart of European history" (27). While Thalaba's love for his adoptive sister Oneiza, along with the character of his protector, Moath, migrate into *Laon and Cythna* through the relationship between its protagonists and in the figure of the Hermit, it is Owenson's focus on this sectarianism that fuels Cythna's indictments of organized religion. In this way Owenson too might be said to participate in what Makdisi calls Shelley's desire to reclaim "Oriental terrain from previous visions and versions of the East" and to fold it "into the emergent space-time of modernity" (*Romantic Imperialism*, 123)—in other words, namely to argue for Western forms of progressive ideals such as religious toleration by showing them either at work or spectacularly failing in fictionalized non-Western lands. Once again, we must address the pressing question of what it means to assert ethical and political norms across a variegated geopolitical context, especially when such assertions may unwittingly sponsor an "imperial world view ... fired by progressivism" (221n46).

On that note, it is worth briefly comparing Shelley's desire for global revolution to his friend Byron's much more cautious negotiation with geopolitical concerns. It has become routine to point out that Byron, unlike Shelley, Southey, or Owenson, actually visited the places he wrote about, and in fact died in Greece fighting for Greek independence. Nonetheless, recent attempts to hold Byron up as a champion of humanitarian intervention before that concept existed in its current form disregard the poet's sophisticated, often despairing take on the uses of military force in the pursuit of seemingly just causes. Like Canto Second of *Laon and Cythna*, Byron's poem *The Giaour* (1813; Appendix F5) opens with an apostrophe to Greece, describing the country's degradation under Ottoman rule and exhorting its "sons" to rebel against their invaders. And yet the much-quoted lines—"For Freedom's battle, once begun, / Bequeathed by bleeding Sire to Son, / Though baffled oft is ever won" (66–68)—take on a sinister meaning in the context of *The Giaour*, which is about a Christian man who, having murdered his Muslim enemy, is cursed to endure a state of monstrous immortality that involves feeding on blood, including that of his own children. This vampiric model of transmission suggests that the inheritance of "Freedom's battle" is at once inexorable and tragic, passively received and mindlessly perpetuated. *The Giaour* is therefore quite a departure from Shelley's simple opposition of non-violent resistance to military action, one that reflects a lived familiarity with war. It is also the case that Shelley uses allegory as an aspirational genre, one that allows readers to see things as they might be in a better world and not as they are. This idealistic scheme of representation seeks to produce clarity around complex issues in order to make evident the difference between good and evil, and what is to be done about the latter; it is, certainly, not without its blind spots.

I have already mentioned Shelley's debt to Peacock's *Ahrimanes*, which Peacock probably abandoned sometime around 1815. In that poem's first canto (Appendix F6), we find the formal as well as thematic elements of Canto First of *Laon and Cythna* vividly rehearsed. In Spenserian stanzas, the poet describes a young man pining, somewhere in Central Asia, for his maiden companion and mourning the current state of society; he is then interrupted by a female spirit who uses the primordial battle of good and evil to explain such ills as private property and religious idolatry before sending him off to make the world a better place, with the help of his lover. Setting the stage for Shelley's poem, *Ahrimanes* introduces erotic love as a mediating term between political despair and revolutionary commitment, all the while continuing to use the Orient as the doubled imaginative locus of present misery and the prospect of change.

Shelley's Revolutions

A romance set in the recent past, a vindication of the rights of women, a troubling appeal to the claims of universalism: *Laon and Cythna* is all these things. It is also a poem, and it uses the resources of form and rhetoric to tell its story and advance its ideas. For Shelley, however, poetry is more than an artistic medium or a genre of literary writing. It, too, is a political action—or, rather, a political action is poetry. As he explains in *A Defence of Poetry*, not only do "architecture, painting, music, the dance, sculpture, [and] philosophy" count as poetry, so do "the forms of civil life" (*Shelley's Poetry and Prose* 518). As for poets, they are not just "authors" of architecture, painting, and so on; they are also "the institutors of laws, and the founders of civil society, and the inventors of the arts of life" (512). The word "poetry" has its origins in the Greek verb *poiein*, meaning to make or to shape, and Shelley has this etymology foremost in his mind when he explains that, in "the earlier epochs of the world," poets were called either "legislators, or prophets," and the identity of the poet "essentially comprises and unites both these characters" (513): the poet, in other words, not only gives shape, direction, and inspiration to his own time, but is also in special imaginative contact with a future only partially visible to the present, a future his own work helps bring into clearer view. Thus we find Laon's songs laying the mental and spiritual foundation for the uprising Cythna brings about, and thus we find Cythna's hymn to Equality describing a better world that swims briefly into existence before it is—for the time being—crushed. The unidentified speaker who begins Canto First, meanwhile, finds himself cast into a prophetic role when he meets Laon and Cythna and hears their story: by transmitting this story to the reader in the next eleven cantos, he offers a brief but memorable lesson in the poetics or, again, the making of revolution itself.

Leigh Hunt faults Shelley for "too great a sameness ... of image and metaphor," but one could also interpret the marked recurrence of particular words in *Laon and Cythna* as an elaboration of these revolutionary poetics. Take "whirlwind," which appears in the poem 26 times, and "multitude," which appears 31 times, counting the Preface. The prevalence of "multitude" makes sense in a poem about a collective revolt against an autocratic state, but the poem is called *Laon and Cythna*, its name taken from the couple whose story organizes its action. If we track Shelley's discrete applications of "multitude" and its variants (e.g., "multitudinous"), we see how the word works to suture the breach between the singularity of the couple and the plurality of the "patriot hosts" (p. 118, V.vii.59), to negotiate, as Godwin puts it, "the due medium between individuality and concert" (*Enquiry* 2.499) by capturing both in one collective noun. Likewise "whirlwind" describes the centripetal movement of solidarity, which pulls different people together towards some shared center, point of focus, or goal. These words dramatize a political power in excess of their meaning, becoming part of the forward motion of Shelley's progressive view of history—something never more obvious than when Shelley styles the revolutionaries a "multitude so moveless" (p. 118, V.liii.568) in a metaphysical continuum with Necessity's "moveless wave." Analyses of this sort might be brought to bear on a large handful of the poem's other recurring tropes, including the many images of tearing, splitting, or rending that disperse Cythna's reference to her "rent soul" (p. 157,

VII.vii.56)—itself the medium through which she speaks to other women—across the text. Meanwhile, the poem's thematic emphasis on Necessity can be felt in Shelley's use of a vocabulary that, once again, anticipates the condensed dialectical argument of "Ode to the West Wind." In alternating between scenes of repose, calm, emptiness or waste, and descriptions of kinetic activity rendered in metaphors of kindling or conflagration, Shelley previews the ode's account of an evolutionary temporality that knits together fast and slow.

Despite Shelley's emphasis on the development and emancipation of human society, his revolution is also an ecological one, and it takes into startling account the web of dependence that exists between human and non-human animals and their habitats. Between the vegetarian celebration of Canto Fifth and the terrifying famine of Canto Tenth, Shelley makes clear that his revolution is one that recognizes the rights of all creatures, as well as the suffering that befalls them when environments are poorly or greedily managed, as the Golden City is during Othman's retrenchment. For all the poem's references to the revolutionary power of attachments between persons, one of the most affecting moments in *Laon and Cythna* is Shelley's description of the City's "mothers" weeping when they hear starving hyenas howling "like starving infants"; when Shelley tells us that these women are "pierced with unnatural pity" (p. 195, X.xv.135), he uses "unnatural" in a now-forgotten sense to mean "outside of the species." In the same way as he deputizes natural phenomena—whirlwinds, whirlpools, waves, fire—as figures for the formation of political and affective bonds between persons, so too does Shelley call upon the idea of "nature" to locate empathy for other species at the heart of his revolutionary program. His simile ("like starving infants") does exactly what the shaping operation of poetry is meant to do: "enlarge the circumference of the imagination" in service of what *Defence of Poetry* defines as "love, or a going out of our own nature" (487).

Shelley had a depressive sensibility, and his idealism could often harden into a distaste or even revulsion for the physical world: in "Adonais," his elegy for John Keats, Keats is said to have "awakened from the dream of life," while the rest of us remain "lost in stormy visions," struggling against "phantoms" and "invulnerable nothings," "decay[ing] / Like corpses in a charnel" as "cold hopes swarm like worms within our living clay" (*Shelley's Poetry and Prose* 344–46, 348–51). He was drawn to poetry because for him it represented the capacity of human beings to think beyond the immediate realities of their material existence while remaining, as they must, bound by its limitations. Poetry, in other words, could try to capture both the dream of life and life itself; it could interpret shadows as a warped but instructive reflection of something real. Even the most hopeful and celebratory moments of *Laon and Cythna* do not abandon an awareness of the necessary imperfection of existence, and in her hymn to Equality Cythna makes clear that, even in utopia, "oft we still must weep, since we are human" (p. 133, V.4.513). This insistence on retaining "sorrow" at the center of an ideal world, much like the poem's insistence that Cythna's suffering is the fount of her power, offers a melancholy but strenuously ethical gloss on the project of utopian politics. It suggests that a good world is not a world without pain, but rather a world where people experience hardship together and equally, as inhabitants of the same fragile planet. To go "out of our own nature" is to leave behind the yearning for personal and private satisfaction, and to seek out the opportunity to bear life with other creatures, human or otherwise.

Percy Bysshe Shelley: A Brief Chronology

1789	The fall of the Bastille begins the French Revolution (14 July).
1791	Thomas Paine's *Rights of Man* published (March).
1792	Mary Wollstonecraft publishes *A Vindication of the Rights of Woman* (January). Birth of Percy Bysshe Shelley (hereafter PBS) at Field Place, West Sussex (4 August). France declares itself a republic (September).
1793	Execution of King Louis XVI (January). France declares war on Britain (February). William Godwin publishes *An Enquiry Concerning Political Justice* (February). Led by Maximilien Robespierre, the so-called Reign of Terror begins in France (September); a period of severe political repression follows in England. Execution of Marie Antoinette (October).
1794–1801	Births of Shelley's five sisters, the second of whom dies in infancy.
1794	Execution of Robespierre (July).
1795	Directory established in France (August).
1797	Marriage of Wollstonecraft and Godwin (March). Birth of Mary Wollstonecraft Godwin, later Mary Shelley and hereafter MWS (30 August), and death of Wollstonecraft from complications related to childbirth (10 September).
1798	William Wordsworth and Samuel Taylor Coleridge publish *Lyrical Ballads*.
1799	Napoleon seizes power (November).
1801	Union of Great Britain and Ireland.
1802	PBS sent to boarding school at Syon House Academy, Isleworth.
1804	PBS enrols in Eton College. Napoleon crowned Emperor of France.
1806	Birth of John Shelley, brother of PBS. Bysshe Shelley (grandfather) created Sir Bysshe Shelley, baronet.
1808	PBS begins romantic correspondence with his cousin, Harriet Grove.
1810	Publishes a Gothic novel, *Zastrozzi* (spring). *Original Poetry by Victor and Cazire* by PBS and sister Elizabeth published and withdrawn (September). Enters University College, Oxford, and meets Thomas Jefferson Hogg (October). Pseudonymous publication of

Posthumous Fragments of Margaret Nicholson, written with Hogg (November).
Another Gothic novel, *St. Irvyne*, published anonymously (December).

1811 Writes *The Necessity of Atheism* with Hogg (February); both are expelled from Oxford (March).
Elopes with Harriet Westbrook (August).
In Keswick (November–February 1812); meets the poet Robert Southey.
George, Prince of Wales, declared Prince Regent, thus beginning the Regency period (February).

1812 Writes *Address to the Irish People* and *Proposals for an Association* after visiting Ireland (February); *Declaration of Rights* (March).
Moves to Wales (April) where he is placed under government surveillance.
The Devil's Walk, a Ballad (August).
Meets William Godwin in London (October).
Meets Thomas Love Peacock and MWS (November).

1813 Returns to London (April).
A Vindication of Natural Diet and *Queen Mab* (April–May).
Birth of daughter Ianthe Shelley (June).

1814 *A Refutation of Deism* (January).
Napoleon exiled to Elba (April).
Accompanied by Clara Mary Jane (Claire) Claremont, PBS and MWS elope and leave for the Continent (July), traveling in France and Switzerland before returning to London (September).
Birth of Charles, son of PBS and Harriet Westbrook (November).

1815 Bysshe Shelley dies (January); PBS negotiates an annual income of £1,000 out of his grandfather's will, with a provision for Harriet.
PBS, MWS, Claire, and Hogg experiment with a "shared household" (January–April).
MWS gives birth to a daughter (February) who dies two weeks later.
Writes *Alastor* (winter).
Napoleon escapes from Elba; his "Hundred Days" reign begins (February); the Battle of Waterloo ends in a decisive defeat of Napoleon's army (June); Napoleon is captured and imprisoned and the Restoration begins in France (July).

1816 "The Year without a Summer" sees record low temperatures all over the world. Birth of William, son of PBS and MWS (January).
Alastor published with other poems (February).

PBS, MWS, and Claire, now Byron's lover, spend the summer in Switzerland, where Byron and Shelley meet. Shelley writes "Hymn to Intellectual Beauty" and "Mont Blanc"; MWS begins *Frankenstein* (May–August).
Suicide of MWS's half-sister Fanny Imlay (October).
Probable suicide of Harriet Westbrook Shelley (November).
Marriage of PBS and MWS; PBS meets John Keats (December).

1817 Birth of Allegra, daughter of Claire and Byron (January).
A Proposal for Putting Reform to the Vote; Chancery Court denies PBS custody of his children with Harriet; Shelleys settle at Albion House, Marlow (March).
Writes *Laon and Cythna* (March–September).
Birth of Clara Everina, daughter of PBS and MWS (September).
An Address to the People on the Death of the Princess Charlotte (November).
Laon and Cythna published and withdrawn, following which PBS revises the poem as *The Revolt of Islam*; publication of *History of a Six-Weeks Tour* by MWS and PBS (November).

1818 *Frankenstein* published anonymously with preface by PBS; "Ozymandias" published; PBS begins *Rosalind and Helen* (January).
The Shelleys, with Claire, leave England permanently (March) and travel in Italy, where they will remain until the death of PBS.
Translates Plato's *Symposium* and writes "On Love" (summer).
Writes "Lines Written among the Euganean Hills"; begins *Julian and Maddalo* and *Prometheus Unbound* (late summer–fall).
Death of Clara Shelley (September).
"Stanzas Written in Dejection" (December).
Birth of Elena Adelaide (December) registered as the child of PBS and (falsely) of MWS at Naples (February 1819).

1819 Work on *Prometheus Unbound* (March–April) and *Julian and Maddalo* (completed by August).
Byron takes Allegra to live with him (April).
Rosalind and Helen published (spring).
Death of William Shelley (June).
Peterloo Massacre near Manchester leaves at least 15 people dead and 300–500 injured (August).
Mask of Anarchy and publication of *The Cenci* (September); "Ode to the West Wind" (October); *Peter Bell the Third* (October–November).
Birth of Percy Florence, son of PBS and MWS; PBS begins

	A Philosophical View of Reform (November).
	"On Life" (November–December).
	"England in 1819" sent to Leigh Hunt for publication in *The Examiner* (December).
1820	Death of George III, ascension of George IV, and official end of the Regency period; Shelleys move to Pisa (January).
	Writes "The Sensitive-Plant," "Ode to Liberty," "To a Sky-Lark," *Letter to Maria Gisbourne*, and "The Cloud" (1819?) (spring–summer).
	Elena Shelley dies while under foster care in Naples (June).
	Publication of *Prometheus Unbound* with other poems of 1820 (August); *The Witch of Atlas*, *Swellfoot the Tyrant*, "Ode to Naples" (late summer–fall).
	Meets Teresa "Emilia" Viviani (November).
	Meets Alexandros Mavrokordatos, leader of the Greek Independence Movement (December).
1821	Meets Edward Williams and his common-law wife Jane (January).
	Writes *Epipsychidion* for Teresa Viviani (January–February) and *A Defence of Poetry* (February–March).
	After learning of the death of John Keats at Rome (February), writes *Adonais* (published July).
	Writes *Hellas* (October).
	The Shelleys are joined in Pisa by Byron (November).
1822	Works on *Charles the First* (January), and writes poems to Jane Williams, including "When the lamp is shattered" and "With a guitar, to Jane" (January–July).
	Allegra Byron dies; the Shelleys and the Willliamses move to Casa Magni near Lerici (April).
	Begins *The Triumph of Life* (May), which will remain unfinished.
	MWS has a miscarriage and nearly dies (June).
	On 1 July, PBS, Edward Williams, and Charles Vivian sail to Livorno to rendezvous with Leigh Hunt and his family; sailing home on 8 July, all three drown during a sudden, violent storm; the bodies of PBS and Williams are identified on 19 July, and PBS is cremated on 16 August.
1823	MWS returns to England with her only surviving child, Percy (July).

A Note on the Text

Laon and Cythna or *The Revolt of Islam*? The choice is a difficult one, and although the number of changes made between the first and second versions of the text is ultimately minimal, even referring to Shelley's poem by one title or another makes a significant difference in how we prepare to read it. Where "Laon and Cythna" foregrounds the love story at the center of the poem, "The Revolt of Islam" places us in a more squarely political context. Nonetheless, Shelley's decision to name his Golden City after the religion of its people creates the misleading expectation that the poem is *about* Islam, which—as Shelley himself pointed out—it certainly is not. My own opinion is that some of the rewritten passages in *The Revolt*, especially at VIII.vii.55–58 and XII.xxx.265, are simply better as poetry than their counterparts in *Laon and Cythna*, and that turning Cythna into Laon's adoptive rather than biological sibling makes the poem's revolutionary theme even more compelling, since it underscores the political significance of elective affiliation—of relationships we choose rather than those we are born into. All the same, this edition offers the reader the text as Shelley wanted it to appear in print the first time and, with it, some of the historical material that will be especially useful to students of Romanticism: this includes the incest trope, which is so prevalent in Romantic literature, and Shelley's strategic use of the concept of atheism to map the contours of progressive identity. If losing this material makes *The Revolt* a more subtle and supple poem, it also makes it less transparent a window onto its time.

The primary copy-text for this edition is the bound volume of *Laon and Cythna* housed at the William Andrews Clark Memorial Library at the University of California, Los Angeles. This is a first edition and second issue of the poem: it contains Shelley's list of errata at the back, and it omits the fly-title leaf—which I have chosen to include here—that occurs in the very rare first issue.[1] Changes to the text—which are indicated in the footnotes—have, for the most part, followed those given by Shelley in his errata, though in difficult cases such as those at IX.ix.80 and XI.xvi.137 I have relied on the collective wisdom of Shelley's editors, and especially on *The Poems of Shelley: Volume Two* (2000) edited by Geoffrey Matthews and Kelvin Everest, with Jack Donovan overseeing *Laon and*

1 Shelley's list of errata is not included in this Broadview Edition, but rather its advisements are incorporated into the text and marked in footnotes. The fly-title leaf, which bears a quotation from Pindar that also finds its way into *The Revolt of Islam*, does appear here, as it appears in the first issue of the first edition of *Laon and Cythna*. For an explanation of this discrepancy, see Thomas J. Wise, *A Shelley Library: A Catalogue of Printed Books, Manuscripts, and Autograph Letters by Percy Bysshe Shelley, Harriet Shelley and Mary Wollstonecraft Shelley* (New York: Haskell House, 1971), 48.

Cythna, and on the third volume of *The Complete Poetry of Percy Bysshe Shelley* (2012) edited by Donald Reiman, Neil Fraistat, Nora Crook, et al.; the facsimile editions of the Bodleian Shelley manuscripts, in particular *BSM VIII* and *BSM XIII*, edited by Tatsuo Tokoo, and *BSM XVII*, edited by Steven Jones, have also been invaluable. At those points where the text of the poem varies from that of *The Revolt of Islam*, the relevant portions of the latter poem are included in footnotes. My copy-texts for *The Revolt of Islam* have been editions of the poem held by the Clark Library and by Columbia University's Rare Book and Manuscript Library, consulted with the guidance of these same editorial and scholarly sources.

This edition is aimed at undergraduate students and graduate students encountering Shelley in coursework. Its first task is to make Shelley's poem accessible to non-specialists; its second task is to avoid overwhelming them. Consequently, the annotations are intended chiefly to aid and enhance basic comprehension of the text: they gloss confusing or archaic uses of words, parse Shelley's challenging syntax, explain obscure plot points, and invite comparisons between various moments in the poem. When it has seemed immediately instructive to consider Shelley's engagement with various literary and philosophical sources, those sources have been cited. When relevant quotations from other sources are included in the footnotes, page numbers are given for prose texts and line numbers (where available) for poetic texts; extracts from classical texts appear in translation and are cited according to convention (e.g., by line, fragment, or chapter number).

When it comes to unfamiliar words or troublesome spellings that are repeated throughout the text (e.g., *bark* or *woof*, *vext* for vexed or *shew* for show) glosses are provided only once. If a word appears more than once but its exact meaning varies (e.g., *hoary*, *waste*), the appropriate or most applicable sense is given each time. Where Shelley uses a non-standard spelling but the sense of the word seems clear—e.g., *inchanted* for enchanted, *thro'* for through—I have trusted the reader to infer Shelley's meaning. Archaic spellings (e.g., *antient* for ancient, *desart* for desert) are retained throughout.

LAON AND CYTHNA; OR, THE REVOLUTION OF THE GOLDEN CITY

PREFACE.

The Poem which I now present to the world, is an attempt from which I scarcely dare to expect success, and in which a writer of established fame might fail without disgrace. It is an experiment on the temper of the public mind, as to how far a thirst for a happier condition of moral and political society survives, among the enlightened and refined, the tempests which have shaken the age in which we live.[1] I have sought to enlist the harmony of metrical language, the etherial combinations of the fancy, the rapid and subtle transitions of human passion, all those elements which essentially compose a Poem, in the cause of a liberal[2] and comprehensive morality, and in the view of kindling within the bosoms of my readers, a virtuous enthusiasm for those doctrines of liberty and justice, that faith and hope in something good, which neither violence, nor misrepresentation, nor prejudice, can ever totally extinguish among mankind.

For this purpose I have chosen a story of human passion in its most universal character, diversified with moving and romantic[3] adventures, and appealing, in contempt of all artificial opinions or institutions, to the common sympathies of every human breast. I have made no attempt to recommend the motives which I would substitute for those at present governing mankind by methodical and systematic argument. I would only awaken the feelings, so that the reader should see the beauty of true virtue, and be incited to those inquiries which have led to my moral and political creed, and that of some of the sublimest intellects in the world. The Poem therefore (with the exception of the first Canto, which is purely introductory) is narrative, not didactic. It is a succession of pictures illustrating the growth and progress of individual mind aspiring after excellence, and devoted to the love of mankind; its influence in refining and making pure the most daring and uncommon impulses of the imagination, the understanding, and the senses; its impatience at "all the oppressions which are done under the sun";[4] its tendency to awaken public hope and to enlighten and improve mankind; the rapid effects of the application of that tendency; the awakening of an immense nation from their slavery and degradation to a true sense of moral dignity and freedom; the

---

1 The totalitarian turn of the French Revolution, followed by the French Revolutionary Wars (1792–1802) and the Napoleonic Wars (1803–15), had left most Britons at best skeptical about the prospects of a better, more democratic political future, and at worst eager to embrace an increasingly repressive government at home.

2 Shelley uses this word both in its primary sense meaning "free" or "unrestrained" and with a political inflection suggesting "open-minded" and "progressive."

3 For a discussion of Shelley's use of romance, see the Introduction above, pp. 20–23.

4 Cf. Ecclesiastes 4:1. "So I returned, and considered all the oppressions that are done under the sun: and behold the tears of *such as were* oppressed, and they had no comforter; and on the side of their oppressors *there was* power; but they had no comforter."

bloodless[1] dethronement of their oppressors, and the unveiling of the religious frauds by which they had been deluded into submission; the tranquillity of successful patriotism, and the universal toleration and benevolence of true philanthropy;[2] the treachery and barbarity of hired soldiers; vice not the object of punishment and hatred, but kindness and pity; the faithlessness of tyrants; the confederacy of the Rulers of the World, and the restoration of the expelled Dynasty by foreign arms; the massacre and extermination of the Patriots, and the victory of established power; the consequences of legitimate despotism, civil war, famine, plague, superstition, and an utter extinction of the domestic[3] affections; the judicial murder of the advocates of Liberty; the temporary triumph of oppression, that secure earnest of its final and inevitable fall; the transient nature of ignorance and error, and the eternity of genius and virtue. Such is the series of delineations of which the Poem consists. And if the lofty passions with which it has been my scope to distinguish this story, shall not excite in the reader a generous impulse, an ardent thirst for excellence, an interest profound and strong, such as belongs to no meaner desires—let not the failure be imputed to a natural unfitness for human sympathy in these sublime and animating themes. It is the business of the Poet to communicate to others the pleasure and the enthusiasm arising out of those images and feelings, in the vivid presence of which within his own mind, consists at once his inspiration and his reward.

The panic which, like an epidemic transport, seized upon all classes of men during the excesses consequent upon the French Revolution, is gradually giving place to sanity. It has ceased to be believed that whole generations of mankind ought to consign themselves to a hopeless inheritance of ignorance and misery, because a nation of men who had been dupes and slaves for centuries, were incapable of conducting themselves with the wisdom and tranquillity of freemen so soon as some of their fetters were partially loosened. That their conduct could not have been marked by any other characters than ferocity and thoughtlessness, is the historical fact from which liberty derives all its recommendations, and falsehood the worst features of its deformity. There is a reflux in the tide of human things which bears the shipwrecked hopes of men into a secure haven, after the storms are past. Methinks, those who now live have survived an age of despair.

The French Revolution may be considered as one of those manifestations of a general state of feeling among civilized mankind, produced by a defect of correspondence between the knowledge existing in society and the improvement, or gradual abolition of political institutions. The year 1788[4] may be assumed as the epoch of one of the most important crises produced

1 I.e., non-violent.

2 Literally, love of mankind.

3 Familial, intimate.

4 Although the beginning of the French Revolution is usually dated 1789, Shelley emphasizes 1788 as the "epoch" in which the "general state of feeling" among the French reached a tipping point that led to the events of the following year.

by this feeling. The sympathies connected with that event extended to every bosom. The most generous and amiable natures were those which participated the most extensively in these sympathies. But such a degree of unmingled good was expected, as it was impossible to realize.[1] If the Revolution had been in every respect prosperous, then misrule and superstition would lose half their claims to our abhorrence, as fetters which the captive can unlock with the slightest motion of his fingers, and which do not eat with poisonous rust into the soul. The revulsion occasioned by the atrocities of the demagogues and the re-establishment of successive tyrannies in France was terrible, and felt in the remotest corner of the civilized world.[2] Could they listen to the plea of reason who had groaned under the calamities of a social state, according to the provisions of which one man riots in luxury whilst another famishes for want of bread? Can he who the day before was a trampled slave, suddenly become liberal-minded,[3] forbearing, and independent? This is the consequence of the habits of a state of society to be produced by resolute perseverance and indefatigable hope, and long-suffering and long-believing courage, and the systematic efforts of generations of men of intellect and virtue. Such is the lesson which experience teaches now. But on the first reverses of hope in the progress of French liberty, the sanguine[4] eagerness for good overleapt the solution of these questions, and for a time extinguished itself in the unexpectedness of their result. Thus many of the most ardent and tender-hearted of the worshippers of public good, have been morally ruined by what a partial glimpse of the events they deplored, appeared to show as the melancholy desolation of all their cherished hopes. Hence gloom and misanthropy have become the characteristics of the age in which we live, the solace of a disappointment that unconsciously finds relief only in the wilful exaggeration of its own despair. This influence has tainted the literature of the age with the hopelessness of the minds from which it flows. Metaphysics,[5] and enquiries into moral and political science, have become little else than vain attempts to

---

1 Achieve.

2 Shelley presumably alludes to the takeover of the Revolutionary government by Maximilien Robespierre (1758–94), Louis Antoine de Saint-Just (1767–94), and other radicals, followed by the ascent of Napoleon Bonaparte (1769–1821) and finally by the Bourbon Restoration in 1814.

3 Fair-minded, objective.

4 Optimistic, confident, or unruffled; literally, bloody. The poem favors the latter usage of the word, but here Shelley may mean deliberately to conflate both meanings, in order to suggest that the revolutionaries' optimism also led them to commit various crimes in the service of what they thought was progress.

5 [Shelley's note:] I ought to except Sir W. Drummond's "Academical Questions;" a volume of very acute and powerful metaphysical criticism. [Sir William Drummond (1770–1828) was a Scottish politician, poet, and philosophical Skeptic, whose *Academical Questions* (1805) helped turn Shelley toward skepticism as, in this case, the belief that our minds do not know or grasp the world in itself, but only encounter it indirectly, through our sense impressions.]

revive exploded superstitions, or sophisms like those[1] of Mr. Malthus,[2] calculated to lull the oppressors of mankind into a security of everlasting triumph. Our works of fiction and poetry have been overshadowed by the same infectious gloom. But mankind appear to me to be emerging from their trance. I am aware, methinks, of a slow, gradual, silent change. In that belief I have composed the following Poem.

I do not presume to enter into competition with our greatest contemporary Poets. Yet I am unwilling to tread in the footsteps of any who have preceded me. I have sought to avoid the imitation of any style of language or versification peculiar to the original minds of which it is the character, designing that even if what I have produced be worthless, it should still be properly my own. Nor have I permitted any system relating to mere words, to divert the attention of the reader from whatever interest I may have succeeded in creating, to my own ingenuity in contriving to disgust them according to the rules of criticism. I have simply clothed my thoughts in what appeared to me the most obvious and appropriate language. A person familiar with nature, and with the most celebrated productions of the human mind, can scarcely err in following the instinct, with respect to selection of language, produced by that familiarity.

There is an education peculiarly fitted for a Poet, without which genius and sensibility can hardly fill the circle of their capacities. No education indeed can entitle to this appellation a dull and unobservant mind, or one, though neither dull nor unobservant, in which the channels of communication between thought and expression have been obstructed or closed. How far it is my fortune to belong to either of the latter classes, I cannot know. I aspire to be something better. The circumstances of my accidental education have been favorable to this ambition.[3] I have been familiar from boyhood

---

1 [Shelley's note:] It is remarkable, as a symptom of the revival of public hope, that Mr. Malthus has assigned, in the later editions of his work, an indefinite dominion to moral restraint over the principle of population. This concession answers all the inferences from his doctrine unfavourable to human improvement, and reduces the "ESSAY ON POPULATION" to a commentary illustrative of the unanswerableness of [William Godwin's] "POLITICAL JUSTICE." [William Godwin (1756–1836), political philosopher and novelist, was Shelley's father-in-law; see Appendix E2.]

2 In 1798 the demographer Thomas Robert Malthus (1766–1834) published the first edition of his *Essay on the Principle of Population*, in which he suggested that all schemes for the improvement of mankind were compromised by the dangerous inevitability of overpopulation. Malthus immediately became the public enemy of progressive writers such as Godwin and William Hazlitt (1778–1830) who, like Shelley, attacked Malthus's promotion of sexual abstinence among the poor. Shelley's most direct engagements with Malthus appear in his *Proposals for an Association of Philanthropists* (1812) and in the unfinished essay *A Philosophical View of Reform* (1819), though we see some of Malthus's views parroted by the "grave and hoary men" of IX.xiv (p. 182).

3 Although *The Prelude* would not be published until 1850, Shelley's list of credentials resembles the experiences William Wordsworth (1770–1850) narrates in that

with mountains and lakes, and the sea, and the solitude of forests: Danger which sports upon the brink of precipices, has been my playmate. I have trodden the glaciers of the Alps, and lived under the eye of Mont Blanc. I have been a wanderer among distant fields. I have sailed down mighty rivers, and seen the sun rise and set, and the stars come forth, whilst I have sailed night and day down a rapid stream among mountains. I have seen populous cities, and have watched the passions which rise and spread, and sink and change amongst assembled multitudes of men. I have seen the theatre of the more visible ravages of tyranny and war, cities and villages reduced to scattered groups of black and roofless houses, and the naked inhabitants sitting famished upon their desolated thresholds. I have conversed with living men of genius. The poetry of an[c]ient Greece and Rome, and modern Italy, and our own country, has been to me like external nature, a passion and an enjoyment. Such are the sources from which the materials for the imagery of my Poem have been drawn. I have considered poetry in its most comprehensive sense, and have read the Poets and the Historians, and the Metaphysicians[1] whose writings have been accessible to me, and have looked upon the beautiful and majestic scenery of the earth as common sources of those elements which it is the province of the Poet to embody and combine. Yet the experience and the feelings to which I refer, do not in themselves constitute men Poets, but only prepares [*sic*] them to be the auditors of those who are. How far I shall be found to possess that more essential attribute of Poetry, the power of awakening in others sensations like those which animate my own bosom, is that which, to speak sincerely, I know not; and which, with an acquiescent and contented spirit, I expect to be taught by the effect which I shall produce upon those whom I now address.

I have avoided, as I have said before, the imitation of any contemporary style. But there must be a resemblance which does not depend upon their own will, between all the writers of any particular age. They cannot escape from subjection to a common influence which arises out of an infinite combination of circumstances belonging to the times in which they live, though each is in a degree the author of the very influence by which his being is thus pervaded. Thus, the tragic Poets of the age of Pericles; the Italian revivers of ancient learning; those mighty intellects of our own country that succeeded the Reformation, the translators of the Bible, Shakspeare [*sic*], Spenser, the Dramatists of the reign of Elizabeth, and Lord Bacon;[2] the

---

autobiographical poem, which is written (or so Wordsworth suggests) to prove his aptitude eventually to write another, never-finished work called *The Recluse*.

1 [Shelley's note:] In this sense there may be such a thing as perfectibility in works of fiction, notwithstanding the concession often made by the advocates of human improvement, that perfectibility is a term applicable only to science.

2 [Shelley's note:] Milton stands alone in the age which he illumined. [John Milton (1608–74), English poet and man of letters, wrote the epic poem *Paradise Lost* (1667) and several important political pamphlets, including tracts on the freedom of the press (*Areopagitica*, 1644), in defense of divorce (*The Doctrine and Discipline of Divorce*, 1643), and on the virtues of popular government and the (*continued*)

colder spirits of the interval[1] that succeeded;—all, resemble each other, and differ from every other in their several classes. In this view of things, Ford[2] can no more be called the imitator of Shakspeare, than Shakspeare the imitator of Ford. There were perhaps few other points of resemblance between these two men, than that which the universal and inevitable influence of their age produced. And this is an influence which neither the meanest scribbler, nor the sublimest genius of any æra[3] can escape; and which I have not attempted to escape.

I have adopted the stanza of Spenser, (a measure inexpressibly beautiful) not because I consider it a finer model of poetical harmony than the blank verse of Shakspeare and Milton, but because in the latter there is no shelter for mediocrity: you must either succeed or fail. This perhaps an aspiring spirit should desire. But I was enticed also, by the brilliancy and magnificence of sound which a mind that has been nourished upon musical thoughts, can produce by a just and harmonious arrangement of the pauses of this measure. Yet there will be found some instances where I have completely failed in this attempt, and one, which I here request the reader to consider as an erratum, where there is left most inadvertently an alexandrine in the middle of a stanza.[4]

But in this, as in every other respect, I have written fearlessly. It is the misfortune of this age that its Writers, too thoughtless of immortality, are exquisitely sensible to temporary praise or blame. They write with the fear of Reviews before their eyes. This system of criticism sprang up in that torpid interval[5] when Poetry was not. Poetry, and the art which professes to regulate and limit its powers, cannot subsist together. Longinus could

---

harms of kingship (*The Tenure of Kings and Magistrates*, 1649). Milton's oeuvre and his biography disclose complex, often contradictory attitudes toward absolutism whether political or theological; to the Romantics, however, his sympathetic portrayal of Satan as a revolutionary in *Paradise Lost* made him an intellectual hero, one who, in the words of Shelley's contemporary William Blake (1757–1827), "was of the Devil's party without knowing it." See William Blake, *The Marriage of Heaven and Hell* (1793), in *The Complete Poetry and Prose of William Blake* 35. A Satan or "Lucifer," clearly based on Milton's, first makes his appearance here at I.xxvi.230 (p. 68).]

1 Given Shelley's note to the preceding phrase, he evidently excepts Milton from the "colder spirits" of the seventeenth century.

2 John Ford (c. 1586–1640), Elizabethan dramatist.

3 Era.

4 In fact, Shelley puts alexandrines in the body of his stanzas at least twice, at IV.xxvii.239 (p. 113) and IX.xxxvi.320 (p. 189), and perhaps three times, depending on how we scan the line at VIII.xxvii.237 (p. 176).

5 The practice of literary criticism became professionalized over the course of the eighteenth century. By the Romantic period, conservative periodicals such as *Blackwood's Edinburgh Magazine* were hugely influential, and tended to support or dismiss writers more on political than aesthetic grounds; they also often published sensationalized accounts of authors' private lives, and Shelley (along with Hazlitt and Leigh Hunt [1784–1859]) was a favorite target.

not have been the contemporary of Homer, nor Boileau of Horace.[1] Yet this species of criticism never presumed to assert an understanding of its own: it has always, unlike true science, followed, not preceded the opinion of mankind, and would even now bribe with worthless adulation some of our greatest Poets to impose gratuitous fetters on their own imaginations, and become unconscious accomplices in the daily murder of all genius either not so aspiring or not so fortunate as their own. I have sought therefore to write, as I believe that Homer, Shakspeare, and Milton wrote, with an utter disregard of anonymous censure. I am certain that calumny and misrepresentation, though it may move me to compassion, cannot disturb my peace. I shall understand the expressive silence of those sagacious enemies who dare not trust themselves to speak. I shall endeavour to extract from the midst of insult, and contempt, and maledictions, those admonitions which may tend to correct whatever imperfections such censurers may discover in this my first serious appeal to the Public. If certain Critics were as clear-sighted as they are malignant, how great would be the benefit to be derived from their virulent writings! As it is, I fear I shall be malicious enough to be amused with their paltry tricks and lame[2] invectives. Should the Public judge that my composition is worthless, I shall indeed bow before the tribunal from which Milton received his crown of immortality, and shall seek to gather, if I live, strength from that defeat, which may nerve me to some new enterprise of thought which may *not* be worthless. I cannot conceive that Lucretius,[3] when he meditated that poem whose doctrines are yet the basis of our metaphysical knowledge, and whose eloquence has been the wonder of mankind, wrote in awe of such censure as the hired sophists[4] of the impure and superstitious noblemen of Rome might affix to what he should produce. It was at the period when Greece was led captive, and Asia made tributary to the Republic, fast verging itself to slavery and ruin, that a multitude of Syrian captives, bigotted to the worship of their obscene Ashtaroth,[5] and the

1 Longinus (first or third century CE), Greek teacher of rhetoric and author of *On the Sublime*, an especially popular and influential text during the eighteenth century; Homer (ninth or eighth century BCE?), Greek poet credited with authorship of the *Iliad* and the *Odyssey*; Nicolas Boileau-Despréaux, known as Boileau (1636–1711), French poet and literary critic; Quintus Horatius Flaccus, known as Horace (65–8 BCE), Roman lyric poet, satirist, and literary critic.

2 Feeble, harmless.

3 Lucretius (c. 99–c. 55 BCE), Epicurean philosopher and poet of Ancient Rome. His *De Rerum Natura* (*On the Nature of Things*) is one of Shelley's major touchstones.

4 Sophism was a pedagogical practice of Ancient Greece, geared toward the teaching of rhetoric in the service of persuasion. Shelley uses the term "sophist" in what, thanks to Plato, has become its derogatory sense to mean "intellectual con-artist."

5 Plural of Astarte, the Greek name for the Babylonian goddess Ishtar. Shelley seems to be using the word to signify "female devils," as Milton does in *Paradise Lost*, 1.419–23.

unworthy successors of Socrates and Zeno, found there a precarious subsistence by administering, under the name of freedmen, to the vices and vanities of the great. These wretched men were skilled to plead, with a superficial but plausible set of sophisms, in favor of that contempt for virtue which is the portion of slaves, and that faith in portents, the most fatal substitute for benevolence in the imaginations of men, which arising from the enslaved communities of the East, then first began to overwhelm the western nations in its stream.[1] Were these the kind of men whose disapprobation the wise and lofty-minded Lucretius should have regarded with a salutary awe? The latest and perhaps the meanest of those who follow in his footsteps, would disdain to hold life on such conditions.

The Poem now presented to the Public occupied little more than six months in the composition. That period has been devoted to the task with unremitting ardour and enthusiasm. I have exercised a watchful and earnest criticism on my work as it grew under my hands. I would willingly have sent it forth to the world with that perfection which long labour and revision is said to bestow. But I found that if I should gain something in exactness by this method, I might lose much of the newness and energy of imagery and language as it flowed fresh from my mind. And although the mere composition occupied no more than six months, the thoughts thus arranged were slowly gathered in as many years.

I trust that the reader will carefully distinguish between those opinions which have a dramatic propriety in reference to the characters which they are designed to elucidate, and such as are properly my own. The erroneous and degrading idea which men have conceived of a Supreme Being, for instance, is spoken against, but not the Supreme Being itself.[2] The belief which some superstitious persons[3] whom I have brought upon the stage entertain of the Deity, as injurious to the character of his benevolence, is widely different from my own. In recommending also a great and important change in the spirit which animates the social institutions of mankind, I have avoided all flattery to those violent and malignant passions of our nature, which are ever on the watch to mingle with and to alloy the most beneficial innovations. There is no quarter given to Revenge, or Envy, or Prejudice. Love is celebrated everywhere as the sole law which should govern the moral world.[4]

---

1 Shelley here gives voice to the widely promulgated claim that as the Roman Empire grew, its moral and philosophical culture was gradually corrupted by the outside influences of "the East."

2 In other words, although Shelley is a vocal critic of religion, he is not necessarily against the idea of God. While most theologians would characterize this position as deist, Shelley prefers to call himself an atheist, at least partly for the word's radical political associations and for its capacity to unsettle his audience.

3 I.e., characters in the poem.

4 In *The Revolt of Islam*, Shelley's preface ends here, omitting the paragraph that follows.

In the personal conduct of my Hero and Heroine, there is one circumstance[1] which was intended to startle the reader from the trance of ordinary life. It was my object to break through the crust of those outworn opinions on which established institutions depend. I have appealed therefore to the most universal of all feelings, and have endeavored to strengthen the moral sense, by forbidding it to waste its energies in seeking to avoid actions which are only crimes of convention. It is because there is so great a multitude of artificial vices, that there are so few real virtues. Those feelings alone which are benevolent or malevolent, are essentially good or bad. The circumstance of which I speak, was introduced, however, merely to accustom men to that charity and toleration which the exhibition of a practice widely differing from their own, has a tendency to promote.[2] Nothing indeed can be more mischievous than many actions innocent in themselves, which might bring down upon individuals the bigotted contempt and rage of the multitude.

---

1 I.e., the sexual relationship between the siblings Laon and Cythna.

2 [Shelley's note:] The sentiments connected with and characteristic of this circumstance, have no personal reference to the Writer. [This caveat may betray Shelley's anxiety over the not-unfounded gossip, circulated in the periodical press, that he was conducting a semi-incestuous ménage with his wife Mary, her stepsister Claire Claremont, and Lord Byron, whose daughter with Claire, Clara Allegra Byron (known as Allegra), was born in January 1817.]

DEDICATION.

—

THERE IS NO DANGER TO A MAN, THAT KNOWS
WHAT LIFE AND DEATH IS: THERE'S NOT ANY LAW
EXCEEDS HIS KNOWLEDGE; NEITHER IS IT LAWFUL
THAT HE SHOULD STOOP TO ANY OTHER LAW.

CHAPMAN.[1]

1 George Chapman (c. 1559–1634), English poet, dramatist, and translator, and the subject of Keats's sonnet "On First Looking into Chapman's Homer" (1816). Shelley's dedication is a slightly altered quotation from Chapman's play, *The Conspiracy and Tragedy of Charles, Duke of Byron, Marshall of France* (1608).

TO
MARY—— ——[1]

1.

So now my summer-task is ended, Mary,
And I return to thee, mine own heart's home;
As to his Queen some victor knight of Faëry,[2]
Earning bright spoils for her inchanted dome;
Nor thou disdain, that ere my fame become
A star among the stars of mortal night,
If it indeed may cleave° its natal gloom, *split, open up*
Its doubtful promise thus I would unite
With thy beloved name, thou Child of love and light.

2.

The toil which stole from thee so many an hour,
Is ended,—and the fruit is at thy feet!
No longer where the woods to frame a bower
With interlaced branches mix and meet,
Or where, with sound like many voices sweet,
Water-falls leap among wild islands green,
Which framed for my lone boat a lone retreat
Of moss-grown trees and weeds, shall I be seen:[3]
But beside thee, where still my heart has ever been.

3.

Thoughts of great deeds were mine, dear Friend, when first
The clouds which wrap this world from youth did pass.
I do remember well the hour which burst
My spirit's sleep: a fresh May-dawn it was,
When I walked forth upon the glittering grass,
And wept, I knew not why; until there rose
From the near school-room, voices, that, alas!
Were but one echo from a world of woes—
The harsh and grating strife of tyrants and of foes.

---

1 Shelley's wife, Mary Wollstonecraft Shelley, née Godwin (1797–1851), is perhaps best known as the author of *Frankenstein* (1818) and *The Last Man* (1826). She became editor of Shelley's works after his death.

2 Fairyland; an allusion to Spenser's *The Faerie Queene* (1590–96) that complements the verse form of the poem.

3 According to Mary Shelley's "Note on *The Revolt of Islam*" (1839), Shelley wrote "the poem ... in his boat, as it floated under the beech-groves of Bisham" (see Appendix G1, p. 290).

4.

And then I clasped my hands and looked around—
—But none was near to mock my streaming eyes,
Which poured their warm drops on the sunny ground—
So without shame, I spake;°—"I will be wise, *spoke*
And just, and free, and mild, if in me lies
Such power, for I grow weary to behold
The selfish and the strong still tyrannise
Without reproach or check." I then controuled
My tears, my heart grew calm, and I was meek and bold.

5.

And from that hour did I with earnest thought
Heap knowledge from forbidden mines of lore,[1]
Yet nothing that my tyrants knew or taught
I cared to learn, but from that secret store
Wrought linked armor for my soul, before
It might walk forth to war among mankind;
Thus power and hope were strengthened more and more
Within me, till there came upon my mind
A sense of loneliness, a thirst with which I pined.

6.

Alas, that love should be a blight and snare
To those who seek all sympathies in one!—[2]
Such once I sought in vain; then black despair,
The shadow of a starless night, was thrown
Over the world in which I moved alone:—
Yet never found I one not false to me,
Hard hearts, and cold, like weights of icy stone
Which crushed and withered mine, that could not be
Aught° but a lifeless clog, until revived by thee. *anything*

---

1 Wisdom. Shelley refers to the controversial philosophy of the Enlightenment, which, insofar as it tends toward materialist accounts of the physical world, seems to support the doctrine of atheism. The Enlightenment period is also associated with anti-monarchical and republican politics as well as with a nascent discourse of human rights, whose various applications included the notion of women's equality and a push for the abolition of the slave trade. Furthermore, key texts of the Enlightenment were often distributed by publishing houses that also sold sexually frank material, and some authors—most notably Denis Diderot (1713–84) and the Marquis de Sade (1740–1814)—mixed philosophy with pornography on a spectrum from the coy and playful to the explicit.

2 Love becomes a "snare" when the ties of marriage are used to bind two people monogamously together for all time. Shelley was still married to Harriet Westbrook when he left England with Mary in 1814. Mary's note on the poem (Appendix G1) suggests that Harriet's recent suicide, in December 1816, was on Shelley's mind during his composition of *Laon and Cythna*.

7.

Thou Friend, whose presence on my wintry heart
Fell, like bright Spring upon some herbless plain;
How beautiful and calm and free thou wert
In thy young wisdom, when the mortal chain
Of Custom thou didst burst and rend in twain,[1]
And walked as free as light the clouds among,
Which many an envious slave[2] then breathed in vain
From his dim dungeon, and my spirit sprung
To meet thee from the woes which had begirt° it long! *surrounded*

8.

No more alone through the world's wilderness,
Although I trod the paths of high intent,
I journeyed now: no more companionless,
Where solitude is like despair, I went.—
There is the wisdom of a stern content
When Poverty can blight the just and good,
When Infamy dares mock the innocent,
And cherished friends turn with the multitude
To trample: this was ours, and we unshaken stood!

9.

Now has descended a serener hour,
And with inconstant fortune, friends return;
Though suffering leaves the knowledge and the power
Which says:—Let scorn be not repaid with scorn.
And from thy side two gentle babes are born[3]
To fill our home with smiles, and thus are we
Most fortunate beneath life's beaming morn;
And these delights, and thou, have been to me
The parents of the Song I consecrate to thee.

10.

Is it, that now my inexperienced fingers
But strike the prelude of a loftier strain?
Or, must the lyre on which my spirit lingers
Soon pause in silence, ne'er to sound again,

---

1 A reference to Mary's decision to leave England with the married Shelley on 28 July 1814.

2 Here and throughout his work, Shelley uses the language of slavery to describe ideological as well as literal enslavement.

3 The Shelleys' children William "Wilmouse" (1816–19) and Clara Everina (1817–18).

Tho' it might shake the Anarch Custom's[1] reign,
And charm the minds of men to Truth's own sway,
Holier than was Amphion's?[2] I would fain
Reply in hope—but I am worn away,
And Death and Love are yet contending for their prey.

11.

And what art thou? I know, but dare not speak:
Time may interpret to his silent years.
Yet in the paleness of thy thoughtful cheek,
And in the light thine ample forehead wears,
And in thy sweetest smiles, and in thy tears,
And in thy gentle speech, a prophecy
Is whispered, to subdue my fondest[3] fears:
And, thro' thine eyes, even in thy soul I see
A lamp of vestal fire[4] burning internally.

12.

They say that thou wert lovely from thy birth,
Of glorious parents,[5] thou aspiring Child.
I wonder not—for One then left this earth[6]
Whose life was like a setting planet mild,
Which clothed thee in the radiance undefiled
Of its departing glory; still her fame
Shines on thee, thro' the tempests dark and wild
Which shake these latter days; and thou canst claim
The shelter, from thy Sire, of an immortal name.[7]

---

1 "Custom" or social convention is, ironically, a lawless "Anarch" because it perverts the laws of nature, including the principle of universal love.

2 Amphion was the son of Zeus and the nymph Antiope, and the husband of Niobe. Pliny (first century CE) credits Amphion with being the inventor of music, and in his *Ars Amatoria* (1 CE) Ovid describes Amphion and his brother Zethus building the walls of Thebes with stones pulled together, as if by magnetic attraction, by the power of Amphion's lyre.

3 Most foolish or weak-minded; alternatively, clung to or cultivated.

4 In ancient Rome, virgin priestesses known as the Vestals kept constant watch over the sacred fire of Vesta, goddess of the hearth. Shelley frequently characterizes his wife as virginal, even asexual, in his poetry; see especially *Epipsychidion* (1821).

5 Godwin and Mary Wollstonecraft (1759–97), political philosopher and novelist.

6 Wollstonecraft died, probably from sepsis, eleven days after giving birth to Mary.

7 On uneasy terms with her father since her involvement with Shelley, Mary can claim the shelter of Godwin's name if not of his household.

13.

One voice[1] came forth from many a mighty spirit,
Which was the echo of three thousand years;
And the tumultuous world stood mute to hear it,
As some lone man who in a desart° hears *desert, wasteland*
The music of his home:—unwonted fears
Fell on the pale oppressors of our race,
And Faith, and Custom, and low-thoughted cares,
Like thunder-stricken dragons, for a space
Left the torn human heart, their food and dwelling-place.

14.

Truth's deathless voice pauses among mankind!
If there must be no response to my cry—
If men must rise and stamp with fury blind
On his pure name who loves them,—thou and I,
Sweet Friend! can look from our tranquillity
Like lamps into the world's tempestuous night,—
Two tranquil stars,[2] while clouds are passing by
Which wrap them from the foundering seaman's sight,
That burn from year to year with unextinguished light.

1 I.e., Godwin's.

2 Shelley introduces the motif of twinning or doubling that will recur throughout the poem. Like Laon and Cythna, Percy and Mary have a relationship that may serve as a model for all other human beings to follow, on a larger scale.

Laon and Cythna.

ΟΣΑΙΣ ΔΕ ΒΡΟΤΟΝ ΕΘΝΟΣ ΑΓΛΑΙΑΙΣ ‘ΑΠΤΟΜΕΣΘΑ,
ΠΕΡΑΙΝΕΙ ΠΡΟΣ ‘ΕΣΧΑΤΟΝ
ΠΛΟΟΝ· ΝΑΥΣΙ Δ’ ΟΥΤΕ ΠΕΖΟΣ ΙΩΝ ΚΕΝ ‘ΕΥΡΟΙΣ
’ΕΣ ‘ΥΠΕΡΒΟΡΕΩΝ ’ΑΓΩΝΑ ΘΑΥΜΑΤΑΝ ‘ΟΔΟΝ.

PIND. *Pyth.* X.[1]

1 These lines from the Greek poet Pindar (c. 518–c. 438 BCE) describe the achievements of the father of Hippokleas, who won the boys’ dialous (a type of stadium race) in the Pythian games held in 498 BCE. Anthony Verity renders the lines from *Pythian* 10 thus:

He will never climb the brazen heaven,
but of all the glories which our mortal race may reach
his voyage takes him to the farthest region.

But neither on foot nor by sea could you discover
the fabulous way leading to the gathering of the Hyperboreans. (26–30)

In Greek myth, the Hyperboreans are people who live (as their name suggests) beyond the “Boreas,” or the North Wind.

Canto First.

I.

WHEN the last hope of trampled France had failed
Like a brief dream of unremaining glory,
From visions of despair I rose, and scaled
The peak of an aërial° promontory, *high*
Whose caverned base with the vext° surge *agitated*
was hoary;° *white or grey*
And saw the golden dawn break forth, and waken
Each cloud and every wave:—but transitory
The calm: for sudden, the firm earth was shaken,
As if by the last wreck[1] its frame[2] were overtaken.

II.

So as I stood, one blast of muttering thunder
Burst in far peals along the waveless deep,
When, gathering fast, around, above and under,
Long trains of tremulous mist began to creep,
Until their complicating lines did steep
The orient° sun in shadow:—not a sound *eastern, in the east*
Was heard; one horrible repose did keep
The forests and the floods, and all around
Darkness more dread than night was poured upon the ground.

III.

Hark! 'tis the rushing of a wind that sweeps
Earth and the ocean. See! the lightnings yawn,
Deluging Heaven with fire, and the lashed deeps
Glitter and boil beneath: it rages on,
One mighty stream, whirlwind and waves upthrown,
Lightning, and hail, and darkness eddying[3] by.
There is a pause—the sea-birds, that were gone
Into their caves to shriek, come forth, to spy
What calm has fall'n on earth, what light is in the sky.

IV.

For, where the irresistible storm had cloven° *split open*
That fearful darkness, the blue sky was seen

---

1 Latest disaster, i.e., the failure of the French Revolution and the restoration of the Bourbon monarchy in 1814.

2 Scaffold, structure; more generally, body.

3 Moving, as a liquid, rapidly in a circle and against some stronger current.

Fretted[1] with many a fair cloud interwoven
Most delicately, and the ocean green,
Beneath that opening spot of blue serene,
Quivered like burning emerald: calm was spread
On all below; but far on high, between
Earth and the upper air, the vast clouds fled,
Countless and swift as leaves on autumn's tempest shed.[2]

V.

For ever, as the war became more fierce
Between the whirlwinds and the rack[3] on high,
That spot grew more serene; blue light did pierce
The woof[4] of those white clouds, which seemed to lie
Far, deep and motionless; while thro' the sky
The pallid semicircle of the moon
Past on, in slow and moving majesty;
Its upper horn arrayed in mists, which soon
But slowly fled, like dew beneath the beams of noon.

VI.

I could not choose but gaze; a fascination
Dwelt in that moon, and sky, and clouds, which drew
My fancy thither, and in expectation
Of what I knew not, I remained:—the hue
Of the white moon, amid that heaven so blue,
Suddenly stained with shadow did appear;
A speck, a cloud, a shape, approaching grew,
Like a great ship in the sun's sinking sphere
Beheld afar at sea, and swift it came anear.

VII.

Even like a bark,° which from a chasm of mountains, *boat*
Dark, vast, and overhanging, on a river
Which there collects the strength of all its fountains,
Comes forth, whilst with the speed its frame doth quiver,
Sails, oars, and stream, tending to one endeavour;
So, from that chasm of light a winged Form

---

1 Carved in a decorative pattern.

2 This image of autumn leaves, accompanied by a comment on their innumerability, is a common epic trope. It occurs memorably in Book 6 of Virgil's *Aeneid* (written 29–19 BCE), in the third canto of Dante's *Inferno* (c. 1314), and in the first book of *Paradise Lost*.

3 A clearing-up, especially of clouds; alternatively, chaos, disorder.

4 The threads that cross from side to side in a weaving; the word may also signify fabric more generally.

On all the winds of heaven approaching ever
Floated, dilating as it came: the storm
Pursued it with fierce blasts, and lightnings swift and warm.

VIII.

A course precipitous, of dizzy speed,
Suspending thought and breath; a monstrous sight!
For in the air do I behold indeed
An Eagle and a Serpent wreathed in fight:[1]—
And now, relaxing its impetuous flight,
Before the aërial rock on which I stood,
The Eagle, hovering, wheeled to left and right,
And hung with lingering wings over the flood,
And startled with its yells the wide air's solitude.

IX.

A shaft of light upon its wings descended,
And every golden feather gleamed therein—
Feather and scale inextricably blended.
The Serpent's mailed° and many-colored skin *armored*
Shone thro' the plumes its coils were twined within
By many a swollen and knotted fold, and high
And far, the neck receding lithe and thin,
Sustained a crested head, which warily
Shifted and glanced before the Eagle's stedfast eye.

X.

Around, around, in ceaseless circles wheeling
With clang of wings and scream, the Eagle sailed
Incessantly—sometimes on high concealing
Its lessening orbs,[2] sometimes as if it failed,
Drooped thro' the air; and still it shrieked and wailed,
And casting back its eager head, with beak
And talon unremittingly assailed
The wreathed Serpent, who did ever seek
Upon his enemy's heart a mortal wound to wreak.° *inflict*

---

1 The eagle is the symbol of Zeus or Jupiter, and Shelley associates it here and elsewhere with political tyranny. By contrast, Shelley uses the snake, symbol of evil in the Judeo-Christian tradition, to represent mankind's struggle against despotism. Meanwhile, the circular shape of the snake suggests continuity and renewal, as the Woman explains below.

2 I.e., the circular motion of its flight, whose course appears smaller ("lessens") as the eagle gets farther away from the speaker.

XI.

What life[,] what power, was kindled and arose
Within the sphere of that appalling fray!
For, from the encounter of those wond'rous foes,
A vapour like the sea's suspended spray
Hung gathered: in the void air, far away,
Floated the shattered plumes; bright scales did leap,
Where'er the Eagle's talons made their way,
Like sparks into the darkness;—as they sweep,
Blood stains the snowy foam of the tumultuous deep.

XII.

Swift chances in that combat—many a check,
And many a change, a dark and wild turmoil;
Sometimes the Snake around his enemy's neck
Locked in stiff rings his adamantine° coil, *unbreakable, unyielding*
Until the Eagle, faint with pain and toil,
Remitted° his strong flight, and near the sea *slackened, slowed down*
Languidly fluttered, hopeless so to foil
His adversary, who then reared on high
His red and burning crest, radiant with victory.

XIII.

Then on the white edge of the bursting surge,
Where they had sunk together, would the Snake
Relax his suffocating grasp, and scourge° *whip*
The wind with his wild writhings; for to break
That chain of torment, the vast bird would shake
The strength of his unconquerable wings
As in despair, and with his sinewy neck,
Dissolve in sudden shock those linked rings,
Then soar—as swift as smoke from a volcano springs.

XIV.

Wile° baffled wile, and strength encountered strength, *strategy*
Thus long, but unprevailing:—the event
Of that portentous fight appeared at length:
Until the lamp of day was almost spent
It had endured, when lifeless, stark, and rent,° *torn*
Hung high that mighty Serpent, and at last
Fell to the sea, while o'er the continent,
With clang of wings and scream the Eagle past,
Heavily borne away on the exhausted blast.

XV.

And with it fled the tempest, so that ocean
And earth and sky shone through the atmosphere—
Only, 'twas strange to see the red commotion
Of waves like mountains o'er the sinking sphere
Of sun-set sweep, and their fierce roar to hear
Amid the calm: down the steep path I wound
To the sea-shore—the evening was most clear
And beautiful, and there the sea I found
Calm as a cradled child in dreamless slumber bound.

XVI.

There was a Woman,[1] beautiful as morning,
Sitting beneath the rocks, upon the sand
Of the waste° sea—fair as one flower adorning *empty*
An icy wilderness[2]—each delicate hand
Lay crossed upon her bosom, and the band
Of her dark hair had fall'n, and so she sate[3]
Looking upon the waves; on the bare strand
Upon the sea-mark[4] a small boat did wait,
Fair as herself, like Love by Hope left desolate.

XVII.

It seemed that this fair Shape had looked upon
That unimaginable fight, and now
That her sweet eyes were weary of the sun,[5]
As brightly it illustrated her woe;
For in the tears which silently to flow
Paused not, its lustre hung: she, watching aye° *still*
The foam-wreaths which the faint tide wove below
Upon the spangled sands, groaned heavily,
And after every groan looked up over the sea.

---

1 Some details of the Woman's story suggest that her character is at least partially based on Mary Wollstonecraft; see below, p. 71, note 2; and p. 74, note 1.

2 Cf. Wordsworth's "She Dwelt among the Untrodden Ways," published in the 1800 edition of *Lyrical Ballads*.

3 Sat. This stanza is reminiscent of Shakespeare, *Twelfth Night*, 2.4.114–15.

4 The highest point on the shore reached by the tide.

5 Cf. Shakespeare, *Macbeth*, 5.5.47–48: "I 'gin to be a-weary of the sun, / And wish the estate o' the world were now undone."

XVIII.

And when she saw the wounded Serpent make
His path between the waves, her lips grew pale,
Parted, and quivered; the tears ceased to break
From her immovable eyes; no voice of wail
Escaped her; but she rose, and on the gale
Loosening her star-bright robe and shadowy hair
Poured forth her voice; the caverns of the vale° *valley*
That opened to the ocean, caught it there,
And filled with silver sounds the overflowing air.

XIX.

She spake in language whose strange melody
Might not belong to earth. I heard, alone,
What made its music more melodious be,
The pity and the love of every tone;
But to the Snake those accents sweet were known
His native tongue and hers;[1] nor did he beat
The hoar spray idly then, but winding on
Thro' the green shadows of the waves that meet
Near to the shore, did pause beside her snowy feet.

XX.

Then on the sands the Woman sate again,
And wept and clasped her hands, and, all between,
Renewed the unintelligible strain
Of her melodious voice and eloquent mien;° *appearance, manner*
And she unveiled her bosom, and the green
And glancing shadows of the sea did play
O'er its marmoreal[2] depth:—one moment seen,
For ere the next, the Serpent did obey
Her voice, and, coiled in rest, in her embrace it lay.

XXI.

Then she arose, and smiled on me with eyes
Serene yet sorrowing,[3] like that planet fair,
While yet the day-light lingereth in the skies,
Which cleaves with arrowy beams the dark-red air,

---

1 Corrected from "her's."

2 Made of or resembling marble.

3 In a note in a draft of this poem, Shelley writes "Demon Lover" beside these lines. The reference is to Samuel Taylor Coleridge's "Kubla Khan" (pub. 1816), which describes a "woman wailing for her demon lover!" (*Poetical Works* 16).

And said: To grieve is wise, but the despair
Was weak and vain[1] which led thee here from sleep:[2]
This shalt thou know, and more, if thou dost dare
With me and with this Serpent, o'er the deep,
A voyage divine and strange, companionship to keep.

XXII.

Her voice was like the wildest, saddest tone,
Yet sweet, of some loved voice heard long ago.
I wept. Shall this fair woman all alone,
Over the sea with that fierce Serpent go?
His head is on her heart, and who can know
How soon he may devour his feeble prey?—
Such were my thoughts, when the tide 'gan to flow;
And that strange boat, like the moon's shade did sway
Amid reflected stars that in the waters lay.

XXIII.

A boat of rare device,[3] which had no sail
But its own curvèd prow of thin moonstone,
Wrought like a web of texture fine and frail,
To catch those gentlest winds which are not known
To breathe, but by the steady speed alone
With which it cleaves the sparkling sea; and now
We are embarked, the mountains hang and frown
Over the starry deep that gleams below
A vast and dim expanse, as o'er the waves we go.

XXIV.

And as we sailed, a strange and awful tale
That Woman told, like such mysterious dream
As makes the slumberer's cheek with wonder pale!
'Twas midnight, and around, a shoreless stream,
Wide ocean rolled, when that majestic theme
Shrined in her heart found utterance, and she bent
Her looks on mine; those eyes a kindling beam
Of love divine into my spirit sent,
And, ere her lips could move, made the air eloquent.

---

1 Devoid of value, pointless; alternatively, foolish; alternatively, excessively self-regarding.

2 Cf. Volney's "[I]f he who loves his fellow creatures be suffered to despair, what will become of nations?" *The Ruins, or a Survey of the Revolutions of Empires*, 126. See also Appendix F2.

3 Making or manufacture. Cf. "Kubla Khan": "It was a miracle of rare device, / A sunny pleasure-dome with caves of ice!" (Coleridge, *Poetical Works* 35–36).

XXV.[1]

Speak not to me, but hear! much shalt thou learn,
Much must remain unthought, and more untold,
In the dark Future's ever-flowing urn:
Know then, that from the depth of ages old,
Two Powers o'er mortal things dominion hold
Ruling the world with a divided lot,
Immortal, all pervading, manifold,
Twin Genii,° equal Gods—when life and thought *spirits, supernatural forces*
Sprang forth, they burst the womb of inessential Nought.[2]

XXVI.

The earliest dweller of the world alone,
Stood on the verge of chaos: Lo! afar
O'er the wide wild abyss two meteors shone,
Sprung from the depth of its tempestuous jar:
A blood red Comet and the Morning Star[3]
Mingling their beams in combat—as he stood,
All thoughts within his mind waged mutual war,
In dreadful sympathy—when to the flood
That fair Star fell, he turned and shed his brother's blood.[4]

XXVII.

Thus evil triumphed, and the Spirit of evil,
One Power of many shapes which none may know,

---

1 Stanzas xxv–xlvii record the Woman's speech.

2 Nothing. The worldview presented here is Manichaeism, which holds that good and evil are always battling one another for control over the universe, and that the outcome of the battle is by no means preordained. As a theology it is similar to and postdates Zoroastrianism, the subject of Thomas Love Peacock's unfinished *Ahrimanes*, which Peacock abandoned in 1816 (see Appendix F6). Similar themes are also treated in Byron's *Manfred* (1816–17).

3 "Morning Star" is a translation of the Hebrew word הֵילֵל or hêlêl, which the King James Bible renders as "Lucifer" in Isaiah 14:12 ("How art thou fallen from heaven, O Lucifer, son of the morning!"); the New American Standard Bible, among other editions, gives the more literal "How you have fallen from heaven, O star of the morning, son of the dawn!" In *Paradise Lost*, Milton characterizes Satan as "the Morning Star that ... with lies, / Drew after him the third part of Heav'ns Host" (5.708–10). Here the Morning Star appears alongside the Snake as another allegorical form taken by what the Woman describes below as the Spirit of Good. The blood-red Comet, along with the Eagle, is the Spirit of Evil, which Shelley associates in particular with political and military violence.

4 The Woman's account of the origins of humanity skips over the narrative of Adam and Eve—and with it, of original sin—and begins with an apparent allusion to the story of Cain, who murders his brother Abel in Genesis 4:8. Moreover, this crime, rather than being in any way precipitated by or associated with the Satanic figure of the Morning Star, is occasioned by his "fall" and the concomitant rise of the despotic Spirit of Evil.

One Shape of many names; the Fiend did revel
In victory, reigning o'er a world of woe,
For the new race of man went to and fro,
Famished and homeless, loathed and loathing, wild,
And hating good—for his immortal foe,
He changed from starry shape, beauteous and mild,
To a dire Snake, with man and beast unreconciled.

XXVIII.

The darkness lingering o'er the dawn of things,
Was Evil's breath and life: this made him strong
To soar aloft with overshadowing wings;
And the great Spirit of Good did creep among
The nations of mankind, and every tongue
Cursed, and blasphemed him as he past;[1] for none
Knew good from evil, tho' their names were hung
In mockery o'er the fane° where many a groan, *temple*
As King, and Lord, and God, the conquering Fiend did own.

XXIX.

The fiend, whose name was Legion;[2] Death, Decay,
Earthquake and Blight, and Want, and Madness pale,
Winged and wan diseases, an array
Numerous as leaves that strew the autumnal gale;[3]
Poison, a snake in flowers, beneath the veil
Of food and mirth, hiding his mortal[4] head;
And, without whom all these might nought avail,
Fear, Hatred, Faith, and Tyranny, who spread
Those subtle nets which snare the living and the dead.

XXX.

His spirit is their power, and they his slaves
In air, and light, and thought, and language dwell;

---

1 Here Shelley inverts the moral and symbolic logic of Genesis 3:14, where the serpent is characterized as the enemy of mankind: "And the Lord God said unto the serpent, Because thou hast done this, thou art cursed above all cattle, and above every beast of the field; upon thy belly shalt thou go, and dust shalt thou eat all the days of thy life." The description of the serpent as "creeping" echoes *Paradise Lost*, where Adam and Eve's transgression brings "forth whatever creeps the ground, / Insect or Worme" (7.475–76).

2 Cf. Mark 5:9: "And [Jesus] asked him, What is thy name? And he answered, saying, My name is Legion: for we are many."

3 Cf. p. 62, I.iv.36.

4 Deadly. Confusingly, here the image of the snake is aligned not with the Spirit of Good but with his enemy, the Fiend.

And keep their state from palaces to graves,
In all resorts° of men—invisible, *dwelling-places*
But, when in ebon[1] mirror, Nightmare fell[2]
To tyrant or impostor bids them rise,
Black winged demon forms—whom, from the hell,
His reign and dwelling beneath nether° skies, *underground*
He loosens to their dark and blasting ministries.

XXXI.

In the world's youth his empire was as firm
As its foundations—soon the Spirit of Good,
Tho' in the likeness of a loathsome worm,[3]
Sprang from the billows of the formless flood,
Which shrank and fled; and with that fiend of blood
Renewed the doubtful° war—thrones then first shook, *of uncertain outcome*
And earth's immense and trampled multitude,
In hope on their own powers began to look,
And Fear, the demon pale, his sanguine shrine forsook.

XXXII.

Then Greece arose, and to its bards and sages,
In dream, the golden-pinioned Genii came,
Even where they slept amid the night of ages,
Steeping their hearts in the divinest flame,
Which thy breath kindled, Power of holiest name![4]
And oft in cycles since, when darkness gave
New weapons to thy foe, their sunlike fame
Upon the combat shone—a light to save,
Like Paradise spread forth beyond the shadowy grave.

XXXIII.

Such is this conflict—when mankind doth strive
With its oppressors in a strife of blood,
Or when free thoughts, like lightnings, are alive;
And in each bosom of the multitude
Justice and truth, with custom's hydra brood,[5]
Wage silent war;—when priests and kings dissemble
In smiles or frowns their fierce disquietude,

---

1 Ebony, black.

2 Terrible, ruthless.

3 See above, p. 69, note 4.

4 The Spirit of Good is credited with having inspired classical Greek philosophy.

5 The hydra is a mythological snake-like animal with multiple heads. When one head is cut off, two—the hydra's "brood" or offspring—immediately grow back in its place.

When round pure hearts, a host of hopes assemble,
The Snake and Eagle meet—the world's foundations tremble!

XXXIV.

Thou hast beheld that fight—when to thy home
Thou dost return, steep not its hearth in tears;
Tho' thou may'st hear that earth is now become
The tyrant's garbage,[1] which to his compeers,° *associates*
The vile reward of their dishonored years,
He will dividing give.—The victor Fiend
Omnipotent of yore,° now quails, and fears *in the past*
His triumph dearly won, which soon will lend
An impulse swift and sure to his approaching end.

XXXV.

List,° stranger list, mine is an human form, *listen*
Like that thou wearest—touch me—shrink not now!
My hand thou feel'st is not a ghost's, but warm
With human blood.—'Twas was many years ago,
Since first my thirsting soul aspired to know
The secrets of this wondrous world, when deep
My heart was pierced with sympathy, for woe
Which could not be mine own—and thought did keep
In dream, unnatural watch beside an infant's sleep.

XXXVI.

Woe could not be mine own, since far from men
I dwelt, a free and happy orphan child,
By the sea-shore, in a deep mountain glen;
And near the waves, and thro' the forests wild,
I roamed, to storm and darkness reconciled:[2]
For I was calm while tempest shook the sky:
But when the breathless heavens in beauty smiled,
I wept, sweet tears, yet too tumultuously
For peace, and clasped my hands aloft in ecstasy.[3]

---

1 Entrails or offal; foul or worthless matter; filth.

2 Wollstonecraft spent some of her childhood and adolescence in Yorkshire and Wales. This description may also draw on Mary Shelley's experiences in Scotland, where she was sent to live at age fifteen, apparently to ease tensions in the Godwin household between herself and her stepmother, Mary Jane Clairmont.

3 Cf. Shelley's "Hymn to Intellectual Beauty" (1817), in which a stanza describing his childhood fascination with ghosts, dark woods, caves, and ruins ends with the line, "I shrieked, and clasped my hands in extacy!" (60).

XXXVII.

These were forebodings of my fate—before
A woman's heart beat in my virgin breast,
It had been nurtured in divinest lore:
A dying poet gave me books, and blest
With wild but holy talk the sweet unrest
In which I watched him as he died away—
A youth with hoary hair—a fleeting guest
Of our lone mountains—and this lore did sway
My spirit like a storm, contending there alway.

XXXVIII.

Thus the dark tale which history doth unfold,
I knew, but not, methinks, as others know,
For they weep not; and Wisdom had unrolled
The clouds which hide the gulf of mortal woe:
To few can she that warning vision shew,° *show*
For I loved all things with intense devotion;
So that when Hope's deep source in fullest flow,
Like earthquake did uplift the stagnant ocean
Of human thoughts—mine shook beneath the wide emotion.

XXXIX.

When first the living blood thro' all these veins
Kindled a thought in sense, great France sprang forth,
And seized, as if to break, the ponderous chains
Which bind in woe the nations of the earth.
I saw, and started from my cottage hearth;
And to the clouds and waves in tameless gladness,
Shrieked, till they caught immeasurable mirth—
And laughed in light and music: soon, sweet madness
Was poured upon my heart, a soft and thrilling sadness.

XL.

Deep slumber fell on me:—my dreams were fire,
Soft and delightful thoughts did rest and hover
Like shadows o'er my brain; and strange desire,
The tempest of a passion, raging over
My tranquil soul, its depths with light did cover,
Which past; and calm, and darkness, sweeter far,
Came—then I loved; but not a human lover!
For when I rose from sleep, the Morning Star
Shone thro' the woodbine wreaths which round my casement° were. *window*

XLI.

'Twas like an eye which seemed to smile on me.
I watched, till by the sun made pale, it sank
Under the billows of the heaving sea;
But from its beams deep love my spirit drank,
And to my brain the boundless world now shrank
Into one thought—one image—yes, for ever!
Even like the dayspring,° poured on vapors dank, *dawn*
The beams of that one Star did shoot and quiver
Thro' my benighted[1] mind—and were extinguished never.

XLII.

The day past thus: at night, methought in dream
A shape of speechless beauty did appear:
It stood like light on a careering° stream *swiftly-moving, hurtling*
Of golden clouds which shook the atmosphere;
A winged youth, his radiant brow did wear
The Morning Star: a wild dissolving bliss
Over my frame he breathed, approaching near,
And bent his eyes of kindling tenderness
Near mine, and on my lips impressed a lingering kiss.

XLIII.

And said: a Spirit loves thee, mortal maiden,
How wilt thou prove thy worth?[2] Then joy and sleep
Together fled, my soul was deeply laden,
And to the shore I went to muse and weep;
But as I moved, over my heart did creep
A joy less soft, but more profound and strong
Than my sweet dream; and it forbade to keep
The path of the sea-shore; that Spirit's tongue
Seemed whispering in my heart, and bore my steps along.

---

1 Ignorant, unenlightened.

2 The story of the Woman and the Morning Star resembles Apuleius' rendering (in his *Metamorphoses,* better known as *The Golden Ass* [second century CE]) of the tale of Cupid and Psyche, another human who must prove she is worthy of divine love. Whereas Psyche's journey leads her ultimately back to Cupid, the Woman's journey takes her into the world of men, and into a life of political action and engagement. The scene may also be compared to that of the Annunciation as described in Luke 1:28.

XLIV.

How, to that vast and peopled city[1] led,
Which was a field of holy warfare then,
I walked among the dying and the dead,
And shared in fearless deeds with evil men.
Calm as an angel in the dragon's den—
How I braved death for liberty and truth,
And spurned at[2] peace, and power, and fame; and when
Those hopes had lost the glory of their youth,
How sadly I returned—might move the hearer's ruth:° *compassion*

XLV.

Warm tears throng fast! the tale may not be said—
Know then, that when this grief had been subdued,
I was not left, like others, cold and dead;
The Spirit whom I loved in solitude
Sustained his child: the tempest-shaken wood,
The waves, the fountains, and the hush of night—
These were his voice, and well I understood
His smile divine, when the calm sea was bright
With silent stars, and Heaven was breathless with delight.

XLVI.

In lonely glens, amid the roar of rivers,
When the dim nights were moonless, have I known
Joys which no tongue can tell; my pale lip quivers
When thought revisits them:—know thou alone,
That after many wondrous years were flown,
I was awakened by a shriek of woe;
And over me a mystic robe was thrown,
By viewless hands, and a bright Star did glow
Before my steps—the Snake then met his mortal foe.

XLVII.

Thou fearest not then the Serpent on thy heart?[3]
Fear it! she said, with brief and passionate cry,
And spake no more: that silence made me start—

1 I.e., Paris. Wollstonecraft lived in and around Paris between 1792 and 1794, during the worst of the Terror. After the breakdown of her relationship with the American writer and businessman Gilbert Imlay (1754–1828), with whom she had a daughter, Fanny (1794–1816), she returned to London in 1795.

2 Rejected, treated with contempt.

3 Here the narrator addresses the Woman; her reply appears in the following line.

I looked, and we were sailing pleasantly,
Swift as a cloud between the sea and sky,
Beneath the rising moon seen far away;
Mountains of ice, like sapphire, piled on high
Hemming the horizon round, in silence lay
On the still waters—these we did approach always.[1]

XLVIII.

And swift and swifter grew the vessel's motion,
So that a dizzy trance fell on my brain—
Wild music woke me: we had passed the ocean
Which girds the pole, Nature's remotest reign—
And we glode° fast o'er a pellucid° plain *glided; clear, translucent*
Of waters, azure with the noon-tide day.
Æthereal mountains shone around—a Fane
Stood in the midst, girt by green isles which lay
On the blue sunny deep, resplendent far away.

XLIX.

It was a Temple, such as mortal hand
Has never built, nor ecstasy, nor dream,
Reared in the cities of inchanted land:
'Twas likest Heaven, ere yet day's purple stream
Ebbs o'er the western forest, while the gleam
Of the unrisen moon among the clouds
Is gathering—when with many a golden beam
The thronging constellations rush in crowds,
Paving with fire the sky and the marmoreal floods.

L.

Like what may be conceived of this vast dome,
When from the depths which thought can seldom pierce
Genius[2] beholds it rise, his native home,
Girt by the desarts of the Universe.
Yet, nor in painting's light, or mightier verse,
Or sculpture's marble language can invest[3]
That shape to mortal sense—such glooms immerse
That incommunicable sight, and rest
Upon the labouring brain and overburthened breast.

---

1 Archaic use of "always," which here means "for a long time" or perhaps "without interruption."

2 Rational thought, the human faculty capable of intuiting the existence of things beyond sense experience.

3 Clothe, i.e., so as to make visible an otherwise invisible "shape."

LI.

Winding among the lawny[1] islands fair,
Whose blosmy° forests starred the shadowy deep, *blossomy, blooming*
The wingless boat paused where an ivory stair
Its fretwork in the crystal sea did steep,
Encircling that vast Fane's aërial heap:
We disembarked, and thro' a portal wide
We past—whose roof of moonstone carved, did keep
A glimmering o'er the forms on every side,
Sculptures like life and thought; immoveable, deep-eyed.

LII.

We came to a vast hall, whose glorious roof
Was diamond, which had drunk the lightning's sheen
In darkness, and now poured it thro' the woof
Of spell-inwoven° clouds hung there to screen *woven together, linked*
Its blinding splendor—thro' such veil was seen
That work of subtlest power, divine and rare;
Orb above orb, with starry shapes between,
And horned moons, and meteors strange and fair,
On night-black columns poised—one hollow hemisphere!

LIII.

Ten thousand columns in that quivering light
Distinct—between whose shafts wound far away
The long and labyrinthine[2] aisles—more bright
With their own radiance than the Heaven of Day;
And on the jasper walls around, there lay
Paintings, the poesy of mightiest thought,
Which did the Spirit's history display;
A tale of passionate change, divinely taught,
Which, in their winged dance, unconscious Genii wrought.

LIV.

Beneath, there sate on many a sapphire throne,
The Great, who had departed from mankind,
A mighty Senate;—some, whose white hair shone
Like mountain snow, mild, beautiful, and blind.[3]
Some, female forms, whose gestures beamed with mind;

---

1 Covered with grass or turf.

2 Maze-like, full of many twists and turns.

3 Opaque, so thick as to be impossible to see through.

And ardent youths, and children bright and fair;
And some had lyres whose strings were intertwined
With pale and clinging flames, which ever there
Waked faint yet thrilling sounds that pierced the crystal air.

LV.

One seat was vacant in the midst, a throne,
Reared on a pyramid like sculptured flame,
Distinct with circling steps which rested on
Their own deep fire—soon as the Woman came
Into that hall, she shrieked the Spirit's name
And fell; and vanished slowly from the sight.
Darkness arose from her dissolving frame,
Which gathering, filled that dome of woven light,
Blotting [its][1] sphered stars with supernatural night.

LVI.

Then first, two glittering lights were seen to glide
In circles on the amethystine[2] floor,
Small serpent eyes trailing from side to side,
Like meteors on a river's grassy shore,
They round each other rolled, dilating more
And more—then rose, commingling into one,
One clear and mighty planet hanging o'er
A cloud of deepest shadow, which was thrown
Athwart the glowing steps and the crystàlline throne.

LVII.

The cloud which rested on that cone of flame
Was cloven; beneath the planet sate a Form,
Fairer than tongue can speak or thought may frame,
The radiance of whose limbs rose-like and warm
Flowed forth, and did with softest light inform
The shadowy dome, the sculptures, and the state
Of those assembled shapes—with clinging charm
Sinking upon their hearts and mine—He sate
Majestic, yet most mild—calm, yet compassionate.

1 Corrected from "it's."

2 Made of amethyst, a violet-colored quartz.

LVIII.

Wonder and joy a passing faintness threw
Over my brow—a hand supported me,
Whose touch was magic strength: an eye of blue
Looked into mine, like moonlight, soothingly;
And a voice said—Thou must a listener be
This day—two mighty Spirits[1] now return,
Like birds of calm, from the world's raging sea,
They pour fresh light from Hope's immortal urn;
A tale of human power—despair not—list and learn!

LIX.

I looked, and lo! one stood forth eloquently,
His eyes were dark and deep, and the clear brow
Which shadowed them was like the morning sky,
The cloudless Heaven of Spring, when in their flow
Thro' the bright air, the soft winds as they blow
Wake the green world—his gestures did obey
The oracular° mind that made his features glow, *far-seeing, prophetic*
And where his curved lips half open lay,
Passion's divinest stream had made impetuous way.

LX.

Beneath the darkness of his outspread hair
He stood thus beautiful: but there was One
Who sate beside him like his shadow there,
And held his hand—far lovelier—she was known
To be thus fair, by the few lines alone
Which thro' her floating locks and gathered cloke,° *cloak*
Glances of soul-dissolving glory, shone:—
None else beheld her eyes—in him they woke
Memories which found a tongue, as thus he silence broke.[2]

1 I.e., Laon and Cythna.

2 Laon ("he") now becomes the principal narrator of the remaining cantos.

Canto Second.

I.

THE star-light smile of children, the sweet looks
Of women, the fair breast from which I fed,
The murmur of the unreposing brooks,
And the green light which shifting overhead,
Some tangled bower of vines around me shed,
The shells on the sea-sand, and the wild flowers,
The lamp-light thro' the rafters cheerly° spread, *cheerily*
And on the twining flax—in life's young hours
These sights and sounds did nurse my spirits' folded powers.

II.

In Argolis,[1] beside the echoing sea,
Such impulses within my mortal frame
Arose, and they were dear to memory,
Like tokens of the dead:—but others came
Soon, in another shape: the wondrous fame
Of the past world, the vital words and deeds
Of minds whom neither time nor change can tame,
Traditions dark and old, whence evil creeds
Start forth, and whose dim shade a stream of poison feeds.

III.

I heard, as all have heard, the various[2] story
Of human life, and wept unwilling tears.
Feeble historians of its shame and glory,
False disputants on all its hopes and fears,
Victims who worshipped ruin,—chroniclers
Of daily scorn, and slaves who loathed their state
Yet flattering power had given its ministers
A throne of judgment in the grave:—'twas fate,
That among such as these my youth should seek its mate.

IV.

The land in which I lived, by a fell bane[3]
Was withered up. Tyrants dwelt side by side,

---

1 A region in Greece on the eastern part of the Peloponnese.

2 Variable in a negative sense; unstable.

3 A terrible misery. Laon presumably refers to the presence of the Ottoman Empire in Greece, which was subject to violent imperial incursions from the fifteenth century until the War of Greek Independence officially ended in 1830.

And stabled in our homes,—until the chain
Stifled the captive's cry, and to abide° *endure, passively accept*
That blasting curse men had no shame—all vied
In evil, slave and despot; fear with lust,
Strange fellowship through mutual hate had tied,
Like two dark serpents tangled in the dust,
Which on the paths of men their mingling poison thrust.[1]

V.

Earth, our bright home, its mountains and its waters,
And the æthereal shapes which are suspended
Over its green expanse, and those fair daughters,
The clouds, of Sun and Ocean, who have blended
The colors of the air since first extended
It cradled the young world, none wandered forth
To see or feel: a darkness had descended
On every heart: the light which shews its worth
Must among gentle thoughts and fearless take its birth.

VI.

This vital world, this home of happy spirits,
Was as a dungeon to my blasted kind,
All that despair from murdered hope inherits
They sought, and in their helpless misery blind,
A deeper prison and heavier chains did find,
And stronger tyrants:[2]—a dark gulph° before, *gulf, chasm*
The realm of a stern Ruler, yawned; behind,
Terror and Time conflicting drove, and bore
On their tempestuous flood the shrieking wretch from shore.

VII.

Out of that Ocean's wrecks had Guilt and Woe
Framed a dark dwelling for their homeless thought,
And, starting at the ghosts which to and fro
Glide o'er its dim and gloomy strand, had brought
The worship thence which they each other taught.
Well might men loathe their life, well might they turn
Even to the ills again from which they sought

1 See the opening lines of Byron's *The Giaour* (Appendix F5).

2 Cf. Coleridge's "France: An Ode" (1798), where the "Sensual and the Dark rebel in vain," for while they may "burst their manacles [they] wear the name / Of Freedom, graven on a heavier chain" (*Poetical Works* 85, 87–88). Laon's "blasted kind" have not rebelled: it is their psychological "misery" and despair that weigh more heavily on them than their own enslavement.

Such refuge after death!—well might they learn
To gaze on this fair world with hopeless unconcern![1]

VIII.

For they all pined in bondage: body and soul,
Tyrant and slave, victim and torturer, bent
Before one Power, to which supreme controul
Over their will by their own weakness lent,
Made all its many names omnipotent;[2]
All symbols of things evil, all divine;
And hymns of blood or mockery, which rent
The air from all its fanes, did intertwine
Imposture's impious toils round each discordant shrine.

IX.

I heard as all have heard, life's various story,
And in no careless heart transcribed the tale;
But, from the sneers of men who had grown hoary
In shame and scorn, from groans of crowds made pale
By famine, from a mother's desolate wail
O'er her polluted[3] child, from innocent blood
Poured on the earth, and brows anxious and pale
With the heart's warfare; did I gather food
To feed my many thoughts: a tameless° multitude! *untameable*

X.

I wandered thro' the wrecks of days departed
Far by the desolated shore,[4] when even
O'er the still sea and jagged islets darted
The light of moonrise; in the northern Heaven,
Among the clouds near the horizon driven,
The mountains lay beneath one[5] planet pale;
Around me, broken tombs and columns riven° *ripped, broken*
Looked vast in twilight, and the sorrowing gale
Waked in those ruins gray its everlasting wail!

---

1 The Ottoman occupation brings not only slavery to the Greek people, but also religion, which teaches people to look forward to life in the next world and discourages them from confronting injustice in this one.

2 Shelley does not distinguish between religions but sees them united in a belief in "one Power" that goes by "many names."

3 Defiled, especially with reference to sexual violence.

4 Cf. Volney 2–3.

5 Originally "our"; corrected from Shelley's list of errata

XI.

I knew not who had framed these wonders then,
Nor, had I heard the story of their deeds;
But dwellings of a race of mightier men,[1]
And monuments of less ungentle creeds
Tell their own tale to him who wisely heeds
The language which they speak; and now, to me,
The moonlight making pale the blooming weeds,
The bright stars shining in the breathless sea,
Interpreted those scrolls of mortal mystery.

XII.

Such man has been, and such may yet become!
Aye, wiser, greater, gentler, even than they
Who on the fragments of yon shattered dome
Have stamped the sign of power—I felt the sway
Of the vast stream of ages bear away
My floating thoughts—my heart beat loud and fast—
Even as a storm let loose beneath the ray
Of the still moon, my spirit onward passed
Beneath truth's steady beams upon its tumult cast.

XIII.

It shall be thus no more! too long, too long,
Sons of the glorious dead, have ye lain bound
In darkness and in ruin.—Hope is strong,
Justice and Truth their winged child[2] have found—
Awake! arise! until the mighty sound
Of your career[3] shall scatter in its gust
The thrones of the oppressor, and the ground
Hide the last altar's unregarded dust,
Whose Idol has so long betrayed your impious trust.

XIV.

It must be so—I will arise and waken
The multitude, and like a sulphurous hill,° *volcano*
Which on a sudden° from its snows has shaken *all of a sudden*
The swoon° of ages, it shall burst and fill *trance, stupor*
The world with cleansing fire; it must, it will—
It may not be restrained!—and who shall stand

---

1 I.e., the Ancient Greeks.

2 I.e., hope.

3 Rapid forward movement; alternatively, course of action.

Amid the rocking earthquake stedfast still,
But Laon?[1] on high Freedom's desart land
A tower whose marble walls the leagued storms withstand!

XV.

One summer night, in commune with the hope
Thus deeply fed, amid those ruins grey
I watched, beneath the dark sky's starry cope;° *cloak, canopy*
And ever from that hour upon me lay
The burthen° of this hope, and night or day, *burden*
In vision or in dream, clove° to my breast: *held closely*
Among mankind, or when gone far away
To the lone shores and mountains, 'twas a guest
Which followed where I fled, and watched when I did rest.

XVI.

These hopes found words thro' which my spirit sought
To weave a bondage of such sympathy,
As might create some response to the thought
Which ruled me now—and as the vapors lie
Bright in the out-spread morning's radiancy,
So were these thoughts invested with the light
Of language: and all bosoms made reply
On which its lustre streamed, whene'er it might
Thro' darkness wide and deep those tranced spirits smite.

XVII.

Yes, many an eye with dizzy tears was dim,
And oft I thought to clasp my own heart's brother,
When I could feel the listener's senses swim,
And hear his breath its own swift gaspings smother
Even as my words evoked them—and another,
And yet another, I did fondly deem,
Felt that we all were sons of one great mother;
And the cold truth such sad reverse did seem,
As to awake in grief from some delightful dream.

1 The male spirit, Laon, at last introduces himself by name. "Laon" is the genitive case of the Greek word *laos* (people), so his name literally means "of the people." Similarly, the creature that overthrows the tyrant Jupiter in Shelley's verse-drama *Prometheus Unbound* (1820) is named Demogorgon, or "people monster."

XVIII.

Yes, oft beside the ruined labyrinth
Which skirts the hoary caves of the green deep,
Did Laon and his friend[1] on one gray plinth,[2]
Round whose worn base the wild waves hiss and leap,
Resting at eve, a lofty converse keep:
And that this friend was false, may now be said
Calmly—that he like other men could weep
Tears which are lies, and could betray and spread
Snares for that guileless heart which for his own had bled.

XIX.

Then, had no great aim recompensed my sorrow,
I must have sought dark respite from its stress
In dreamless rest, in sleep that sees no morrow[3]—
For to tread life's dismaying wilderness
Without one smile to cheer, one voice to bless,
Amid the snares and scoffs of human kind,
Is hard—but I betrayed it not, nor less
With love that scorned return, sought to unbind
The interwoven clouds which make its wisdom blind.

XX.

With deathless minds, which leave where they have past
A path of light, my soul communion knew;
Till from that glorious intercourse, at last,
As from a mine of magic store, I drew
Words which were weapons;—round my heart there grew
The adamantine armor of their power,
And from my fancy wings of golden hue
Sprang forth—yet not alone from wisdom's tower,
A minister of truth, these plumes young Laon bore.

---

1 This friend may be based, at least partially, on Thomas Jefferson Hogg (1792–1862), who fell out with Shelley in 1811; like Laon and his companion, they were later reconciled. Laon does not elaborate here on the nature of his friend's faults, though the source of the conflict between Shelley and Hogg was apparently the latter's attempt to seduce Shelley's first wife Harriet.

2 A pedestal, especially at the base of a column.

3 I.e., had Laon not found a political cause toward which to direct himself, he might have committed suicide.

XXI.

I had a little sister, whose fair eyes[1]
Were lodestars° of delight, which drew me home — *beacons, guides*
When I might wander forth; nor did I prize
Aught human thing beneath Heaven's mighty dome
Beyond this child: so when sad hours were come,
And baffled hope like ice still clung to me,
Since kin were cold, and friends had now become
Heartless and false, I turned from all, to be,
Cythna,[2] the only source of tears and smiles to thee.

XXII.

What wert thou then? A child most infantine,° — *childlike, guileless*
Yet wandering far beyond that innocent age
In all but its sweet looks and mien divine;
Even then, methought, with the world's tyrant rage
A patient warfare thy young heart did wage,
When those soft eyes of scarcely conscious thought,
Some tale, or thine own fancies would engage
To overflow with tears, or converse fraught
With passion, o'er their depths its fleeting light had wrought.

XXIII.

She moved upon this earth a shape of brightness,
A power, that from its objects scarcely drew
One impulse of her being—in her lightness
Most like some radiant cloud of morning dew,
Which wanders thro' the waste air's pathless blue,
To nourish some far desart: she did seem
Beside me, gathering beauty as she grew,
Like the bright shade of some immortal dream
Which walks, when tempest sleeps, the wave of life's dark stream.

XXIV.

As mine own shadow was this child to me,
A second self, far dearer and more fair;
Which clothed in undissolving radiancy,

---

1 In *The Revolt of Islam* (hereafter *RoI*), this line is changed to read "An orphan with my parents lived, whose eyes [...]."

2 Shelley's draft shows that he considered naming his heroine Zia, the Arabic word for light, before settling on Cythna. In their notes to the poem, Reiman, Fraistat, and Crook give many possible sources for the name, including Cytherea, the birthplace of Aphrodite, Greek goddess of love and beauty. See *The Complete Poetry of Percy Bysshe Shelley* 603.

All those steep paths which languor and despair
Of human things, had made so dark and bare,
But which I trod alone—nor, till bereft
Of friends, and overcome by lonely care,
Knew I what solace for that loss was left,
Though by a bitter wound my trusting heart was cleft.

XXV.

Once she was dear, now she was all I had
To love in human life—this sister[1] sweet,
This child of twelve years old—so she was made
My sole associate, and her willing feet
Wandered with mine where earth and ocean meet,
Beyond the aërial mountains whose vast cells
The unreposing billows ever beat,
Thro' forests wide and old, and lawny dells° *valleys*
Where boughs of incense droop over the emerald wells.

XXVI.

And warm and light I felt her clasping hand
When twined in mine: she followed where I went,
Thro' the lone paths of our immortal land.
It had no waste, but some memorial lent
Which strung me to my toil[2]—some monument
Vital° with mind: then, Cythna by my side, *alive, animated*
Until the bright and beaming day were spent,
Would rest, with looks entreating to abide,
Too earnest and too sweet ever to be denied.

XXVII.

And soon I could not have refused her—thus
For ever, day and night, we two were ne'er
Parted, but when brief sleep divided us:
And when the pauses of the lulling air
Of noon beside the sea, had made a lair
For her soothed senses, in my arms she slept,
And I kept watch over her slumbers there,
While, as the shifting visions o'er her swept,
Amid her innocent rest by turns she smil'd and wept.

---

1 *RoI* has "playmate."

2 I.e., there is no part of Laon's homeland, even its "wastes" or empty places, that does not inspire him in his efforts to secure its liberty.

XXVIII.

And, in the murmur of her dreams was heard
Sometimes the name of Laon:—suddenly
She would arise, and, like the secret bird[1]
Whom sunset wakens, fill the shore and sky
With her sweet accents—a wild melody!
Hymns which my soul had woven to Freedom, strong
The source of passion whence they rose, to be;
Triumphant strains, which, like a spirit's tongue,
To the inchanted waves that child of glory sung.

XXIX.

Her white arms lifted thro' the shadowy stream
Of her loose hair—oh, excellently great
Seemed to me then my purpose, the vast theme
Of those impassioned songs, when Cythna sate
Amid the calm which rapture doth create
After its tumult, her heart vibrating,
Her spirit o'er the ocean's floating state
From her deep eyes far wandering, on the wing
Of visions that were mine, beyond its utmost spring.

XXX.

For, before Cythna loved it, had my song
Peopled with thoughts the boundless universe,
A mighty congregation, which were strong,
Where'er they trod the darkness, to disperse
The cloud of that unutterable curse
Which clings upon mankind:—all things became
Slaves to my holy and heroic verse,[2]
Earth, sea and sky, the planets, life and fame
And fate, or whate'er else binds the world's wondrous frame.

XXXI.

And this beloved child thus felt the sway
Of my conceptions, gathering like a cloud
The very wind on which it rolls away:
[Hers][3] too were all my thoughts, ere yet endowed
With music and with light, their fountains flowed

1 I.e., the owl.
2 Cf. "To Mary" above, p. 55, note 2.
3 Corrected from "Her's."

In poesy; and her still and earnest face,
Pallid with feelings which intensely glowed
Within, was turned on mine with speechless grace,
Watching the hopes which there her heart had learned to trace.

XXXII.

In me, communion with this purest being
Kindled intenser zeal, and made me wise
In knowledge, which in [hers][1] mine own mind seeing,[2]
Left in the human world few mysteries:
How without fear of evil or disguise
Was Cythna!—what a spirit strong and mild,
Which death, or pain or peril could despise,
Yet melt in tenderness! what genius wild,
Yet mighty, was inclosed within one simple child!

XXXIII.

New lore was this—old age with its grey hair,
And wrinkled legends of unworthy things,
And icy sneers, is nought: it cannot dare
To burst the chains which life forever flings
On the entangled soul's aspiring wings,
So is it cold and cruel, and is made
The careless slave of that dark power which brings
Evil, like blight on man, who still betrayed,
Laughs o'er the grave in which his living hopes are laid.

XXXIV.

Nor are the strong and the severe to keep
The empire of the world:[3] thus Cythna taught
Even in the visions of her eloquent sleep,
Unconscious of the power thro' which she wrought
The woof of such intelligible thought,

---

1 Corrected from "her's."

2 This phrase and several other passages in the poem, most notably IV.xxx.262–70 (pp. 113–14), recall the finale of Wordsworth's "Lines Written a Few Miles above Tintern Abbey" (1798), which closes with the speaker's address to his sister:

[I]n thy voice I catch
The language of my former heart, and read
My former pleasures in the shooting lights
Of thy wild eyes. Oh! yet a little while
May I behold in thee what I was once,
My dear, dear Sister! (117–22)

3 Cf. Matthew 5:5: "Blessed are the meek: for they shall inherit the earth."

As from the tranquil strength which cradled lay
In her smile-peopled[1] rest, my spirit sought
Why the deceiver and the slave has sway
O'er heralds so divine of truth's arising day.

XXXV.

Within that fairest form, the female mind
Untainted by the poison clouds which rest
On the dark world, a sacred home did find:
But else, from the wide earth's maternal breast,
Victorious Evil, which had dispossest
All native power, had those fair children torn,
And made them slaves to soothe his vile unrest,
And minister to lust its joys forlorn,
Till they had learned to breathe the atmosphere of scorn.

XXXVI.

This misery was but coldly felt, 'till she
Became my only friend, who had indued
My purpose with a wider sympathy;[2]
Thus Cythna mourned with me the servitude
In which the half of humankind were mewed° *confined*
Victims of lust and hate, the slaves of slaves,[3]
She mourned that grace and power were thrown as food
To the hyena lust, who, among graves,
Over his loathed meal, laughing in agony, raves.

XXXVII.

And I, still gazing on that glorious child,
Even as these thoughts flushed o'er her:—"Cythna sweet,
Well with the world art thou unreconciled;
Never will peace and human nature meet
Till free and equal man and woman greet
Domestic peace; and ere this power can make

---

1 I.e., full of smiles.

2 Before his intimacy with Cythna, Laon has had a detached, impersonal view of the suffering of women. She teaches him to cast the net of his compassion more widely, to include the female "half of humankind."

3 The language here is partially borrowed from Wollstonecraft, who continually refers to women as slaves in her *Vindication of the Rights of Woman* (1792; see Appendix E1). Like her, Cythna insists that universal human freedom cannot be achieved without, and must be preceded by, the emancipation of women. See also Byron's description in the *Giaour* of the Greeks as "the bondsmen of a slave" (Appendix F5, p. 277), where the slave is the head eunuch of the Imperial Harem of the Ottoman Sultans.

In human hearts its calm and holy seat;
This slavery must be broken"—as I spake,
From Cythna's eyes a light of exultation brake.° *broke*

XXXVIII.

She replied earnestly:—"It shall be mine,
This task, mine, Laon!—thou hast much to gain;
Nor wilt thou at poor Cythna's pride repine,° *complain, express dissatisfaction*
If she should lead a happy female train
To meet thee over the rejoicing plain,
When myriads at thy call shall throng around
The Golden City."—Then the child did strain
My arm upon her tremulous heart, and wound
Her own about my neck, till some reply she found.

XXXIX.

I smiled, and spake not—"wherefore dost thou smile
At what I say? Laon, I am not weak,
And, though my cheek might become pale the while,
With thee, if thou desirest, will I seek
Through their array of banded° slaves to wreak *in league, allied*
Ruin upon the tyrants. I had thought
It was more hard to turn my unpractised cheek
To scorn and shame, and this beloved spot
And thee, O dearest friend, to leave and murmur not.

XL.

"Whence came I what I am? thou, Laon, knowest
How a young child should thus undaunted be;
Methinks it is a power which thou bestowest,
Through which I seek, by most resembling thee,
So to become most good, and great and free,
Yet far beyond this Ocean's utmost roar
In towers and huts are many like to me,
Who, could they see thine eyes, or feel such lore
As I have learnt from them, like me would fear no more.

XLI.

"Think'st thou that I shall speak unskilfully,
And none will heed me? I remember now,
How once a slave in tortures doomed to die,
Was saved, because in accents sweet and low
He sung a song his Judge loved long ago,

As he was led to death.[1]—All shall relent
Who hear me—tears as mine have flowed, shall flow,
Hearts beat as mine now beats, with such intent
As renovates the world; a will omnipotent!

XLII.

"Yes, I will tread Pride's golden palaces,
Thro' Penury's° roofless huts and squalid cells *Poverty's*
Will I descend, where'er in abjectness° *wretchedness, misery*
Woman with some vile slave her tyrant dwells,
There with the music of thine own sweet spells
Will disinchant° the captives, and will pour *break the spell on*
For the despairing, from the crystal wells
Of thy deep spirit, reason's mighty lore,
And power shall then abound, and hope arise once more.

XLIII.

"Can man be free if woman be a slave?
Chain one who lives, and breathes this boundless air
To the corruption[2] of a closed grave!
Can they whose mates are beasts, condemned to bear
Scorn, heavier far than toil or anguish, dare
To trample their oppressors? in their home,
Among their babes, thou knowest a curse would wear
The shape of woman—hoary° crime would come *moldy, corrupt*
Behind, and fraud rebuild religion's tottering dome.

XLIV.

"I am a child:—I would not yet depart.
When I go forth alone, bearing the lamp
Aloft which thou hast kindled in my heart,
Millions of slaves from many a dungeon damp
Shall leap in joy, as the benumbing cramp
Of ages leaves their limbs—no ill may harm
Thy Cythna ever—truth its radiant stamp
Has fixed, as an invulnerable charm,
Upon her children's brow, dark falsehood to disarm.

---

1 This story originates in Plutarch's (45–120 CE) *Life of Nicias*, in which a group of captured Athenians recites from memory the works of Euripides to their Sicilian captors. Around the same time Shelley was writing his poem, Byron was completing the fourth and final canto of *Childe Harold's Pilgrimage* (1812–18), in which the same story is used to compare the Athenians and the Venetians, whose "love of Tasso" alone "should ... cut the knot / Which ties" them to "tyrants" (*Complete Poetical Works* 2.4.145–49).

2 Rot, the disintegration of the body after death.

XLV.

"Wait yet awhile for the appointed day—
Thou wilt depart, and I with tears shall stand
Watching thy dim sail skirt the ocean grey;
Amid the dwellers of this lonely land
I shall remain alone—and thy command
Shall then dissolve the world's unquiet° trance, *restless*
And, multitudinous as the desart sand[1]
Borne on the storm, its millions shall advance,
Thronging round thee, the light of their deliverance.

XLVI.

"Then, like the forests of some pathless mountain,
Which from remotest glens two warring winds
Involve° in fire, which not the loosened fountain *wrap, surround*
Of broadest floods might quench, shall all the kinds
Of evil, catch from our uniting minds
The spark which must consume them;—Cythna then
Will have cast off the impotence that binds
Her childhood now, and thro' the paths of men
Will pass, as the charmed bird that haunts the serpent's den.[2]

XLVII.

"We part!—O Laon, I must dare nor tremble
To meet those looks no more!—Oh, heavy stroke,
Sweet brother of my soul! can I dissemble
The agony of this thought?"—As thus she spoke
The gathered sobs her quivering accents broke,
And in my arms she hid her beating breast.
I remained still for tears—sudden she woke
As one awakes from sleep, and wildly prest
My bosom, her whole frame impetuously possest.

XLVIII.

"We part to meet again—but yon blue waste,[3]
Yon desart wide and deep holds no recess,
Within whose happy silence, thus embraced

---

1 Originally "sands"; corrected from Shelley's list of errata.

2 "There is a story that with the coming of spring the winged serpents fly from Arabia to Egypt, and the ibis birds meet the serpents at this pass and will not suffer the snakes to come through, but kill them." Herodotus, *Historia* [*The History*] (440 BCE), 2.76.

3 An empty or unpopulated place.

We might survive all ills in one caress:
Nor doth the grave—I fear 'tis passionless—
Nor yon cold vacant Heaven:—we meet again
Within the minds of men, whose lips shall bless
Our memory, and whose hopes its light retain
When these dissevered° bones are trodden in the plain." *separated*

XLIX.

I could not speak, tho' she had ceased, for now
The fountains of her feeling, swift and deep,
Seemed to suspend the tumult of their flow;
So we arose, and by the star-light steep
Went homeward—neither did we speak nor weep,
But pale, were calm with passion—thus subdued,
Like evening shades that o'er the mountains creep,
We moved towards our home; where, in this mood,
Each from the other sought refuge in solitude.

Canto Third.

I.

WHAT thoughts had sway o'er my sister's slumber[1]
That night, I know not; but my own did seem
As if they might ten thousand years outnumber
Of waking life, the visions of a dream,
Which hid in one dim gulf the troubled stream
Of mind;[2] a boundless chaos wild and vast,
Whose limits yet were never memory's theme:
And I lay struggling as its whirlwinds past,
Sometimes for rapture sick, sometimes for pain aghast.

II.

Two hours, whose mighty circle did embrace
More time than might make grey the infant world,
Rolled thus, a weary and tumultuous space:
When the third came, like mist on breezes curled,
From my dim sleep a shadow was unfurled:
Methought, upon the threshold of a cave
I sate with Cythna; drooping briony,[3] pearled
With dew from the wild streamlet's shattered wave,
Hung, where we sate to taste the joys which Nature gave.

III.

We lived a day as we were wont to live,
But Nature had a robe of glory on,
And the bright air o'er every shape did weave
Intenser hues, so that the herbless stone,
The leafless bough among the leaves alone,
Had being clearer than its own could be,
And Cythna's pure and radiant self was shown
In this strange vision, so divine to me,
That if I loved before, now love was agony.

IV.

Morn fled, noon came, evening, then night descended,
And we prolonged calm talk beneath the sphere
Of the calm moon—when, suddenly was blended
With our repose a nameless sense of fear;

---

1 *RoI* has "Cythna's lonely slumber."

2 Cf. p. 85, II.xxiii.207.

3 A flowering plant with emetic and purgative properties, native to Eurasia.

And from the cave behind I seemed to hear
Sounds gathering upwards!—accents incomplete,
And stifled shrieks,—and now, more near and near,
A tumult and a rush of thronging feet
The cavern's secret depths beneath the earth did beat.

V.

The scene was changed, and away, away, away!
Through the air and over the sea we sped,
And Cythna in my sheltering bosom lay,
And the winds bore me—thro' the darkness spread
Around, the gaping earth then vomited
Legions of foul and ghastly shapes, which hung
Upon my flight; and ever as we fled,
They plucked at Cythna—soon to me then clung
A sense of actual things those monstrous dreams among.

VI.

And I lay struggling in the impotence
Of sleep, while outward life had burst its bound,
Tho', still deluded, strove the tortured sense
To its dire wanderings to adapt the sound
Which in the light of morn was poured around
Our dwelling—breathless, pale, and unaware
I rose, and all the cottage crowded found
With armed men, whose glittering swords were bare,
And whose degraded limbs the tyrant's garb[1] did wear.

VII.

And ere with rapid lips and gathered brow
I could demand the cause—a feeble shriek—
It was a feeble shriek, faint, far and low,
Arrested me—my mien grew calm and meek,
And grasping a small knife, I went to seek
That voice among the crowd—'twas Cythna's cry!
Beneath most calm resolve did agony wreak
Its whirlwind rage:—so I past quietly
Till I beheld, where bound, that dearest child did lie.

VIII.

I started to behold her, for delight
And exultation, and a joyance° free, *enjoyment, merrymaking*

1 The men are soldiers, dressed in the uniform of the Sultan Othman's army.

Solemn, serene and lofty, filled the light
Of the calm smile with which she looked on me:
So that I feared some brainless ecstacy,° *insanity*
Wrought from that bitter woe, had wildered° her— *bewildered, confused*
"Farewell! farewell!" she said, as I drew nigh.
"At first my peace was marred by this strange stir,
Now I am calm as truth—its chosen minister.

IX.

"Look not so, Laon—say farewell in hope,
These bloody[1] men are but the slaves who bear
Their mistress to her task—it was my scope° *purpose, aim*
The slavery where they drag me now, to share,
And among captives willing chains to wear
Awhile—the rest thou knowest—return, dear friend!
Let our first triumph trample the despair
Which would ensnare us now, for in the end,
In victory or in death our hopes and fears must blend."

X.

These words had fallen on my unheeding ear,
Whilst I had watched the motions of the crew
With seeming careless glance; not many were
Around her, for their comrades just withdrew
To guard some other victim—so I drew
My knife, and with one impulse, suddenly
All unaware three of their number slew,
And grasped a fourth by the throat, and with loud cry
My countrymen invoked to death or liberty.

XI.

What followed then, I know not—for a stroke
On my raised arm and naked head, came down,
Filling my eyes with blood—when I awoke,
I felt that they had bound me in my swoon,
And up a rock which overhangs the town,
By the steep path were bearing me: below,
The plain was filled with slaughter,—overthrown
The vineyards and the harvests, and the glow
Of blazing roofs shone far o'er the white Ocean's flow.

1 Guilty of or implicated by association with violence and crime.

XII.

Upon that rock a mighty column stood,
Whose capital[1] seemed sculptured in the sky,
Which to the wanderers o'er the solitude
Of distant seas, from ages long gone by,
Had made a landmark; o'er its height to fly
Scarcely the cloud, the vulture, or the blast,
Has power—and when the shades of evening lie
On Earth and Ocean, its carv'd summits cast
The sunken daylight far thro' the aërial waste.

XIII.

They bore me to a cavern in the hill
Beneath that column, and unbound me there:
And one did strip me stark;° and one did fill *naked*
A vessel from the putrid pool; one bare° *bore*
A lighted torch, and four with friendless care
Guided my steps the cavern-paths along,
Then up a steep and dark and narrow stair
We wound, until the torch's fiery tongue
Amid the gushing day beamless and pallid hung.

XIV.

They raised me to the platform of the pile,
That column's dizzy height:—the grate of brass
Thro' which they thrust me, open stood the while,
As to its ponderous and suspended mass,
With chains which eat into the flesh, alas!
With brazen links, my naked limbs they bound:
The grate, as they departed to repass,
With horrid clangour fell, and the far sound
Of their retiring steps in the dense gloom was drowned.[2]

XV.

The noon was calm and bright:—around that column
The overhanging sky and circling sea
Spread forth in silentness profound and solemn
The darkness of brief frenzy° cast on me, *madness, delirium*
So that I knew not my own misery:
The islands and the mountains in the day

---

1 The topmost section of a column.

2 Laon's torture resembles the trials of the unfortunate Verezzi in Shelley's Gothic novel *Zastrozzi: A Romance* (1810), and those of Prometheus in *Prometheus Unbound* (1820).

Like clouds reposed afar; and I could see
The town among the woods below that lay,
And the dark rocks which bound the bright and glassy bay.

XVI.

It was so calm, that scarce the feathery weed
Sown by some eagle on the topmost stone
Swayed in the air:—so bright, that noon did breed
No shadow in the sky beside mine own—
Mine, and the shadow of my chain alone.
Below, the smoke of roofs involved in flame
Rested like night, all else was clearly shewn
In that broad glare, yet sound to me none came,
But of the living blood that ran within my frame.

XVII.

The peace of madness fled, and ah, too soon!
A ship was lying on the sunny main,° *the open sea*
Its sails were flagging in the breathless noon—
Its shadow lay beyond—that sight again
Waked, with its presence, in my tranced° brain *dazed*
The stings of a known sorrow, keen and cold:
I knew that ship bore Cythna o'er the plain
Of waters, to her blighting slavery sold,
And watched it with such thoughts as must remain untold.

XVIII.

I watched until the shades of evening wrapt
Earth like an exhalation—then the bark
Moved, for that calm was by the sunset snapt.
It moved a speck upon the Ocean dark:
Soon the wan stars came forth, and I could mark
Its path no more!—I sought to close mine eyes,
But like the balls, their lids were stiff and stark;
I would have risen, but ere that I could rise,
My parched skin was split with piercing agonies.

XIX.

I gnawed my brazen° chain, and sought to sever *made of brass*
Its adamantine links, that I might die:
O Liberty! forgive the base endeavour,
Forgive me, if reserved for victory,
The Champion of thy faith e'er sought to fly.°— *escape*

That starry night, with its clear silence, sent
Tameless resolve which laughed at misery
Into my soul—linked remembrance lent
To that such power, to me such a severe content.

XX.

To breathe, to be, to hope, or to despair
And die, I questioned not; nor, though the Sun
Its shafts of agony kindling thro' the air
Moved over me, nor though in evening dun,° *dull, dingy*
Or when the stars their visible courses run,
Or morning, the wide universe was spread
In dreary calmness round me, did I shun
Its presence, nor seek refuge with the dead
From one faint hope whose flower a dropping poison shed.

XXI.

Two days thus past—I neither raved nor died—
Thirst raged within me, like a scorpion's nest
Built in mine entrails: I had spurned° aside *kicked*
The water-vessel, while despair possest
My thoughts, and now no drop remained! The uprest° *rising*
Of the third sun brought hunger—but the crust
Which had been left, was to my craving breast
Fuel, not food. I chewed the bitter dust,
And bit my bloodless arm, and licked the brazen rust.[1]

XXII.

My brain began to fail when the fourth morn
Burst o'er the golden isles—a fearful sleep,
Which through the caverns dreary and forlorn
Of the riven soul, sent its foul dreams to sweep
With whirlwind swiftness—a fall far and deep,—
A gulph, a void, a sense of senselessness—
These things dwelt in me, even as shadows keep
Their watch in some dim charnel's° loneliness, *cemetery's*
A shoreless sea, a sky sunless and planetless!

---

1 Cf. Coleridge, *The Rime of the Ancyent Marinere*, in the 1798 edition of *Lyrical Ballads*:
With throat unslack'd, with black lips bak'd
  Ne could we laugh, ne wail:
Then while thro' drouth all dumb they stood
I bit my arm and suck'd the blood
  And cry'd, A sail! a sail! (3.149–53)

XXIII.

The forms which peopled this terrific° trance *frightening or severe*
I well remember—like a quire° of devils, *choir*
Around me they involved a giddy dance;
Legions seemed gathering from the misty levels
Of Ocean, to supply those ceaseless revels,
Foul, ceaseless shadows:—thought could not divide
The actual world from these entangling evils,
Which so bemocked themselves, that I descried° *made out, perceived*
All shapes like mine own self, hideously multiplied.

XXIV.

The sense of day and night, of false and true,
Was dead within me. Yet two visions burst
That darkness—one, as since that hour I knew,
Was not a phantom of the realms accurst,
Where then my spirit dwelt—but of the first
I know not yet,[1] was it a dream or no.
But both, tho' not distincter,[2] were immersed
In hues which, when thro' memory's waste they flow,
Make their divided streams more bright and rapid now.

XXV.

Methought that grate was lifted, and the seven
Who brought me thither, four stiff corpses bare,
And from the frieze to the four winds of Heaven
Hung them on high by the entangled hair:
Swarthy were three—the fourth was very fair:[3]
As they retired, the golden moon upsprung,
And eagerly, out in the giddy air,
Leaning that I might eat,[4] I stretched and clung
Over the shapeless depth in which those corpses hung.

---

1 I.e, "I still do not know."

2 I.e., the dreams are not any more distinct now, in recollection, than they were when Laon experienced them.

3 The three "swarthy" or dark-skinned corpses represent the guards Laon had slain. The fourth corpse is Cythna, whom Laon imagines is or will soon be dead; he may also consider her imprisonment in the Sultan's harem to be a fate comparable to death.

4 The suggestion of cannibalism in the next several lines prefigures the description of famine in Canto Tenth.

XXVI.

A woman's shape, now lank and cold and blue,
The dwelling of the many-colored worm
Hung there, the white and hollow cheek I drew
To my dry lips—What radiance did inform
Those horny° eyes? whose was that withered form? *dull, semi-opaque*
Alas, alas! it seemed that Cythna's ghost
Laughed in those looks, and that the flesh was warm
Within my teeth!—a whirlwind keen as frost
Then in its sinking gulphs my sickening spirit tost.

XXVII.

Then seemed it that a tameless hurricane
Arose, and bore me in its dark career
Beyond the sun, beyond the stars that wane
On the verge of formless space—it languished there,
And dying, left a silence lone and drear,° *lonely and dreary*
More horrible than famine:—in the deep
The shape of an old man did then appear,
Stately and beautiful, that dreadful sleep
His heavenly smiles dispersed, and I could wake and weep.

XXVIII.

And when the blinding tears had fallen, I saw
That column, and those corpses, and the moon,
And felt the poisonous tooth of hunger gnaw
My vitals, I rejoiced, as if the boon° *favor, gift*
Of senseless death would be accorded soon;—
When from that stony gloom a voice arose,
Solemn and sweet as when low winds attune
The midnight pines; the grate did then unclose,
And on that reverend form the moonlight did repose.

XXIX.

He struck my chains, and gently spake and smiled:
As they were loosened by that Hermit old,[1]
Mine eyes were of their madness half beguiled

1 Mary Shelley claimed that the Hermit was based on Dr. James Lind, a kindly and politically progressive physician at Eton College, which Shelley attended between 1804 and 1810 (Appendix G1, p. 290). Coleridge's Mariner is also rescued by a hermit in *The Rime of the Ancyent Marinere*, 6.541–46.

To answer those kind looks,[1]—he did infold° *wrap*
His giant arms around me, to uphold
My wretched frame, my scorched limbs he wound
In linen moist and balmy, and as cold
As dew to drooping leaves;—the chain, with sound
Like earthquake, thro' the chasm of that steep stair did bound,

XXX.

As lifting me, it fell!—What next I heard
Were billows leaping on the harbour bar,
And the shrill sea-wind, whose breath idly stirred
My hair;—I looked abroad, and saw a star
Shining beside a sail, and distant far
That mountain and its column, the known mark
Of those who in the wide deep wandering are,
So that I feared some Spirit, fell and dark,
In trance had lain° me thus within a fiendish bark. *laid*

XXXI.

For now indeed, over the salt sea billow
I sailed: yet dared not look upon the shape
Of him who ruled the helm, altho' the pillow
For my light head was hollowed in his lap,
And my bare limbs his mantle° did enwrap, *cloak*
Fearing it was a fiend: at last, he bent
O'er me his aged face, as if to snap
Those dreadful thoughts the gentle grandsire° bent, *grandfather, older man*
And to my inmost soul his soothing looks he sent.

XXXII.

A soft and healing potion to my lips
At intervals he raised—now looked on high,
To mark if yet the starry giant dips
His zone[2] in the dim sea—now cheeringly,
Though he said little, did he speak to me.
"It is a friend beside thee—take good cheer,
Poor victim, thou art now at liberty!"
I joyed as those a human tone to hear,
Who in cells deep and lone have languished many a year.

---

1 I.e., in meeting the Hermit's gaze, Laon's eyes, and Laon himself, lose (are "beguiled" of) some of their madness.

2 Belt. The Hermit is navigating by the constellation of Orion (the "starry giant") and specifically by Orion's belt, the three stars that mark the constellation's midsection.

XXXIII.

A dim and feeble joy, whose glimpses oft
Were quenched in a relapse of wildering° dreams, *bewildering, confusing*
Yet still methought we sailed, until aloft
The stars of night grew pallid, and the beams
Of morn descended on the ocean streams,
And still that aged man, so grand and mild,
Tended me, even as some sick mother seems
To hang in hope over a dying child,
Till in the azure East darkness again was piled.

XXXIV.

And then the night-wind steaming from the shore,
Sent odours dying sweet across the sea,
And the swift boat the little waves which bore,
Were cut by its keen keel,[1] tho' slantingly;
Soon I could hear the leaves sigh, and could see
The myrtle blossoms starring the dim grove,
As past the pebbly beach the boat did flee
On sidelong wing, into a silent cove,
Where ebon pines[2] a shade under the starlight wove.

---

1 I.e., the waves are cut by the keel of the boat they bear.

2 Ebony, a dense, black wood commonly (though not exclusively) yielded by deciduous and evergreen trees of the genus Diospyros, or "Zeus's wheat."

Canto Fourth.

I.

THE old man took the oars, and soon the bark
Smote° on the beach beside a tower of stone; *struck*
It was a crumbling heap whose portal dark
With blooming ivy-trails was overgrown;
Upon whose floor the spangling° sands were strown,° *shining; scattered*
And rarest sea-shells, which the eternal flood,
Slave to the mother of the months,[1] had thrown
Within the walls of that grey tower, which stood
A changeling of man's art, nursed amid Nature's brood.

II.

When the old man his boat had anchored,
He wound me in his arms with tender care,
And very few, but kindly words he said,
And bore me through the tower adown° a stair, *down*
Whose smooth descent some ceaseless step to wear
For many a year had fallen—We came at last
To a small chamber, which with mosses rare
Was tapestried, where me his soft hands placed
Upon a couch° of grass and oak-leaves interlaced. *bed*

III.

The moon was darting through the lattices
Its yellow light, warm as the beams of day—
So warm, that to admit the dewy breeze,
The old man opened them; the moonlight lay
Upon a lake whose waters wove[2] their play
Even to the threshold of that lonely home:
Within was seen in the dim wavering ray,
The antique sculptured roof, and many a tome[3]
Whose lore had made that sage all that he had become.

IV.

The rock-built barrier of the sea was past,—
And I was on the margin of a lake,
A lonely lake, amid the forests vast

1 I.e., the moon.

2 Originally "wore"; corrected from Shelley's list of errata.

3 Book, especially a large, heavy book.

And snowy mountains:—did my spirit wake
From sleep, as many-coloured as the snake
That girds eternity?[1] in life and truth,
Might not my heart its cravings ever slake?
Was Cythna then a dream, and all my youth,
And all its hopes and fears, and all its joy and ruth?° *sorrow, grief*

V.

Thus madness came again,—a milder madness,
Which darkened nought but time's unquiet flow
With supernatural shades of clinging sadness;
That gentle Hermit, in my helpless woe,
By my sick couch was busy to and fro,
Like a strong spirit ministrant of° good: *ministering, bringing*
When I was healed, he led me forth to shew
The wonders of his sylvan[2] solitude,
And we together sate by that isle-fretted flood.[3]

VI.

He knew his soothing words to weave with skill
From all my madness told; like mine own heart,
Of Cythna would he question me, until
That thrilling name had ceased to make me start,
From his familiar lips—it was not art,
Of wisdom and of justice when he spoke—
When mid soft looks of pity, there would dart
A glance as keen as is the lightning's stroke
When it doth rive° the knots of some ancestral oak. *tear apart*

VII.

Thus slowly from my brain the darkness rolled,
My thoughts their due array did re-assume
Thro' the inchantments of that Hermit old;
Then I bethought me of the glorious doom° *destiny, vocation*
Of those who sternly struggle to relume° *relight*
The lamp of Hope o'er man's bewildered lot,

1 Many cultures, including those of ancient Egypt and Greece, use images of the ouroboros—a snake eating its own tail—to symbolize the eternal re-creation of the world. In the *Timaeus* (written c. 360 BCE), Plato describes such a creature as the first living thing in the universe, and Volney speaks of the "theological philosophers" of antiquity picturing the continuity and conservation of matter as "a great round serpent ... devouring his tail—that is, folding and unfolding himself eternally, like the revolutions of the spheres" (271).

2 Belonging to or characteristic of a forest.

3 The lake on which the Hermit dwells is dotted ("fretted") with small islands.

And, sitting by the waters, in the gloom
Of eve, to that friend's heart I told my thought—
That heart which had grown old, but had corrupted not.

VIII.

That hoary° man had spent his livelong age *gray-bearded*
In converse with the dead, who leave the stamp
Of ever-burning thoughts on many a page,
When they are gone into the senseless damp
Of graves;—his spirit thus became a lamp
Of splendour, like to those on which it fed
Thro' peopled haunts, the City and the Camp,° *army encampment*
Deep thirst for knowledge had his footsteps led,
And all the ways of men among mankind he read.

IX.

But custom maketh blind and obdurate
The loftiest hearts:—he had beheld the woe
In which mankind was bound,[1] but deemed that fate
Which made them abject, would preserve them so;
And in such faith, some stedfast joy to know,
He sought this cell: but when fame went abroad,
That one[2] in Argolis did undergo
Torture for liberty, and that the crowd
High truths from gifted lips had heard and understood;

X.

And that the multitude was gathering wide;
His spirit leaped within his aged frame,
In lonely peace he could no more abide,
But to the land on which the victor's flame
Had fed, my native land, the Hermit came:
Each heart was there a shield, and every tongue
Was as a sword of truth—young Laon's name
Rallied their secret hopes, tho' tyrants sung
Hymns of triumphant joy our scattered tribes among.

XI.

He came to the lone column on the rock,
And with his sweet and mighty eloquence
The hearts of those who watched it did unlock,

1 Cf. p. 89, II.xxxvi.319–20.

2 I.e., Laon.

And made them melt in tears of penitence.
They gave him entrance free to bear me thence.
Since this, the old man said, seven years are spent,
While slowly truth on thy benighted sense[1]
Has crept; the hope which wildered it has lent
Meanwhile, to me the power of a sublime intent.

XII.[2]

"Yes, from the records of my youthful state,
And from the lore of bards and sages old,
From whatsoe'er my wakened thoughts create
Out of the hopes of thine aspirings bold,
Have I collected language to unfold
Truth to my countrymen; from shore to shore
Doctrines of human power my words have told,
They have been heard, and men aspire to more
Than they have ever gained or ever lost of yore.

XIII.

"In secret chambers parents read, and weep,
My writings to their babes, no longer blind;
And young men gather when their tyrants sleep,
And vows of faith each to the other bind;
And marriageable maidens, who have pined
With love, till life seemed melting tho' their look,[3]
A warmer zeal,[4] a nobler hope, now find;
And every bosom thus is rapt and shook,
Like autumn's myriad leaves in one swoln° mountain brook.[5] *swollen*

XIV.

"The tyrants of the Golden City tremble
At voices which are heard about the streets;
The ministers of fraud can scarce dissemble
The lies of their own heart; but when one meets
Another at the shrine, he inly weets,[6]

---

1 "Benighted" literally means covered in darkness or night. The Hermit means that Laon has spent the last seven years not in his right mind, his "sense" or mental capacity having been compromised by his various ordeals.

2 The Hermit speaks from xii.100 to xxviii.249.

3 Originally "looks"; corrected from Shelley's list of errata.

4 That is, they have replaced their romantic interests with political ones. Also note the echo of p. 88, II.xxxii.281.

5 Cf. p. 62, I.iv.36; and p. 69, I.xxix.256.

6 He knows within himself.

Though he says nothing, that the truth is known;
Murderers are pale upon the judgment seats,
And gold grows vile even to the wealthy crone,[1]
And laughter fills the Fane, and curses shake the Throne.

XV.

"Kind thoughts, and mighty hopes, and gentle deeds
Abound, for fearless love, and the pure law
Of mild equality and peace, succeeds
To faiths which long have held the world in awe,
Bloody and false, and cold:—as whirlpools draw
All wrecks of Ocean to their chasm, the sway
Of thy strong genius, Laon, which foresaw
This hope, compels all spirits to obey,
Which round thy secret strength now throng in wide array.[2]

XVI.

"For I have been thy passive instrument"[3]—
(As thus the old man spake, his countenance
Gleamed on me like a spirit's)—"thou hast lent
To me, to all, the power to advance
Towards this unforeseen deliverance
From our ancestral chains—aye, thou didst rear
That lamp of hope on high, which time nor chance,
Nor change may not extinguish, and my share
Of good was o'er the world its gathered beams to bear.

XVII.

"But I, alas! am both unknown and old,
And though the woof of wisdom I know well
To dye in hues of language, I am cold
In seeming, and the hopes which inly dwell,
My[4] manners note that I did long repel;
But Laon's name to the tumultuous throng

---

1 An elderly person, usually female.

2 This image of Laon's "genius" functioning as a whirlpool to draw people to his cause foreshadows the very similar image applied to Cythna in VII.vii.55–60 (p. 157). The phrase "secret strength" also appears in Shelley's poem "Mont Blanc," in *Shelley's Poetry and Prose*, 5.139.

3 Cf. Shelley's "Ode to the West Wind" (1820), in which the speaker enjoins the wind: "Make me thy lyre, even as the forest is." Like the Hermit's speech, "Ode to the West Wind" exemplifies Shelley's attraction to passivity as a revolutionary posture, one that enables the individual to be used as the "instrument" or tool of historical change. See "Ode to the West Wind," in *Shelley's Poetry and Prose* 5.57.

4 Originally "Thy"; corrected from Shelley's list of errata.

Were like the star whose beams the waves compel
And tempests, and his soul-subduing tongue
Were as a lance to quell the mailed crest[1] of wrong.

XVIII.

"Perchance° blood need not flow, if thou at length *maybe*
Wouldst rise, perchance the very slaves would spare
Their brethren and themselves; great is the strength
Of words—for lately did a maiden[2] fair,
Who from her childhood has been taught to bear
The tyrant's heaviest yoke, arise, and make
Her sex the law of truth and freedom hear,
And with these quiet words—'for thine own sake
I prithee spare me,'—did with ruth so take[3]

XIX.

"All hearts, that even the torturer who had bound
Her meek calm frame, ere it was yet impaled,
Loosened her weeping then;[4] nor could be found
One human hand to harm her—unassailed
Therefore she walks thro' the great City, veiled
In virtue's adamantine eloquence,
'Gainst scorn, and death and pain thus trebly° mailed, *triply*
And blending in the smiles of that defence,
The Serpent and the Dove, Wisdom and Innocence.[5]

XX.

"The wild-eyed women throng around her path:
From their luxurious dungeons, from the dust
Of meaner thralls,[6] from the oppressor's wrath,
Or the caresses of his sated lust,
They congregate:—in her they put their trust;
The tyrants send their armed slaves to quell
Her power;—they, even like a thunder gust

---

1 Armored helmet. The Hermit casts Laon as a knight who uses words as weapons against evil.

2 The maiden's true identity as Cythna is hardly concealed by the poem.

3 The alexandrine that should form the last line of the stanza is two syllables short.

4 Recall Cythna's prophecy from pp. 90–91, II.xli.362–66, in which she plans to use her powers of speech to persuade her captors to let her go.

5 Cf. Matthew 10:16: "Behold, I send you forth as sheep in the midst of wolves: be ye therefore wise as serpents, and harmless as doves."

6 I.e., places of sexual oppression ("thralls") less lavish than those "luxurious dungeons." The Hermit means to say, effectively, that the movement of "wild-eyed women" includes women of all social and economic circumstances.

Caught by some forest, bend beneath the spell
Of that young maiden's speech, and to their chiefs rebel.

XXI.

"Thus she doth equal laws and justice teach
To woman, outraged and polluted long;
Gathering the sweetest fruit in human reach
For those fair hands now free, while armed wrong
Trembles before her look, tho' it be strong;
Thousands thus dwell beside her, virgins bright
And matrons with their babes, a stately throng!
Lovers renew the vows which they did plight° *pledge, promise*
In early faith, and hearts long parted now unite,

XXII.

"And homeless orphans find a home near her,
And those poor victims of the proud, no less,
Fair wrecks, on whom the smiling world with stir,° *commotion, excitement*
Thrusts the redemption of its wickedness:—
In squalid huts, and in its palaces,
Sits Lust alone, while o'er the land is borne
Her voice, whose awful sweetness doth repress
All evil, and her foes relenting turn,
And cast the vote of love in hope's abandoned urn.[1]

XXIII.

"So in the populous City, a young maiden
Has baffled havock of the prey which he
Marks as his own,[2] whene'er with chains o'erladen
Men make them arms to hurl down tyranny,
False arbiter between the bound and free;
And o'er the land, in hamlets and in towns
The multitudes collect tumultuously,
And throng in arms; but tyranny disowns
Their claim, and gathers strength around its trembling thrones.

---

1 In the democracy of ancient Athens, men would cast votes by depositing pebbles in urns.

2 The antecedent of "he" is "Lust" in the previous stanza. The mysterious maiden has thwarted ("baffled") Lust's seizure ("havock") of the women of the City, a phrase that might mean either that she has prevented the Sultan Othman (himself the personification of Lust) from taking any more women for his harem, or that she has protected the City's women in general from sexual assault.

XXIV.

"Blood soon, altho' unwillingly to shed,
The free cannot forbear—the Queen of Slaves,
The hood-winked° Angel of the blind and dead, *duped, fooled*
Custom, with iron mace points to the graves
Where her own standard desolately waves
Over the dust of Prophets and of Kings.
Many yet stand in her array—'she paves
Her path with human hearts,' and o'er it flings
The wildering gloom of her immeasurable wings.[1]

XXV.

"There is a plain beneath the City's wall,
Bounded by misty mountains, wide and vast,
Millions there lift at Freedom's thrilling call
Ten thousand standards wide, they load the blast
Which bears one sound of many voices past,
And startles on his throne their sceptred foe:
He sits amid his idle pomp° aghast, *useless wealth*
And that his power hath passed away, doth know—
Why pause the victor swords to seal his overthrow?

XXVI.

"The tyrant's guards resistance yet maintain:
Fearless, and fierce, and hard as beasts of blood;
They stand a speck amid the peopled plain;
Carnage and ruin have been made their food
From infancy—ill has become their good,[2]
And for its hateful sake their will has wove
The chains which eat their hearts[3]—the multitude
Surrounding them, with words of human love,
Seek from their own decay their stubborn minds to move.

---

1 Custom resembles both the winged goddess Rumor ("Fama") in Book 4 of Virgil's *Aeneid* and Até (Ἄτη), who is described by Homer in *The Iliad* as the goddess or spirit of delusion and folly. Richmond Lattimore's translation of *The Iliad* is helpful here:

> Delusion is the eldest daughter of Zeus, the accursed
> who deludes all; her feet are delicate and they step not
> on the firm earth, but she walks the air above men's heads
> and leads them astray. (19.91–94)

2 Cf. *Paradise Lost*, 4.110.

3 Cf. p. 98, III.xiv.122.

XXVII.

"Over the land is felt a sudden pause,
As night and day those ruthless bands around
The watch of love is kept:—a trance which awes
The thoughts of men with hope—as when the sound
Of whirlwind, whose fierce blasts the waves and clouds confound,[1]
Dies suddenly, the mariner in fear
Feels silence sink upon his heart—thus bound,
The conquerors pause, and oh! may freemen ne'er
Clasp the relentless knees of Dread, the murderer!

XXVIII.

"If blood be shed, 'tis but a change and choice
Of bonds,—from slavery to cowardice
A wretched fall!—uplift thy charmed voice,
Pour on those evil men the love that lies
Hovering within those spirit-soothing eyes—
Arise, my friend, farewell!"—As thus he spake,
From the green earth lightly I did arise,
As one out of dim dreams that doth awake,
And looked upon the depth of that reposing° lake. *at rest, still*

XXIX.

I saw my countenance reflected there;—
And then my youth fell on me like a wind
Descending on still waters—my thin hair
Was prematurely gray, my face was lined
With channels, such as suffering leaves behind,
Not age;—my brow was pale, but in my cheek
And lips a flush of gnawing fire did find
Their food and dwelling; tho' mine eyes might speak
A subtle mind and strong within a frame thus weak.

XXX.

And tho' their lustre now was[2] spent and faded,
Yet in my hollow looks and withered mien
The likeness of a shape for which was braided
The brightest woof of genius, still was seen—
One who, methought, had gone from the world's scene,
And left it vacant—'twas her brother's face[3]—

---

1 One of the stray alexandrines to which Shelley refers in his preface, p. 46.

2 Originally "were"; corrected from Shelley's list of errata.

3 *RoI* has "her lover's face."

It might resemble her—it once had been
The mirror of her thoughts, and still the grace
Which her mind's shadow cast, left there a lingering trace.

XXXI.

What then was I? She slumbered with the dead.
Glory and joy and peace, had come and gone.
Doth the cloud perish, when the beams are fled
Which steeped its skirts in gold? or dark and lone,
Doth it not thro' the paths of night unknown,
On outspread wings of its own wind upborne
Pour rain upon the earth? the stars are shewn,
When the cold moon sharpens her silver horn
Under the sea, and make the wide night not forlorn.

XXXII.

Strengthened in heart, yet sad, that aged man
I left, with interchange of looks and tears,
And lingering speech, and to the Camp[1] began
My war. O'er many a mountain chain which rears
Its hundred crests aloft, my spirit bears
My frame; o'er many a dale° and many a moor,[2] *valley*
And gaily now me seems° serene earth wears *it seems to me*
The blosmy spring's star-bright investiture,° *garb*
A vision which aught sad from sadness might allure.

XXXIII.

My powers revived within me, and I went
As one whom winds waft o'er the bending grass,
Thro' many a vale of that broad continent.
At night when I reposed, fair dreams did pass
Before my pillow;—my own Cythna was
Not like a child of death, among them ever;
When I arose from rest, a woeful mass
That gentlest sleep seemed from my life to sever,
As if the light of youth were not withdrawn forever.

1 I.e., the camp where the maiden's band has gathered.

2 Either a wet marshland or a dried-up one, which leaves behind a low-lying plain of grass.

XXXIV.

Aye as I went, that maiden who had reared
The torch of Truth afar, of whose high deeds
The Hermit in his pilgrimage had heard,
Haunted my thoughts.—Ah, Hope its sickness feeds
With whatsoe'er it finds, or flowers or weeds!
Could she be Cythna?—Was that corpse a shade
Such as self-torturing thought from madness breeds?
Why was this hope not torture? yet it made
A light around my step which would not ever fade.

Canto Fifth.

I.

OVER the utmost hill at length I sped,
A snowy steep:—the moon was hanging low
Over the Asian mountains, and outspread
The plain, the City, and the Camp below,
Skirted the midnight Ocean's glimmering flow,
The City's moon-lit spires and myriad lamps,
Like stars in a sublunar[1] sky did glow,
And fires blazed far amid the scattered camps,
Like springs of flame, which burst where'er swift Earthquake stamps.

II.

All slept but those in watchful arms who stood,
And those who sate tending the beacon's light,
And the few sounds from that vast multitude
Made silence more profound—Oh, what a might
Of human thought was cradled in that night!
How many hearts impenetrably veiled,
Beat underneath its shade, what secret fight
Evil and good, in woven passions mailed,
Waged thro' that silent throng; a war that never failed!

III.

And now the Power of Good held victory
So, thro' the labyrinth of many a tent,
Among the silent millions who did lie
In innocent sleep, exultingly I went;
The moon had left Heaven desert° now, but lent *empty, deserted*
From eastern morn the first faint lustre showed
An armed youth—over his spear he bent
His downward face—"A friend!" I cried aloud,
And quickly common hopes made freemen understood.

IV.

I sate beside him while the morning beam
Crept slowly over Heaven, and talked with him
Of those immortal hopes, a glorious theme!
Which led us forth, until the stars grew dim:

---

1 Literally, beneath the moon; figuratively, of this world. In other words, the city lights appear to be stars in a sky anchored to the ground, not above our heads

And all the while, methought, his voice did swim,
As if it drowned in remembrance were
Of thoughts which make the moist eyes overbrim:
At last, when daylight 'gan to fill the air,
He looked on me, and cried in wonder—"thou art here!"

V.

Then, suddenly, I knew it was the youth
In whom its earliest hopes my spirit found;[1]
But envious tongues had stained his spotless truth,
And thoughtless pride his love in silence bound,
And shame and sorrow mine in toils had wound,
Whilst he was innocent, and I deluded;
The truth now came upon me, on the ground
Tears of repenting joy, which fast intruded,
Fell fast—and o'er its peace our mingling spirits brooded.[2]

VI.

Thus, while with rapid lips and earnest eyes
We talked, a sound of sweeping conflict spread,
As from the earth did suddenly arise;
From every tent roused by that clamour dread,
Our bands outsprung and seized their arms—we sped
Towards the sound: our tribes were gathering far,
Those sanguine° slaves amid ten thousand dead — *bloody, bloodthirsty*
Stabbed in their sleep, trampled in treacherous war,
The gentle hearts whose power their lives had sought to spare.

VII.

Like rabid snakes, that sting some gentle child
Who brings them food, when winter false and fair
Allures them forth with its cold smiles, so wild
They rage among the camp;—they overbear° — *overwhelm, outnumber*
The patriot hosts—confusion, then despair,
Descends like night—when "Laon!" one did cry:
Like a bright ghost from Heaven that shout did scare
The slaves, and, widening thro' the vaulted sky,
Seemed sent from Earth to Heaven in sign of victory.

---

1 The youth is Laon's "false" friend from Canto Second (p. 84, II.xviii.159).

2 Hovered, protected; usually said of birds sitting ("brooding") on their eggs to keep them warm.

VIII.

In sudden panic those false murderers fled,
Like insect tribes before the northern gale:
But swifter still, our hosts encompassed
Their shattered ranks, and in a craggy vale,
Where even their fierce despair might nought avail
Hemmed° them around!—and then revenge and fear *shut in, surrounded*
Made the high virtue of the patriots fail:
One pointed on his foe the mortal spear—
I rushed before its point, and cried "Forbear, forbear!"[1]

IX.

The spear transfixed my arm that was uplifted
In swift expostulation,[2] and the blood
Gushed round its point: I smiled, and—"Oh! thou gifted
With eloquence which shall not be withstood,
Flow thus!"—I cried in joy, "thou vital flood,
Until my heart be dry, ere thus the cause
For which thou wert aught worthy be subdued—
Ah, ye are pale,—ye weep,—your passions pause,—
'Tis well! ye feel the truth of love's benignant° laws. *benevolent*

X.

"Soldiers, our brethren and our friends are slain.
Ye murdered them, I think, as they did sleep!
Alas, what have ye done? The slightest pain
Which ye might suffer, there were eyes to weep;
But ye have quenched them—there were smiles to steep
Your hearts in balm, but they are lost in woe;
And those whom love did set his watch to keep
Around your tents truth's freedom to bestow,
Ye stabbed as they did sleep—but they forgive ye now.

XI.

"O wherefore should ill ever flow from ill,
And pain still keener pain forever breed?
We all are brethren—even the slaves who kill
For hire, are men; and to avenge misdeed

---

1 Endure; alternatively, to abstain from injuring. Laon seems to be using both meanings at once—which may be why he repeats the word—exhorting his comrades not to hurt their enemies and to bear patiently the hurt those enemies inflict on them.

2 Reproof, objection. I.e., Laon's comrade stabs his arm with a spear in protest of Laon's endorsement of non-violence.

On the misdoer, doth but Misery feed
With her own broken heart! O Earth, O Heaven!
And thou, dread Nature, which to every deed
And all that lives, or is, to be hath given,[1]
Even as to thee have these done ill, and are forgiven.

XII.

"Join then your hands and hearts, and let the past
Be as a grave which gives not up its dead
To evil thoughts"—a film then overcast
My sense with dimness, for the wound, which bled
Freshly, swift shadows o'er mine eyes had shed.
When I awoke, I lay 'mid friends and foes,
And earnest countenances on me shed
The light of questioning looks, whilst one did close
My wound with balmiest[2] herbs, and soothed me to repose;

XIII.

And one, whose spear had pierced me, leaned beside
With quivering lips and humid° eyes;—and all[3] *wet*
Seemed like some brothers on a journey wide
Gone forth, whom now strange meeting did befall
In a strange land, round one whom they might call
Their friend, their chief, their father, for assay
Of peril,[4] which had saved them from the thrall
Of death, now suffering. Thus the vast array
Of those fraternal bands were reconciled that day.

XIV.

Lifting the thunder of their acclamation,
Towards the City then the multitude,
And I among them, went in joy—a nation
Made free by love;—a mighty brotherhood
Linked by a jealous° interchange of good; *passionate, intense*
A glorious pageant, more magnificent

---

1 This line seems to invite an alternative punctuation, namely, "And all that lives, or is to be, hath given," and some editions amend the line this way. However, as confusing as it sounds, what Shelley apparently means is that Nature has brought every deed, along with all that lives or is, into existence—Nature has "given" those things "to be."

2 Especially fragrant or soothing.

3 I.e., both the patriot revolutionaries and Othman's soldiers.

4 Trial of danger. Laon has put himself in harm's way to illustrate the mortal and moral dangers of physical violence.

Than kingly slaves arrayed in gold and blood,
When they return from carnage, and are sent
In triumph bright beneath the populous battlement.

XV.

Afar, the city walls were thronged on high,
And myriads on each giddy turret clung,
And to each spire far lessening in the sky,
Bright pennons° on the idle winds were hung; *flags*
As we approached a shout of joyance sprung
At once from all the crowd, as if the vast
And peopled Earth its boundless skies among
The sudden clamor of delight had cast,
When from before its face some general wreck had past.

XVI.

Our armies thro' the City's hundred gates
Were poured, like brooks which to the rocky lair
Of some deep lake, whose silence them awaits,
Throng from the mountains when the storms are there;
And as we past thro' the calm sunny air
A thousand flower-inwoven crowns were shed,
The token flowers of truth and freedom fair,
And fairest hands bound them on many a head,
Those angels of love's heaven, that over all was spread.

XVII.

I trod as one tranced in some rapturous vision:
Those bloody bands so lately reconciled,
Were, ever as they went, by the contrition
Of anger turned to love from ill beguiled,
And every one on them more gently smiled
Because they had done evil:—the sweet awe
Of such mild looks made their own hearts grow mild,
And did with soft attraction ever draw
Their spirits to the love of freedom's equal law.

XVIII.

And they, and all, in one loud symphony
My name with Liberty commingling, lifted,
"The friend and the preserver of the free!
The parent of this joy!" and fair eyes gifted
With feelings, caught from one who had uplifted

The light of a great spirit, round me shone;
And all the shapes of this grand scenery shifted
Like restless clouds before the steadfast sun,—
Where was that Maid? I asked, but it was known of none.

XIX.

Laone[1] was the name her love[2] had chosen,
For she was nameless, and her birth none knew:
Where was Laone now?—The words were frozen
Within my lips with fear; but to subdue
Such dreadful hope, to my great task was due,
And when at length one brought reply, that she
To-morrow would appear, I then withdrew
To judge what need for that great throng might be,
For now the stars came thick over the twilight sea.

XX.

Yet need was none for rest or food to care,
Even though that multitude was passing great,
Since each one for the other did prepare
All kindly succor—Therefore to the gate
Of the Imperial House, now desolate,
I past, and there was found aghast, alone,
The fallen Tyrant!—silently he sate
Upon the footstool of his golden throne,
Which, starred with sunny gems, in its own lustre shone.

XXI.

Alone, but for one child, who led before him
A graceful dance: the only living thing
Of all the crowd, which thither to adore him
Flocked yesterday, who solace sought to bring
In his abandonment!—she knew the King
Had praised her dance of yore, and now she wove
Its circles, aye weeping and murmuring,
'Mid her sad task of unregarded° love, *ignored, unappreciated*
That to no smiles it might his speechless sadness move.

---

1 The female form of Laon.

2 The phrase "her love" is ambiguous. Most obviously, it means something like "her preference," but it also suggests that the maiden (whom the reader has guessed is Cythna) has been motivated by "her love" for Laon to choose his name for her own.

XXII.

She fled to him, and wildly clasped his feet
When human steps were heard:—he moved nor spoke,
Nor changed his hue, nor raised his looks to meet
The gaze of strangers—our loud entrance woke
The echoes of the hall, which circling broke
Th[e][1] calm of its recesses,—like a tomb
Its sculptured walls vacantly to the stroke° *strike, blow*
Of footfalls answered, and the twilight's gloom,
Lay like a charnel's mist within the radiant dome.

XXIII.

The little child stood up when we came nigh;
Her lips and cheeks seemed very pale and wan,
But on her forehead, and within her eye
Lay beauty, which makes hearts that feed thereon
Sick with excess of sweetness; on the throne
She leaned;—the King with gathered brow, and lips
Wreathed° by long scorn, did inly sneer and frown *twisted*
With hue like that when some great painter dips
His pencil in the gloom of earthquake and eclipse.

XXIV.

She stood beside him like a rainbow braided
Within some storm, when scarce its shadows vast
From the blue paths of the swift sun have faded;
A sweet and solemn smile, like Cythna's, cast
One moment's light, which made my heart beat fast,
O'er that child's parted lips—a gleam of bliss,
A shade of vanished days,—as the tears past
Which wrapt it, even as with a father's kiss
I pressed those softest eyes in trembling tenderness.

XXV.

The sceptred wretch then from that solitude
I drew, and of his change compassionate,[2]
With words of sadness soothed his rugged° mood. *turbulent, rough*
But he, while pride and fear held deep debate,
With sullen guile of ill-dissembled hate
Glared on me as a toothless snake might glare:

---

1 The text has "Thee," which is certainly an error.

2 I.e., sympathetic to the difficulty of his new situation.

Pity, not scorn I felt, tho' desolate
The desolator now,[1] and unaware
The curses which he mocked had caught him by the hair.

XXVI.

I led him forth from that which now might seem
A gorgeous grave:[2] thro' portals sculptured deep
With imagery beautiful as dream
We went, and left the shades which tend on sleep
Over its unregarded gold to keep
Their silent watch.—The child trod faintingly,
And as she went, the tears which she did weep
Glanced in the star-light; wildered seemed she,
And when I spake, for sobs she could not answer me.

XXVII.

At last the tyrant cried, "She hungers, slave,
Stab her, or give her bread!"—It was a tone
Such as sick fancies in a new made grave
Might hear. I trembled, for the truth was known,
He with this child had thus been left alone,
And neither had gone forth for food,—but he
In mingled pride and awe cowered near his throne,
And she a nursling[3] of captivity
Knew nought beyond those walls, nor what such change might be.

XXVIII.

And he was troubled at a charm withdrawn
Thus suddenly; that scepters ruled no more—
That even from gold the dreadful strength was gone,
Which once[4] made all things subject to its power—
Such wonder seized him, as if hour by hour
The past had come again; and the swift fall
Of one so great and terrible of yore,
To desolateness, in the hearts of all
Like wonder stirred, who saw such awful change befal.

1 Othman, the "desolater" or destroyer, is now himself destroyed.

2 I.e., the imperial palace.

3 A child, especially a foster child.

4 Originally "Whileom"; corrected from Shelley's list of errata.

XXIX.

A mighty crowd, such as the wide land pours
Once in a thousand years, now gathered round
The fallen tyrant;—like the rush of showers
Of hail in spring, pattering along the ground,
Their many footsteps fell, else came no sound
From the wide multitude: that lonely man
Then knew the burthen of his change, and found,
Concealing in the dust his visage wan,
Refuge from the keen looks which thro' his bosom ran.

XXX.

And he was faint withal: I sate beside him
Upon the earth, and took that child so fair
From his weak arms, that ill might none betide° him — *happen to, befall*
Or her;—when food was brought to them, her share
To his averted lips the child did bear,
But, when she saw he had enough, she ate
And wept the while;—the lonely man's despair
Hunger then overcame, and of his state
Forgetful, on the dust as in a trance he sate.

XXXI.

Slowly the silence of the multitudes
Past, as when far is heard in some lone dell
The gathering of a wind among the woods—
And he is fallen! they cry, he who did dwell
Like famine or the plague, or aught more fell
Among our homes, is fallen! the murderer
Who slaked his thirsting soul as from a well
Of blood and tears with ruin! he is here!
Sunk in a gulph of scorn from which none may him rear!

XXXII.

Then was heard—He who judged, let him be brought
To judgment![1] blood for blood cries from the soil
On which his crimes have deep pollution wrought![2]
Shall Othman only unavenged despoil?

---

1 Cf. Matthew 7:1–2: "Judge not, that ye be not judged. For with what judgment ye judge, ye shall be judged: and with what measure ye mete, it shall be measured to you again."

2 Cf. Genesis 4:10: "And [God] said, What hast thou done? the voice of thy brother's blood crieth unto me from the ground."

Shall they, who by the stress of grinding toil
Wrest from the unwilling earth his luxuries,[1]
Perish for crime, while his foul blood may boil,
Or creep within his veins at will?—Arise!
And to high justice make her chosen sacrifice!

XXXIII.

"What do ye seek? what fear ye?" then I cried,[2]
Suddenly starting forth, "that ye should shed
The blood of Othman—if your hearts are tried
In the true love of freedom, cease to dread
This one poor lonely man—beneath Heaven spread
In purest light above us all, thro' earth[,]
Maternal earth, who doth her sweet smiles shed[3]
For all, let him go free; until the worth
Of human nature win from these a second birth.

XXXIV.

"What call ye *justice*? Is there one who ne'er
In secret thought has wished another's ill?—
Are ye all pure? let those stand forth who hear,
And tremble not.[4] Shall they insult and kill,
If such they be? their mild eyes can they fill
With the false anger of the hypocrite?
Alas, such were not pure—the chastened will
Of virtue sees that justice is the light
Of love, and not revenge, and terror and despite."° *scorn*

XXXV.

The murmur of the people slowly dying,
Paused as I spake; then those who near me were
Cast gentle looks where[5] the lone man was lying
Shrouding his head, which now that infant fair
Clasped on her lap in silence;—through the air
Sobs were then heard, and many kissed my feet

---

1 I.e., by mining gold and other precious metals.

2 Laon now answers the anonymous speaker of the previous stanza.

3 Originally "spread"; corrected from Shelley's list of errata.

4 Cf. John 8:7: "So when they continued asking him, he lifted up himself, and said unto them, He that is without sin among you, let him first cast a stone[.]" Reiman, Fraistat, and Crook offer persuasive evidence that Laon's speech is inspired by Shelley's reading of accounts of the execution of Louis XVI and of the pleas for mercy made on his behalf by the likes of Paine to France's revolutionary government. See *The Complete Poetry of Percy Bysshe Shelley* 756–57.

5 Originally "when"; corrected from Shelley's list of errata.

In pity's madness, and to the despair
Of him whom late they cursed, a solace sweet
His very victims brought—soft looks and speeches
meet.° *matching, appropriate to*

XXXVI.

Then to a home for his repose assigned,
Accompanied by the still throng he went
In silence, where to soothe his rankling[1] mind,
Some likeness of his antient° state was lent; *ancient*
And if his heart could have been innocent
As those who pardoned him, he might have ended
His days in peace; but his straight lips were bent,
Men said, into a smile which guile portended,
A sight with which that child, like hope with fear, was blended.

XXXVII.

'Twas midnight now, the eve of that great day
Whereon the many nations at whose call
The chains of earth like mist melted away,
Decreed to hold a sacred Festival,
A rite to attest the equality of all
Who live. So to their homes, to dream or wake
All went. The sleepless silence did recal
Laone to my thoughts, with hopes that make
The flood recede from which their thirst they seek to slake.

XXXVIII.

The dawn flowed forth, and from its purple fountains
I drank those hopes which make the spirit quail,° *tremble*
As to the plain between the misty mountains
And the great City, with a countenance pale
I went:—it was a sight which might avail
To make men weep exulting tears, for whom
Now first from human power the reverend veil
Was torn, to see Earth from her general womb
Pour forth her swarming sons to a fraternal doom:[2]

---

1 Festering, e.g., with resentment.

2 Destiny. The word is used here in a neutral sense, though perhaps with some foreshadowing of the disasters to follow in subsequent cantos. The imagery of this stanza recalls Matthew 27:51–53: "And, behold, the veil of the temple was rent in twain from the top to the bottom; and the earth did quake, and the rocks rent; And the graves were opened; and many bodies of the saints which slept arose, And came out of the graves after his resurrection, and went into the holy city, and appeared unto many."

XXXIX.

To see, far glancing in the misty morning,
The signs of that innumerable host,
To hear one sound of many made, the warning
Of Earth to Heaven from its free children tost,
While the eternal hills, and the sea lost
In wavering light, and, starring the blue sky
The city's myriad spires of gold, almost
With human joy made mute society,
Its witnesses with men who must hereafter be.

XL.[1]

To see like some vast island from the Ocean,
The Altar of the Federation[2] rear
Its pile i' the midst; a work, which the devotion
Of millions in one night created there,
Sudden, as when the moonrise makes appear
Strange clouds in the east; a marble pyramid
Distinct with steps: that mighty shape did wear
The light of genius; its still shadow hid
Far ships: to know its height the morning mists forbid!

XLI.

To hear the restless multitudes forever
Around the base of that great Altar flow,
As on some mountain islet burst and shiver
Atlantic waves; and solemnly and slow
As the wind bore that tumult to and fro,
To feel the dreamlike music, which did swim
Like beams thro' floating clouds on waves below
Falling in pauses, from that Altar dim
As silver-sounding tongues breathed an aërial hymn.

XLII.

To hear, to see, to live, was on that morn
Lethean joy![3] so that all those assembled
Cast off their memories of the past outworn;

---

1 Stanzas xl to xliii are incorrectly numbered in the original text. The correct numbers are given here.

2 This seems to allude to the Fête de la Fédération (the Festival of the Federation) held in France on 14 July 1790, the one-year anniversary of the fall of the Bastille. For the Fête, an altar was erected in the center of the Champ de Mars in Paris, and citizens and officials swore oaths upon it during the celebration. For an eyewitness description of the Fête, see Williams, *Letters Written in France* 5–17.

3 In Greek mythology, Lethe is the stream of forgetfulness.

Two only bosoms with their own life trembled,
And mine was one,—and we had both dissembled;[1]
So with a beating heart I went, and one,
Who having much, covets yet more, resembled;
A lost and dear possession, which not won,
He walks in lonely gloom beneath the noonday sun.

XLIII.

To the great Pyramid I came: its stair
With female quires was thronged: the loveliest
Among the free, grouped with its sculptures rare;
As I approached, the morning's golden mist,
Which now the wonder-stricken breezes kist
With their cold lips, fled, and the summit shone
Like Athos seen from Samothracia,[2] drest
In earliest light, by vintagers,[3] and one
Sate there, a female Shape upon an ivory throne.

XLIV.

Form most like the imagined habitant° *inhabitant, dweller*
Of silver exhalations sprung from dawn,
By winds which feed on sunrise woven, to inchant
The faiths of men: all mortal eyes were drawn,
As famished mariners thro' strange seas gone
Gaze on a burning watch-tower, by the light
Of those divinest lineaments[4]—alone
With thoughts which none could share, from that fair sight
I turned in sickness, for a veil shrouded her countenance bright.

XLV.

And, neither did I hear the acclamations,
Which from brief silence bursting, filled the air
With her strange name and mine, from all the nations

---

1 Presumably the two bosoms belong to Cythna, who has actually disguised ("dissembled") herself as Laone, and to Laon, whose "dissembling" is harder to identify. Perhaps Laon means that, unlike the members of the crowd united in fellow-feeling, he and Cythna are set apart by their preoccupation with their own, personal concerns, namely their desire to locate each other. Laon would then be a dissembler insofar as he is projecting more excitement about the Festival than he can fully feel, since his mind is more on Cythna than on the celebration. Cythna (or so Laon suggests) is in a similar position, and is disguising both her identity and her emotional state.

2 Athos is a mountain in Greece, Samothracia an island in the Aegean Sea.

3 Laborers, usually in a vineyard.

4 Lines, features especially of a face or body.

Which we, they said, in strength had gathered there
From the sleep of bondage; nor the vision fair
Of that bright pageantry beheld,—but blind
And silent, as a breathing corpse did fare,
Leaning upon my friend, till like a wind
To fevered cheeks, a voice flowed o'er my troubled mind.

XLVI.

Like music of some minstrel heavenly gifted,
To one whom fiends inthrall, this voice to me;
Scarce did I wish her veil to be uplifted,
I was so calm and joyous.—I could see
The platform where[1] we stood, the statues three
Which kept their marble watch on that high shrine,
The multitudes, the mountains, and the sea;
As, when eclipse hath past, things sudden shine
To men's astonished eyes most clear and crystalline.

XLVII.

At first Laone spoke most tremulously:
But soon her voice the calmness which it shed
Gathered, and—"thou art whom I sought to see,
And thou art our first votary[2] here," she said:
"I had a dear friend once, but he is dead!—
And of all those on the wide earth who breathe,
Thou dost resemble him alone—I spread
This veil between us two that thou beneath
Shouldst image[3] one who may have been long lost in death.

XLVIII.

"For this wilt thou not henceforth pardon me?
Yes, but those joys which silence well requite
Forbid reply;—why men have chosen me
To be the Priestess of this holiest rite
I scarcely know, but that the floods of light
Which flow over the world, have borne me hither
To meet thee, long most dear; and now unite
Thine hand with mine, and may all comfort wither
From both the hearts whose pulse in joy now beat together,

1 Originally "when"; corrected from Shelley's list of errata.

2 A person who has taken a (usually religious) vow.

3 Imagine, project an image of.

XLIX.

"If our own will as others' law we bind,
If the foul worship trampled here we fear;
If as ourselves we cease to love our kind!"—
She paused, and pointed upwards—sculptured there
Three shapes around her ivory throne appear;
One was a Giant, like a child asleep
On a loose rock, whose grasp crushed, as it were
In dream, sceptres and crowns; and one did keep
Its watchful eyes in doubt whether to smile or weep;

L.

A Woman sitting on the sculptured disk
Of the broad earth, and feeding from one breast
A human babe and a young basilisk;[1]
Her looks were sweet as Heaven's when loveliest
In Autumn eves.—The third Image was drest
In white wings swift as clouds in winter skies,
Beneath his feet, 'mongst ghastliest forms, represt° *repressed, pushed down*
Lay Faith, an obscene worm, who sought to rise,
While calmly on the Sun he turned his diamond eyes.[2]

LI.

Beside that Image then I sate, while she
Stood, 'mid the throngs which ever ebbed and flowed
Like light amid the shadows of the sea
Cast from one cloudless star, and on the crowd
That touch which none who feels forgets, bestowed;
And whilst the sun returned the stedfast gaze
Of the great Image as o'er Heaven it glode,
That rite had place; it ceased when sunset's blaze
Burned o'er the isles; all stood in joy and deep amaze.
When in the silence of all spirits there
Laone's voice was felt, and thro' the air
Her thrilling gestures spoke, most eloquently fair.

---

1 A mythical reptilian creature with a lethal gaze.

2 The three figures—the Giant, the Woman, and the winged Image—represent Equality, Love, and Wisdom. They revise the French Revolutionary slogan of "*Liberté, Egalité, Fraternité*" (Liberty, Equality, Fraternity or brotherhood) in terms that better suit Shelley's philosophical vision, in which equality between persons fosters love among all mankind, while love for others—as Plato predicts in the *Symposium* (c. 385–370 BCE)—ultimately encourages the love of wisdom necessary to human happiness. Cythna addresses each of these deities, in reverse order, in her hymn that follows the next stanza.

1.[1]

"Calm art thou as yon sunset! swift and strong
As new-fledged Eagles,[2] beautiful and young,
That float among the blinding beams of morning;
And underneath thy feet writhe Faith, and Folly,
Custom, and Hell, and mortal Melancholy—
Hark! the Earth starts to hear the mighty warning
Of thy voice sublime and holy;
Its free spirits here assembled,
See thee, feel thee, know thee now,—
To thy voice their hearts have trembled
Like ten thousand clouds which flow
With one wide wind as it flies!—
Wisdom! thy irresistible children rise
To hail thee, and the elements they chain[3]
And their own will to swell the glory of thy train[.]

2.

"O Spirit vast and deep as Night and Heaven!
Mother and soul of all to which is given
The light of life, the loveliness of being,
Lo! thou dost re-ascend the human heart,
Thy throne of power, almighty as thou wert
In dreams of Poets old grown pale by seeing
The shade of thee:—now, millions start
To feel thy lightnings thro' them burning:
Nature, or God, or Love, or Pleasure,
Or Sympathy the sad tears turning
To mutual smiles, a drainless° treasure, *bottomless, inexhaustible*
Descends amidst us;—Scorn, and Hate,
Revenge and Selfishness are desolate°— *destroyed*
A hundred nations swear that there shall be
Pity and Peace and Love, among the good and free!

---

1 Shelley uses Arabic numerals to denote the six stanzas of Cythna's hymn. Unlike the Spenserian form of the rest of the poem, this ode is composed of fifteen-line stanzas, each with six, ten-, or eleven-syllable lines followed by six shorter, highly irregular tetrameter lines, two pentameter lines, and then (as in the Spenserian stanza) a final alexandrine; note that line 520 of Stanza 4 has eleven syllables, and that Stanza 5 alters the ode's form somewhat, with five tetrameter lines instead of six, and closing with three pentameter lines instead of two. The content of the hymn may usefully be compared in its entirety to Shelley's "Ode to the West Wind."

2 In stark contrast to the allegory of the Snake and the Eagle in Canto First, here the image of "new-fledged Eagles" (i.e., young eagles that have just acquired adult feathers) seems to have only positive associations.

3 Shelley may refer here to the Enlightenment ambition to use scientific knowledge to "chain" or harness the natural elements, and to find in them the means of making life easier and more humane.

3.

"Eldest of things, divine Equality!
Wisdom and Love are but the slaves of thee,
The Angels of thy sway, who pour around thee
Treasures from all the cells of human thought,
And from the Stars, and from the Ocean brought,
And the last living heart whose beatings bound thee:[1]
    The powerful and the wise had sought
    Thy coming, thou in light descending
    O'er the wide land which is thine own
    Like the spring whose breath is blending
    All blasts of fragrance into one,
    Comest upon the paths of men!—
Earth bares her general bosom to thy ken,
And all her children here in glory meet
To feed upon thy smiles, and clasp thy sacred feet.

4.

"My brethren we are free! the plains and mountains,
The gray sea shore, the forests and the fountains,
Are haunts of happiest dwellers;—man and woman,
Their common bondage burst, may freely borrow
From lawless[2] love a solace for their sorrow;
For oft we still must weep, since we are human.
    A stormy night's serenest morrow,
    Whose showers are pity's gentle tears,
    Whose clouds are smiles of those that die
    Like infants without hopes or fears,
    And whose beams are joys that lie
    In blended hearts, now holds dominion;
The dawn of mind, which, upwards on a pinion
Borne, swift as sun-rise, far illumines space,
And clasps this barren world in its own bright embrace!

---

1 The meaning of this line is difficult to parse, but the gist seems to be that the "last living heart" contains (like the cosmos, the ocean, and the human mind) valuable things that Wisdom and Love bring as gifts to Equality. The heart in question might also be said to have "bound" or confined Equality before the revolution set her loose, but Shelley may be suggesting that the human heart and Equality share the same boundaries or limits. If the former interpretation holds, it suggests another, darker meaning for the line as well—that only when the heart of the last living member of the human race stops beating, and the race itself is extinct, will Equality truly reign over the earth.

2 Free love, love not bound by legal marriage. In a more general sense, love is "lawless" because it cannot be regulated or contained.

5.

"My brethren, we are free! the fruits are glowing
Beneath the stars, and the night winds are flowing
O'er the ripe corn, the birds and beasts are dreaming—
Never again may blood of bird or beast
Stain with its venomous stream a human feast,[1]
To the pure skies in accusation steaming,
  Avenging poisons shall have ceased
  To feed disease and fear and madness,
  The dwellers of the earth and air
  Shall throng around our steps in gladness
  Seeking their food or refuge there.
Our toil from thought all glorious forms shall cull,
To make this Earth, our home, more beautiful,
  And Science, and her sister Poesy,
  Shall clothe in light the fields and cities of the free!

6.

"Victory, Victory to the prostrate nations!
Bear witness Night, and ye mute Constellations
Who gaze on us from your crystalline cars![2]
Thoughts have gone forth whose powers can sleep no more!
Victory! Victory! Earth's remotest shore,
Regions which groan beneath the Antarctic stars,
    The green lands cradled in the roar
    Of western waves, and wildernesses
    Peopled and vast, which skirt the oceans
    Where morning dyes her golden tresses,
    Shall soon partake our high emotions:
    Kings shall turn pale! Almighty Fear
The Fiend-God, when our charmed name he hear,
Shall fade like shadow from his thousand fanes,
While Truth with Joy enthroned o'er his[3] lost empire reigns!"

LII.

Ere she had ceased, the mists of night intwining
Their dim woof, floated o'er the infinite throng;
She, like a spirit thro' the darkness shining,
In tones whose sweetness silence did prolong,
As if to lingering winds they did belong,

---

1 The principles of the vegetarian diet are here laid out in a manner similar to that of Shelley's *Vindication of Natural Diet* (see Appendix A1).

2 Chariots made of crystal. Many mythic traditions describe constellations being driven around the sky by god-helmed chariots.

3 I.e., Fear's.

Poured forth her inmost soul: a passionate speech
With wild and thrilling pauses woven among,
Which whoso° heard, was mute, for it could teach *whosoever, whoever*
To rapture° like her own all listening hearts to reach. *carry away, enchant*

LIII.

Her voice was as a mountain stream which sweeps
The withered leaves of Autumn[1] to the lake,
And in some deep and narrow bay then sleeps
In the shadow of the shores; as dead leaves wake
Under the wave, in flowers and herbs which make
Those green depths beautiful when skies are blue,
The multitude so moveless° did partake *without moving, passively*
Such living change, and kindling murmurs flew
As o'er that speechless calm delight and wonder grew.

LIV.

Over the plain the throngs were scattered then
In groups around the fires, which from the sea
Even to the gorge of the first mountain glen
Blazed wide and far: the banquet of the free
Was spread beneath many a dark cypress tree,
Beneath whose spires, which swayed in the red flame,[2]
Reclining as they ate, of Liberty
And Hope, and Justice, and Laone's name,
Earth's children did a woof of happy converse frame.

LV.

Their feast was such as Earth, the general mother,
Pours from her fairest bosom, when she smiles
In the embrace of Autumn; to each other
As when some parent fondly reconciles
Her warring children, she their wrath beguiles
With her[3] own sustenance; they relenting weep:
Such was this Festival, which from their isles
And continents, and winds, and oceans deep,
All shapes might throng to share, that fly, or walk, or creep.

---

1 Cf. p. 62, I.iv.36; p. 69, I.xxix.256; and p. 108, IV.xiii.117.

2 The original text has "light," which clearly violates the rhyme scheme of the Spenserian stanza. In the manuscript version of *Laon and Cythna*, Shelley had first written "light," then "flames," then finally "flame," suggesting that "the copy transcribed for the press must inadvertently have reintroduced 'light'"; see *The Complete Poetry of Percy Bysshe Shelley* 1.773–74. This edition follows previous ones in substituting "flame."

3 Originally "their"; corrected from Shelley's list of errata.

LVI.

Might share in peace and innocence, for gore
Or poison[1] none this festal° did pollute, *festival*
But piled on high, an overflowing store
Of pomegranates, and citrons, fairest fruit,
Melons, and dates, and figs, and many a root
Sweet and sustaining, and bright grapes ere yet
Accursed fire their mild juice could transmute
Into a mortal bane,[2] and brown corn set
In baskets; with pure streams their thirsting lips they wet.

LVII.

Laone had descended from the shrine,
And every deepest look and holiest mind
Fed on her form, though now those tones divine
Were silent as she past; she did unwind
Her veil, as with the crowds of her own kind
She mixed; some impulse made my heart refrain
From seeking her that night, so I reclined
Amidst a group, where on the utmost plain
A festal watch-fire burned beside the dusky main.

LVIII.

And joyous was our feast; pathetic° talk, *like-minded, sympathetic*
And wit, and harmony of choral strains,
While far Orion o'er the waves did walk
That flow among the isles, held us in chains
Of sweet captivity, which none disdains
Who feels: but when his zone grew dim in mist
Which clothes the Ocean's bosom,[3] o'er the plains
The multitudes went homeward, to their rest,
Which that delightful day with its own shadow blest.

---

1 I.e., animal meat or wine.

2 I.e., before the grapes could be used to make wine.

3 Cf. p. 103, III.xxxii.281–83.

Canto Sixth.

I.

BESIDE the dimness of the glimmering sea,
Weaving swift language from impassioned themes,
With that dear friend[1] I lingered, who to me
So late had been restored, beneath the gleams
Of the silver stars; and ever in soft dreams
Of future love and peace sweet converse lapt° *lulled or sheltered*
Our willing fancies, 'till the pallid beams
Of the last watchfire fell, and darkness wrapt
The waves, and each bright chain of floating fire was snapt.

II.

And till we came even to the City's wall
And the great gate, then, none knew whence or why,
Disquiet on the multitudes did fall:
And first, one pale and breathless passed us by,
And stared and spoke not;—then with piercing cry
A troop of wild-eyed women, by the shrieks
Of their own terror driven,—tumultuously
Hither and thither hurrying with pale cheeks,
Each one from fear unknown a sudden refuge seeks—

III.

Then, rallying cries of treason and of danger
Resounded: and—"they come! to arms! to arms!
The Tyrant is amongst us, and the stranger
Comes to enslave us in his name! to arms!"
In vain: for Panic, the pale fiend who charms
Strength to forswear° her right, those millions swept *abandon*
Like waves before the tempest—these alarms
Came to me, as to know their cause I leapt
On the gate's turret, and in rage and grief and scorn I wept!

IV.

For to the North I saw the town on fire,
And its red light made morning pallid now,
Which burst over wide Asia;—louder, higher,
The yells of victory and the screams of woe
I heard approach, and saw the throng below

1 Laon's friend from Cantos Second and Fifth.

Stream through the gates like foam-wrought[1] waterfalls
Fed from a thousand storms—the fearful glow
Of bombs flares[2] overhead—at intervals
The red artillery's bolt[3] mangling among them falls.

V.

And now the horsemen come—and all was done
Swifter than I have spoken—I beheld
Their red swords flash in the unrisen sun.
I rushed among the rout° to have repelled *crowd*
That miserable flight—one moment quelled
By voice, and looks, and eloquent despair,
As if reproach from their own hearts withheld
Their steps, they stood; but soon came pouring there
New multitudes, and did those rallied bands o'erbear.° *overwhelm*

VI.

I strove, as drifted on some cataract° *waterfall*
By irresistible streams, some wretch might strive
Who hears its fatal roar:—the files compact
Whelmed me,[4] and from the gate availed to drive
With quickening impulse, as each bolt did rive
Their ranks with bloodier chasm:—into the plain
Disgorged° at length the dead and the alive *vomited*
In one dread mass, were parted, and the stain
Of blood, from mortal steel fell o'er the fields like rain.

VII.

For now the despot's bloodhounds with their prey,
Unarmed and unaware, were gorging deep
Their gluttony of death; the loose array
Of horsemen o'er the wide fields murdering sweep,
And with loud laughter for their tyrant reap
A harvest sown with other hopes, the while,
Far overhead, ships from Propontis[5] keep
A killing rain of fire:—when the waves smile
As sudden earthquakes light many a volcano isle.

---

1 Made of or covered with foam.

2 Shelley presumably meant something like "bombs' flares" or "bomb's flare."

3 Arrow, especially one discharged from a crossbow.

4 I.e., the tightly-clustered groups of foot-soldiers ("files") knocked me over.

5 Ancient name for the Sea of Marmara, an inland sea within the borders of Turkey, which links the Black Sea to the Aegean.

VIII.

Thus sudden, unexpected feast was spread
For the carrion fowls° of Heaven.—I saw the sight[—] *scavenger birds*
I moved—I lived—as o'er the heaps of dead,
Whose stony eyes glared in the morning light
I trod;—to me there came no thought of flight,° *retreat, escape*
But with loud cries of scorn, which whoso heard
That dreaded death, felt in his veins the might
Of virtuous shame return, the crowd I stirred,
And desperation's hope in many hearts recurred.

IX.

A band of brothers[1] gathering round me, made,
Although unarmed, a stedfast front, and still
Retreating, with stern looks beneath the shade
Of gathered eyebrows, did the victors fill
With doubt even in success; deliberate will
Inspired our growing troop, not overthrown
It gained the shelter of a grassy hill,
And ever still our comrades were hewn° down, *cut*
And their defenceless limbs beneath our footsteps strown.

X.

Immovably we stood—in joy I found,
Beside me then, firm as a giant pine
Among the mountain vapours driven around,
The old man[2] whom I loved—his eyes divine
With a mild look of courage answered mine,
And my young friend was near, and ardently
His hand grasped mine a moment—now the line
Of war extended, to our rallying cry
As myriads[3] flocked in love and brotherhood to die.

XI.

For ever while the sun was climbing Heaven
The horseman hewed our unarmed myriads down
Safely, tho' when by thirst of carnage driven
Too near, those slaves were swiftly overthrown

---

1 Cf. the famous lines from the St. Crispin's Day speech in Shakespeare's *Henry V*: "We few, we happy few, we band of brothers" (4.3.60).

2 I.e., the Hermit.

3 Large numbers, from the Ancient Greek for "ten thousand."

By hundreds leaping on them:—flesh and bone
Soon made our ghastly ramparts; then the shaft
Of the artillery from the sea was thrown
More fast and fiery, and the conquerors laugh'd
In pride to hear the wind our screams of torment waft.

XII.

For on one side alone the hill gave shelter,
So vast that phalanx[1] of unconquered men,
And there the living in the blood did welter° *writhe, struggle*
Of the dead and dying, which, in that green glen
Like stifled torrents, made a plashy fen[2]
Under the feet—thus was the butchery waged
While the sun clombe° Heaven's eastern steep—but when *climbed*
It 'gan to sink, a fiercer combat raged,
For in more doubtful strife the armies were engaged.

XIII.

Within a cave upon the hill were found
A bundle of rude pikes,[3] the instrument
Of those who war but on their native ground
For natural rights:[4] a shout of joyance sent
Even from our hearts the wide air pierced and rent,
As those few arms the bravest and the best
Seized, and each sixth, thus armed, did now present
A line which covered and sustained the rest,
A confident phalanx, which the foes on every side invest.[5]

XIV.

That onset turned the foes to flight almost
But soon they saw their present strength, and knew
That coming night would to our resolute host
Bring victory, so dismounting close they drew

---

1 A group of heavily-armed soldiers organized into rows, with the soldiers in front pointing their spears forward, and each subsequent row of soldiers holding their spears at oblique angles to the front line.

2 Swampy or splashing marsh.

3 Primitive spears, or even just sharpened sticks.

4 I.e., rights that every person has simply by virtue of being a person, such as the right to defend oneself. Note that Shelley implicitly contrasts the protection of "native ground" to war conducted for reasons that, we can assume, include the desire to take other people's land.

5 Enclose, lay siege to. The line is irregular, having fifteen syllables instead of the alexandrine's customary twelve.

Their glittering files, and then the combat grew
Unequal but most horrible;—and ever
Our myriads, whom the swift bolt overthrew,
Or the red sword, failed like a mountain river
Which rushes forth in foam to sink in sands forever.

XV.

Sorrow and shame, to see with their own kind
Our human brethren mix, like beasts of blood,
To mutual ruin armed by one behind
Who sits and scoffs!—That friend so mild and good,
Who like its shadow near my youth had stood,
Was stabbed!—my old preserver's hoary hair
With the flesh clinging to its roots, was strewed
Under my feet!—I lost all sense or care,
And like the rest I grew desperate and unaware.

XVI.

The battle became ghastlier—in the midst
I paused, and saw, how ugly and how fell
O Hate! thou art, even when thy life thou shed'st
For love. The ground in many a little dell
Was broken, up and down whose steeps befell
Alternate victory and defeat, and there
The combatants with rage most horrible
Strove, and their eyes started with cracking° stare, *mad, wild*
And impotent their tongues they lolled into the air,

XVII.

Flaccid and foamy, like a mad dog's hanging;
Want, and Moon-madness, and the pest's swift Bane[1]
When its shafts smite—while yet its bow is twanging—
Have each their mark and sign—some ghastly stain;
And this was thine, O War! of hate and pain
Thou loathed slave. I saw all shapes of death
And ministered to many, o'er the plain
While carnage in the sun-beam's warmth did seethe,
Till twilight o'er the east wove her serenest wreath.

---

1 Famine and poverty, and the madness triggered by the full moon, and the swiftly moving (because highly contagious) misery of the plague.

XVIII.

The few who yet survived, resolute and firm
Around me fought. At the decline of day
Winding above the mountain's snowy term,
New banners shone: they quivered in the ray
Of the sun's unseen orb—ere night the array° *ranks*
Of fresh troops hemmed us in—of those brave bands
I soon survived alone—and now I lay
Vanquished and faint, the grasp of bloody hands
I felt, and saw on high the glare of falling brands:° *torches*

XIX.

When on my foes a sudden terror came,
And they fled, scattering—lo! with reinless speed
A black Tartarian horse[1] of giant frame
Comes trampling over the dead, the living bleed
Beneath the hoofs of that tremendous steed,
On which, like to an Angel, robed in white,
Sate one waving a sword;—the hosts recede
And fly, as thro' their ranks, with awful might,
Sweeps in the shadow of eve that Phantom swift and bright;

XX.

And its path made a solitude.—I rose
And marked its coming: it relaxed its course
As it approached me, and the wind that flows
Thro' night, bore accents to mine ear whose force
Might create smiles in death—the Tartar horse
Paused, and I saw the shape its might which swayed,
And heard her musical pants, like the sweet source
Of waters in the desart, as she said,
"Mount with me, Laon, now"—I rapidly obeyed.

XXI.

Then: "Away! away!" she cried, and stretched her sword
As 'twere a scourge over the courser's° head, *battle horse's*
And lightly shook the reins:[2]—We spake no word

---

1 Tartars are a native people of eastern Europe and northern Asia, known for their skill on horseback.

2 Cythna's appearance in stanzas xix–xxi calls to mind a number of warrior women from antiquity through the Renaissance, from the Celtic queen Boadicea, who led a revolt against the Roman Empire, to Virgil's Camilla and Juturna, who defend Latium from the invasion of Aeneas' army in Books 11 and 12 of the *Aeneid*, to Spenser's female knight Britomart to Tasso's heroic maiden

But like the vapour of the tempest fled
Over the plain; her dark hair was dispread° *spread out*
Like the pine's locks upon the lingering blast;
Over mine eyes its shadowy strings it spread
Fitfully, and the hills and streams fled fast,
As o'er their glimmering forms the steed's broad shadow past.

XXII.

And his hoofs ground the rocks to fire and dust,
His strong sides made the torrents rise in spray,
And turbulence, as of a whirlwind's gust,
Surrounded us;—and still away! away!
Thro' the desart night we sped, while she alway
Gazed on a mountain which we neared, whose crest
Crowned with a marble ruin, in the ray
Of the obscure stars gleamed;—its rugged breast
The steed strained up, and then his impulse° did arrest. *forward motion*

XXIII.

A rocky hill which overhung the Ocean:—
From that lone ruin, when the steed that panted
Paused, might be heard the murmur of the motion
Of waters, as in spots forever haunted
By the choicest winds of Heaven, which are inchanted
To music, by the wand of Solitude,
That wizard wild, and the far tents implanted° *fixed, embedded*
Upon the plain, be seen by those who stood
Thence marking the dark shore of Ocean's curved flood.

XXIV.

One moment these were heard and seen—another
Past; and the two who stood beneath that night,
Each only heard, or saw, or felt the other;
As from the lofty steed she did alight,
Cythna, (for, from the eyes whose deepest light
Of love and sadness made my lips feel pale
With influence strange of mournfullest delight,
My own sweet sister[1] looked), with joy did quail,
And felt her strength in tears of human weakness fail.

Clorinda in *Gerusalemme Liberata* (1581). The allusion to Clorinda is especially suggestive here, since it is she who saves the lovers Sophronia and Olindo from burning at the stake, the fate of Laon and Cythna in Canto Twelfth.

1 *RoI* has "Cythna."

XXV.

And, for a space in my embrace she rested,
Her head on my unquiet heart reposing,
While my faint arms her languid frame invested:
At length she looked on me, and, half unclosing
Her tremulous lips, said: "Friend, thy bands were losing
The battle, as I stood before the King
In bonds.—I burst them then, and, swiftly choosing
The time, did seize a Tartar's sword, and spring
Upon his horse, and swift as on the whirlwind's wing,

XXVI.

"Have thou and I been borne beyond pursuer,
And we are here."—Then turning to the steed,
She pressed the white moon on his front with pure
And rose-like lips, and many a fragrant weed
From the green ruin plucked, that he might feed;—
But I to a stone seat that Maiden led,
And kissing her fair eyes, said, "Thou hast need
Of rest," and I heaped up the courser's bed
In a green mossy nook, with mountain flowers dispread.

XXVII.

Within that ruin, where a shattered portal
Looks to the eastern stars, abandoned now
By man, to be the home of things immortal,
Memories, like awful ghosts which come and go,
And must inherit all he builds below,
When he is gone, a hall stood; o'er whose roof
Fair clinging weeds with ivy pale did grow,
Clasping its gray rents with a verdurous woof,
A hanging dome of leaves, a canopy moon-proof.[1]

XXVIII.

The autumnal winds, as if spell-bound, had made
A natural couch of leaves in that recess,
Which seasons none disturbed, but in the shade
Of flowering parasites,[2] did spring love to dress
With their sweet blooms the wintry loneliness

1 I.e., the ivy weaves a leafy ("verdurous") awning over the roof's crumbling stones, blocking out the moon's rays.

2 Flowering parasitic plants native to Western Asia include sandalwood, dodder, and mistletoe.

Of those dead leaves, shedding their stars, whene'er
The wandering wind her nurslings might caress;
Whose intertwining fingers ever there,
Made music wild and soft that filled the listening air.

XXIX.

We know not where we go, or what sweet dream
May pilot° us thro' caverns strange and fair *drive, steer*
Of far and pathless passion, while the stream
Of life, our bark doth on its whirlpools bear,
Spreading swift wings as sails to the dim air;
Nor should we seek to know, so the devotion
Of love and gentle thoughts be heard still there
Louder and louder from the utmost Ocean
Of universal life, attuning its commotion.

XXX.

To the pure all things are pure! Oblivion wrapped
Our spirits, and the fearful overthrow
Of public hope was from our being snapt,
Tho' linked years had bound it there; for now
A power, a thirst, a knowledge, which below
All thoughts, like light beyond the atmosphere,
Clothing its clouds with grace, doth ever flow,
Came on us, as we sate in silence there,
Beneath the golden stars of the clear azure air.

XXXI.

In silence which doth follow talk that causes
The baffled heart to speak with sighs and tears,
When wildering passion swalloweth up the pauses
Of inexpressive speech:—the youthful years
Which we together past, their hopes and fears,
The blood itself which ran within our frames,
That likeness of the features which endears
The thoughts expressed by them, our very names,
And all the winged hours which speechless memory claims,

XXXII.

Had found a voice:—and ere that voice did pass,
The night grew damp and dim, and thro' a rent
Of the ruin where we sate, from the morass,° *marshland*
A wandering Meteor by some wild wind sent,

Hung high in the green dome, to which it lent
A faint and pallid lustre; while the song
Of blasts, in which its[1] blue hair quivering bent,
Strewed strangest sounds the moving leaves among;
A wondrous light, the sound as of a spirit's tongue.

XXXIII.

The Meteor shewed the leaves on which we sate,
And Cythna's glowing arms, and the thick ties
Of her soft hair, which bent with gathered weight
My neck near hers, her dark and deepening eyes,
Which, as twin phantoms of one star that lies
O'er a dim well, move, though the star reposes,
Swam in our mute and liquid ecstasies,
Her marble brow, and eager lips, like roses,
With their own fragrance pale, which Spring but half uncloses.

XXXIV.

The meteor to its far morass returned:
The beating of our veins one interval
Made still; and then I felt the blood that burned
Within her frame, mingle with mine, and fall
Around my heart like fire; and over all
A mist was spread, the sickness of a deep
And speechless swoon of joy, as might befall
Two disunited spirits[2] when they leap
In union from this earth's obscure and fading sleep.

XXXV.

Was it one moment that confounded thus
All thought, all sense, all feeling, into one
Unutterable power, which shielded us
Even from our own cold looks, when we had gone
Into a wide and wild oblivion
Of tumult and of tenderness? or now
Had ages, such as make the moon and sun,

---

1 I.e., the meteor's.

2 The idea that Laon and Cythna's spirits are not naturally separate but have rather been "dis-united" may allude to Aristophanes' speech in the *Symposium*, where the playwright famously recounts a creation myth in which all humans used to come in bodies with two heads, four arms, and four legs. Zeus, concerned that these humans would grow too powerful, cut them all in two, leaving each half of the original body to search for its missing piece. The desire for and the pursuit of this original whole, according to Aristophanes, is what we call love. See Plato, *Symposium*, 189d5–191d5.

The seasons, and mankind their changes know,
Left fear and time unfelt by us alone below?

XXXVI.

I know not. What are kisses whose fire clasps
The failing heart in languishment, or limb
Twined within limb? or the quick dying gasps
Of the life meeting, when the faint eyes swim
Thro' tears of a wide mist boundless and dim,
In one caress? What is the strong controul[1]
Which leads the heart that dizzy steep to climb,
Where far over the world those vapours roll,
Which blend two restless frames in one reposing soul?

XXXVII.

It is the shadow which doth float unseen,
But not unfelt, o'er blind mortality,
Whose divine darkness fled not, from that green
And lone recess, where lapt in peace did lie
Our linked frames; till, from the changing sky,
That night and still another day had fled;
And then I saw and felt. The moon was high,
And clouds, as of a coming storm, were spread
Under its orb,—loud winds were gathering overhead.

XXXVIII.

Cythna's sweet lips seemed lurid[2] in the moon,
Her fairest limbs with the night wind were chill,
And her dark tresses were all loosely strewn
O'er her pale bosom:—all within was still,
And the sweet peace of joy did almost fill
The depth of her unfathomable look;—
And we sate calmly, though that rocky hill,
The waves contending in its caverns strook,° *struck*
For they foreknew[3] the storm, and the gray ruin shook.

---

1 Control. Used ambiguously here, the word might mean either "self-restraint" or "self-assertion." These competing interpretations allow Shelley's defense of sexual love to dovetail with his notion of "passivity" as a form of political resistance—and poetic inspiration—at once non-violent and forceful.

2 Shining, especially with a reddish light.

3 Had foreknowledge of, predicted or sensed.

XXXIX.

There we unheeding sate, in the communion
Of interchanged vows, which, with a rite
Of faith most sweet and sacred, stamped our union.—
Few were the living hearts which could unite
Like ours, or celebrate a bridal night[1]
With such close sympathies, for to each other
Had high and solemn hopes, the gentle might
Of earliest love, and all the thoughts which smother,
Cold Evil's power, now linked a sister and a brother.[2]

XL.

And such is Nature's modesty,[3] that those
Who grow together cannot choose but love,
If faith or custom do not interpose,
Or common slavery mar what else might move
All gentlest thoughts; as in the sacred grove
Which shades the springs of Æthiopian Nile,
That living tree, which, if the arrowy dove
Strike with her shadow, shrinks in fear awhile,[4]
But its own kindred leaves clasps while the sun-beams smile;

XLI.

And clings to them, when darkness may dissever
The close caresses of all duller plants
Which bloom on the wide earth—thus we forever
Were linked, for love had nurst us in the haunts
Where knowledge, from its secret source inchants
Young hearts with the fresh music of its springing,

---

1 Shelley uses the language of marriage somewhat ironically here, for what makes Laon and Cythna's union "sacred" is that, in its rebuff of custom and convention—including the convention of marriage—it honors love's right to be free.

2 In *RoI,* lines 348–51 are rendered thus:

With such close sympathies, for they had sprung
From linked youth, and from the gentle might
Of earliest love, delayed and cherished long,
Which common hopes and fears made, like a tempest, strong.

3 *RoI* has "law divine."

4 The mimosa plant, or *mimosa pudica* ("shy"), shrinks back when it is touched. It is sometimes called "the sensitive plant," and in his 1820 poem by that same name, Shelley describes its "fan-like leaves" closing "beneath the kisses of Night" as the "living tree" mentioned here recoils from the dove's shadow (see Shelley, *The Sensitive-Plant,* in *Shelley's Poetry and Prose* 1.3–4). For this description, Shelley is probably indebted to Erasmus Darwin's *Loves of the Plants*: "Weak with nice sense, the chaste MIMOSA stands, / From each rude touch withdraws her timid hands" (1.301–02).

Ere yet its gathered flood feeds human wants,
As the great Nile feeds Egypt; ever flinging
Light on the woven boughs which o'er its waves are swinging.

XLII.

The tones of Cythna's voice like echoes were
Of those far murmuring streams; they rose and fell,
Mixed with mine own in the tempestuous air,—
And so we sate, until our talk befel
Of° the late ruin, swift and horrible, *turned to*
And how those seeds of hope might yet be sown,
Whose fruit is evil's mortal poison: well,
For us, this ruin[1] made a watch-tower lone,
But Cythna's eyes looked faint, and now two days were gone° *had passed*

XLIII.

Since she had food:—therefore I did awaken
The Tartar steed, who, from his ebon mane,
Soon as the clinging slumbers he had shaken,
Bent his thin head to seek the brazen rein,
Following me obediently; with pain
Of heart, so deep and dread, that one caress,
When lips and heart refuse to part again,
Till they have told their fill, could scarce express
The anguish of her mute and fearful tenderness,

XLIV.

Cythna beheld me part, as I bestrode
That willing steed—the tempest and the night,
Which gave my path its safety as I rode
Down the ravine of rocks, did soon unite
The darkness and the tumult of their might
Borne on all winds.—Far thro' the streaming rain
Floating, at intervals the garments white
Of Cythna gleamed, and her voice once again
Came to me on the gust, and soon I reached the plain.

XLV.

I dreaded not the tempest, nor did he
Who bore me, but his eyeballs wide and red

---

1 While "the late ruin" of line 374 refers to the defeat of the revolutionary army, here Laon is talking about the abandoned hall where he and Cythna have taken shelter.

Turned on the lightning's cleft[1] exultingly;
And when the earth beneath his tameless tread,
Shook with the sullen thunder, he would spread
His nostrils to the blast, and joyously
Mock the fierce peal[2] with neighings;—thus we sped
O'er the lit plain, and soon I could descry
Where Death and Fire had gorged° the spoil of victory. *eaten greedily*

XLVI.

There was a desolate village in a wood
Whose bloom-inwoven leaves now scattering fed
The hungry storm; it was a place of blood,
A heap of hearthless walls;—the flames were dead
Within those dwellings now,—the life had fled
From all those corpses now,—but the wide sky
Flooded with lightning was ribbed overhead
By the black rafters, and around did lie
Women, and babes, and men, slaughtered confusedly.

XLVII.

Beside the fountain in the market-place
Dismounting, I beheld those corpses stare
With horny eyes upon each other's face,
And on the earth, and on the vacant air,
And upon me, close to the waters where
I stooped to slake my thirst;—I shrank to taste,
For the salt bitterness of blood was there;
But tied the steed beside, and sought in haste
If any yet survived amid that ghastly waste.[3]

XLVIII.

No living thing was there beside one woman,
Whom I found wandering in the streets, and she
Was withered from a likeness of aught human
Into a fiend, by some strange misery:
Soon as she heard my steps she leaped on me,
And glued her burning lips to mine, and laughed
With a loud, long, and frantic laugh of glee,

---

1 I.e., the lightning's splitting ("cleft") of the sky's darkness.

2 A ringing sound, in this case of thunder.

3 A region that has been devastated, for example by war.

And cried, "Now, Mortal, thou hast deeply quaffed° *drunk*
The Plague's blue[1] kisses—soon millions shall pledge the draught![2]

XLIX.

"My name is Pestilence—this bosom dry,
Once fed two babes—a sister and a brother—
When I came home, one in the blood did lie
Of three death-wounds—the flames had ate the other!
Since then I have no longer been a mother,
But I am Pestilence;—hither and thither
I flit about, that I may slay and smother:—
All lips which I have kissed must surely wither,
But Death's—if thou art he, we'll go to work together!

L.

"What seek'st thou here? the moonlight comes in flashes,—
The dew is rising dankly from the dell—
'Twill moisten her![3] and thou shalt see the gashes
In my sweet boy, now full of worms—but tell
First what thou seek'st."—"I seek for food."—"'Tis well,
Thou shalt have food; Famine, my paramour,° *lover*
Waits for us at the feast—cruel and fell
Is Famine, but he drives not from his door
Those whom these lips have kissed, alone. No more, no more!"

LI.

As thus she spake, she grasped me with the strength
Of madness, and by many a ruined hearth
She led, and over many a corpse:—at length
We came to a lone hut, where on the earth
Which made its floor, she in her ghastly mirth
Gathering from all those homes now desolate,
Had piled three heaps of loaves, making a dearth
Among the dead[4]—round which she set in state
A ring of cold, stiff babes; silent and stark they sate.

---

1 I.e., like the lips of a corpse.

2 Toast, i.e., with the drink ("draught") of the "Plague's blue kisses."

3 I.e., moisten her burnt body.

4 I.e., a scarcity of bread in the homes of those already dead, whose food Pestilence has seized. This line may allude to Thucydides' discussion of a prophecy that haunts the Athenians once their city is overcome with the plague during the Peloponnesian War: "A Dorian war shall come and with it death." Thucydides records that "there had been a controversy as to whether the word in this ancient verse was 'dearth' rather than 'death'; but in the present state of affairs the *(continued)*

LII.

She leaped upon a pile, and lifted high
Her mad looks to the lightning, and cried: "Eat!
Share the great feast—to-morrow we must die!"[1]
And then she spurned the loaves with her pale feet,
Towards her bloodless guests;—that sight to meet,
Mine eyes and my heart ached, and but that she
Who loved me, did with absent looks defeat
Despair, I might have raved in sympathy;
But now I took the food that woman offered me;

LIII.

And vainly having with her madness striven° *struggled*
If I might win° her to return with me, *persuade*
Departed. In the eastern beams of Heaven
The lightning now grew pallid—rapidly,
As by the shore of the tempestuous sea
The dark steed bore me, and the mountain grey
Soon echoed to his hoofs, and I could see
Cythna among the rocks, where she alway
Had sate, with anxious eyes fixed on the lingering day.

LIV.

And joy was ours to meet: she was most pale,
Famished, and wet and weary, so I cast
My arms around her, lest her steps should fail
As to our home we went, and, thus embraced,
Her full heart seemed a deeper joy to taste
Than e'er the prosperous know; the steed behind
Trod peacefully along the mountain waste,° *uncultivated*
We reached our home ere morning could unbind
Night's latest veil, and on our bridal couch reclin'd.

---

view that the word was 'death' naturally prevailed; it was a case of people adapting their memories to suit their sufferings" (2.54).

1 Cf. Isaiah 22:13: "And behold joy and gladness, slaying oxen, and killing sheep, eating flesh, and drinking wine: let us eat and drink; for to morrow we shall die."

LV.

Her chilled heart having cherished in my bosom,
And sweetest kisses past, we two did share
Our peaceful meal:—as an autumnal blossom
Which spreads its shrunk leaves in the sunny air,
After cold showers, like rainbows woven there,
Thus in her lips and cheeks the vital spirit
Mantled,° and in her eyes, an atmosphere *adorned*
Of health, and hope; and sorrow languished near it,
And fear, and all that dark despondence doth inherit.

Canto Seventh.

I.

SO we sate joyous as the morning ray
Which fed upon the wrecks of night and storm
Now lingering on the winds; light airs did play
Among the dewy weeds, the sun was warm,
And we sate linked in the inwoven charm
Of converse and caresses sweet and deep,
Speechless caresses, talk that might disarm
Time, tho' he wield the darts of death and sleep,
And those thrice mortal barbs in his own poison steep.

II.

I told her of my sufferings and my madness,
And how, awakened from that dreamy mood
By Liberty's uprise, the strength of gladness
Came to my spirit in my solitude;
And all that now I was, while tears pursued
Each other down her fair and listening cheek
Fast as the thoughts which fed them, like a flood
From sunbright dales; and when I ceased to speak,
Her accents soft and sweet the pausing air did wake.

III.

She told me a strange tale of strange endurance,
Like broken memories of many a heart
Woven into one; to which no firm assurance,
So wild were they, could her own faith impart.[1]
She said that not a tear did dare to start
From the swoln brain, and that her thoughts were firm
When from all mortal hope she did depart,
Borne by those slaves across the Ocean's term,° *boundary, border*
And that she reached the port without one fear infirm.[2]

IV.

One was she among many there, the thralls° *slaves*
Of the cold tyrant's cruel lust: and they

---

1 I.e., Cythna herself is not certain that the events she recounts in the following stanzas actually happened.

2 Weak. It is not clear if Shelley means that Cythna had not been weakened (made "infirm") by fear, or if she arrived there free of "fear infirm"—that is, the kind of fear that, in being itself weak, betrays a weakness in the person who harbors it.

Laughed mournfully in those polluted halls;
But she was calm and sad, musing alway
On loftiest enterprise, till on a day
The Tyrant heard her singing to her lute
A wild, and sad, and spirit-thrilling lay,
Like winds that die in wastes°—one moment mute *deserts, unpopulated areas*
The evil thoughts it made, which did his breast pollute.[1]

V.

Even when he saw her wonderous loveliness,
One moment to great Nature's sacred power[2]
He bent, and was no longer passionless;
But when he bade her to his secret bower
Be borne, a loveless victim, and she tore
Her locks in agony, and her words of flame
And mightier looks availed not; then he bore
Again his load of slavery, and became
A king, a heartless beast, a pageant and a name.[3]

VI.

She told me what a loathsome agony
Is that when selfishness mocks love's delight,
Foul as in dreams most fearful imagery
To dally with the mowing° dead—that night *grimacing*
All torture, fear, or horror made seem light
Which the soul dreams or knows, and when the day
Shone on her awful frenzy, from the sight
Where like a Spirit in fleshly chains she lay
Struggling, aghast and pale the Tyrant fled away.

---

1 Note that both Othman's halls and his "breast" or heart are polluted, as if the affliction Shelley calls Lust spreads germ-like from a person to his environment, and from an environment to the person who inhabits it. The idea that a mentality and a location might be mutually constitutive recalls Satan's famous declaration in *Paradise Lost*: "The mind is its own place, and in itself / Can make a Heaven of Hell, a Hell of Heaven" (1.254–55).

2 I.e., love.

3 The argument of the stanza is that Othman's attraction to Cythna is natural and laudable; it is an expression of the love that links all human beings in a universal quest for the beautiful and the good. However, when Othman forces himself on Cythna, he betrays this love, and falls back into the unfortunate state where he is no longer a human being, but rather a hollow abstraction ("a pageant and a name") crossed dangerously with the powers of kingship and the uncontrolled appetite of a "beast."

VII.

Her madness was a beam of light, a power
Which dawned thro' the rent soul; and words it gave
Gestures and looks, such as in whirlwinds bore
Which might not be withstood, whence none could save
All who approached their sphere, like some calm wave
Vexed into whirlpools by the chasms beneath;
And sympathy made each attendant slave
Fearless and free, and they began to breathe
Deep curses, like the voice of flames far underneath.

VIII.

The King felt pale upon his noon-day throne:
At night two slaves he to her chamber sent,
One was a green and wrinkled eunuch,[1] grown
From human shape into an instrument
Of all things ill—distorted, bowed and bent.
The other was a wretch from infancy
Made dumb[2] by poison; who nought knew or meant
But to obey; from the fire-isles came he,
A diver lean and strong, of Oman's coral sea.[3]

IX.

They bore her to a bark, and the swift stroke
Of silent rowers clove the blue moonlight seas,
Until upon their path the morning broke;
They anchored then, where, be there calm or breeze,

---

1 A man who has been castrated, usually before puberty. Eunuchs were traditionally used to guard harems, since they were thought to present neither sexual threat nor sexual appeal to the women who were kept there.

2 Mute. This description may be taken literally or figuratively. Perhaps, as the following clause explains, the guard has been indoctrinated into and so silenced by the "poison" of Othman's regime. Perhaps he has actually been made mute by the use of some kind of toxin.

3 Oman is a country on the southeast coast of the Arabian peninsula, though by "Oman's coral sea" Shelley likely refers to both the Persian Gulf and the Gulf of Oman. When Shelley was writing his poem, the Omani Empire controlled the southern and much of the eastern coast of the Persian Gulf, as well as portions of East Africa. The Empire's African holdings included the Zanzibar archipelago, hub of the slave trade; combined with Shelley's identification of the "diver" as an "Æthiop," below, this reference to Oman seems to imply that the diver has been captured and sold in Zanzibar before ending up ultimately in Othman's service. Cf. the opening lines of Thomas Moore's 1817 poem *Lalla Rookh*:

'Tis moonlight over OMAN's Sea;—
  Her banks of pearl and palmy isles
Bask in the night-beam beauteously,
  And her blue waters sleep in smiles.

The gloomiest of the drear Symplegades[1]
Shakes with the sleepless surge;—the Æthiop[2] there
Wound his long arms around her, and with knees
Like iron clasped her feet, and plunged with her
Among the closing waves out of the boundless air.

X.[3]

"Swift as an eagle stooping from the plain
Of morning light, into some shadowy wood,
He plunged thro' the green silence of the main,
Thro' many a cavern which the eternal flood
Had scooped, as dark lairs for its monster brood;
And among mighty shapes which fled in wonder,
And among mightier shadows which pursued
His heels, he wound: until the dark rocks under
He touched a golden chain—a sound arose like thunder,

XI.

"A stunning clang of massive bolts redoubling
Beneath the deep—a burst of waters driven
As from the roots of the sea, raging and bubbling:
And in that roof of crags a space was riven
Thro' which there[4] shone the emerald beams of heaven,
Shot thro' the lines of many waves inwoven,
Like sunlight thro' acacia woods at even,
Thro' which, his way the diver having cloven,
Past like a spark sent up out of a burning oven.

XII.

"And then," she said, "he laid me in a cave
Above the waters, by that chasm of sea,
A fountain round and vast, in which the wave
Imprisoned, boiled and leaped perpetually,
Down which, one moment resting, he did flee,
Winning the adverse depth;[5] that spacious cell

---

1 According to Greek mythology, the Symplegades, known to the Romans as the Cyanean Rocks, were two islands located at the entrance to the Bosphorus, a famous strait in what is now Turkey. They would smash together periodically, crushing any ship that tried to pass between them. They were at last subdued by Jason and the Argonauts, who needed to get past the Symplegades in order to reach the Hellespont, and to return home to Greece.

2 I.e., the diver. In the nineteenth century, "Aethiop" referred to black Africans in general.

3 The quotation marks indicate that Cythna takes over the narration of her own story.

4 Originally "these"; corrected from Shelley's list of errata.

5 In other words, the diver goes back in the direction from whence he brought Cythna to her prison.

Like an upaithric[1] temple wide and high,
Whose aëry dome is inaccessible,
Was pierced with one round cleft thro' which the sun-beams fell.

XIII.

"Below, the fountain's brink was richly paven
With the deep's wealth, coral, and pearl, and sand
Like spangling gold, and purple shells engraven
With mystic legends by no mortal hand,
Left there, when thronging to the moon's command,
The gathering waves rent the Hesperian[2] gate
Of mountains, and on such bright floor did stand
Columns, and shapes like statues, and the state
Of kingless thrones, which Earth did in her heart create.

XIV.

"The fiend of madness which had made its prey
Of my poor heart, was lulled to sleep awhile:
There was an interval of many a day,
And a sea-eagle brought me food the while,
Whose nest was built in that untrodden isle,
And who, to be the jailor had been taught,
Of that strange dungeon; as a friend whose smile
Like light and rest at morn and even is sought,
That wild bird was to me, till madness misery brought.[3]

XV.

"The misery of a madness slow and creeping,
Which made the earth seem fire, the sea seem air,
And the white clouds of noon which oft were sleeping,
In the blue heaven so beautiful and fair,
Like hosts of ghastly shadows hovering there;
And the sea-eagle looked a fiend, who bore
Thy mangled limbs for food![4]—thus all things were

---

1 Open-air (from the Greek *hypaithros*, exposed, uncovered).

2 I.e., western, in the west like Hesperus, the Evening Star.

3 Like Prometheus, Cythna is visited by an eagle in her prison. Unlike Prometheus, however, she is fed by the eagle. The eagle of Aeschylus' *Prometheus Bound* (fifth century BCE)—which Shelley would rewrite as *Prometheus Unbound*—would peck out and eat his liver, which would regenerate to be pecked out again on a daily basis.

4 Cf. Laon's vision in III.xxvi.226–34 (p. 102).

Transformed into the agony which I wore
Even as a poisoned robe[1] around my bosom's core.

XVI.

"Again I knew the day and night fast fleeing,
The eagle, and the fountain, and the air;
Another frenzy came—there seemed a being
Within me—a strange load my heart did bear,
As if some living thing had made its lair
Even in the fountains of my life:—a long
And wondrous vision wrought from my despair,
Then grew, like sweet reality among
Dim visionary woes, an unreposing throng.° *restless crowd*

XVII.

"Methought I was about to be a mother—
Month after month went by, and still I dreamed
That we should soon be all to one another,
I and my child; and still new pulses seemed
To beat beside my heart, and still I deemed
There was a babe within—and when the rain
Of winter thro' the rifted cavern streamed,
Methought, after a lapse of lingering pain,
I saw that lovely shape, which near my heart had lain.

XVIII.

"It was a babe, beautiful from its birth,—
It was like thee, dear love, its eyes were thine,
Its brow, its lips, and so upon the earth
It laid its fingers as now rest on mine
Thine own beloved:—'twas a dream divine;
Even to remember how it fled, how swift,
How utterly, might make the heart repine,—
Tho 'twas a dream."—Then Cythna did uplift
Her looks on mine, as if some doubt she sought to shift:

XIX.

A doubt which would not flee, a tenderness
Of questioning grief, a source of thronging tears;
Which, having past, as one whom sobs opprest,

---

1 There are many poisoned robes in the classical tradition, including the Shirt of Nessus that killed Heracles, and the dress Medea gives to Glauce, her husband Jason's bride-to-be, whose flesh is melted off by the enchanted garment.

She spoke: "Yes, in the wilderness of years
Her memory, aye, like a green home appears,
She sucked her fill even at this breast, sweet love,
For many months. I had no mortal fears;[1]
Methought I felt her lips and breath approve,[2]—
It was a human thing which to my bosom clove.

XX.

"I watched the dawn of her first smiles, and soon
When zenith-stars were trembling on the wave,[3]
Or when the beams of the invisible moon,
Or sun, from many a prism within the cave
Their gem-born shadows to the water gave,
Her looks would hunt them, and with outspread hand,
From the swift lights which might that fountain pave,
She would mark one, and laugh, when that command
Slighting, it lingered there, and could not understand.

XXI.

"Methought her looks began to talk with me;
And no articulate sounds, but something sweet
Her lips would frame,[4]—so sweet it could not be,
That it was meaningless; her touch would meet
Mine, and our pulses calmly flow and beat
In response while we slept; and on a day
When I was happiest in that strange retreat,
With heaps of golden shells we two did play,—
Both infants, weaving wings for time's perpetual way.[5]

XXII.

"Ere night, methought, her waning eyes were grown
Weary with joy, and tired with our delight,
We, on the earth, like sister twins lay down
On one fair mother's bosom:—from that night
She fled;—like those illusions clear and bright,
Which dwell in lakes, when the red moon on high

---

1 Cf. Wordsworth's lines, "A slumber did my spirit seal; / I had no human fears," from "A Slumber Did My Spirit Seal," the 1800 edition of *Lyrical Ballads*, lines 1–2.

2 Prove. Cythna means that the physical feeling of the baby's lips and breath on her own breast seemed to verify that the baby was not a dream, but real.

3 I.e., when the reflection of those stars that seem to be the highest ("zenith-stars") in the sky was "trembling" or shimmering on the waves that come into Cythna's cave.

4 Give structure to; supply.

5 I.e., for time to use to fly along his eternal journey into the future.

Pause ere it wakens tempest;—and her flight,
Tho' 'twas the death of brainless phantasy,° *hallucination*
Yet smote my lonesome heart more than all misery.[1]

XXIII.

"It seemed that in the dreary night, the diver
Who brought me thither, came again, and bore
My child away. I saw the waters quiver,
When he so swiftly sunk, as once before:
Then morning came—it shone even as of yore,
But I was changed—the very life was gone
Out of my heart—I wasted more and more,
Day after day, and sitting there alone,
Vexed° the inconstant waves with my perpetual moan. *harassed*

XXIV.

"I was no longer mad, and yet methought
My breasts were swoln and changed:[2]—in every vein
The blood stood still one moment, while that thought
Was passing—with a gush of sickening pain
It ebbed even to its withered springs again:
When my wan° eyes in stern resolve I turned *dark, gloomy*
From that most strange delusion, which would fain
Have waked the dream[3] for which my spirit yearned
With more than human love,—then left it unreturned.

XXV.

"So now my reason was restored to me,
I struggled with that dream, which, like a beast
Most fierce and beauteous, in my memory
Had made its lair, and on my heart did feast;
But all that cave and all its shapes possest
By thoughts which could not fade, renewed each one
Some smile, some look, some gesture which had blest

---

1 Mary and Percy's first child, a girl, was born two months prematurely on 22 February 1815, and died two weeks later. Cythna's loss of her daughter almost certainly reflects something of this experience.

2 I.e., filled with milk, as though Cythna had actually been pregnant and given birth. In a letter to Hogg written on 6 March 1815, Mary reports, "Shelley is afraid of a fever from the milk" that, left undrunk, plugs up her breasts, "for I am no longer a mother now" (*Letters of Mary Wollstonecraft Shelley* 1.68–71).

3 In other words, Cythna tries to ignore the "strange delusion" that her breasts seem recently to have contained milk, a fantasy that would be likely to revive "the dream" of her child.

Me heretofore: I, sitting there alone,
Vexed the inconstant waves with my perpetual moan.

XXVI.

"Time past, I know not whether months or years;
For day, nor night, nor change of seasons made
Its note, but thoughts and unavailing tears:
And I became at last even as a shade,° *ghost*
A smoke, a cloud on which the winds have preyed,
'Till it be thin as air; until, one even,° *evening*
A Nautilus[1] upon the fountain played,
Spreading his azure sail where breath of Heaven
Descended not, among the waves and whirlpools driven.

XXVII.

"And when the Eagle came, that lovely thing,
Oaring with rosy feet its silver boat,
Fled near me as for shelter; on slow wing,
The Eagle, hovering o'er his prey did float;
But when he saw that I with fear did note
His purpose, proffering my own food to him,
The eager plumes subsided on his throat—
He came where that bright child of sea did swim,
And o'er it cast in peace his shadow broad and dim.

XXVIII.

"This wakened me, it gave me human strength
And hope, I know not whence or wherefore, rose,
But I resumed my ancient° powers at length; *old, previous*
My spirit felt again like one of those
Like thine, whose fate it is to make the woes
Of humankind their prey—what was this cave?
Its deep foundation no firm purpose knows
Immutable, resistless,° strong to save, *irresistible*
Like mind while yet it mocks the all-devouring grave.

---

1 A nautilus is a mollusk with a purplish, spiral-shaped shell, but Shelley may be thinking of the pelagic octopus or paper nautilus, which is native to the Mediterranean. Pelagic octopuses (genus *Argonauta*) are known as argonauts, which is appropriate since Cythna has been imprisoned near the Symplegades, the moving islands that Jason and his Argonauts made stand still (see above, p. 158, note 1).

XXIX.

"And where was Laon? might my heart be dead,
While that far dearer heart could move and be?
Or whilst over the earth the pall° was spread, *burial shroud*
Which I had sworn to rend? I might be free,
Could I but win that friendly bird to me,
To bring me ropes; and long in vain I sought
By intercourse of mutual imagery
Of objects,[1] if such aid he could be taught;
But fruit, and flowers, and boughs, yet never ropes he brought.

XXX.

"We live in our own world, and mine was made
From glorious phantasies of hope departed:
Aye, we are darkened with their floating shade,
Or cast a lustre on them—time imparted
Such power to me, I became fearless-hearted,
My eye and voice grew firm, calm was my mind,
And piercing, like the morn, now it has darted
Its lustre on all hidden things, behind
Yon dim and fading clouds which load the weary wind.

XXXI.

"My mind became the book through which I grew
Wise in all human wisdom, and its cave,
Which like a mine I rifled through and through,
To me the keeping of its secrets gave—
One mind, the type of all, the moveless wave
Whose calm reflects all moving things that are,[2]
Necessity,[3] and love, and life, the grave,

---

1 I.e., by showing the eagle objects that looked similar to ropes.

2 Cf. Wordsworth, *The Prelude* 6.624–40.

3 "Necessity" is an important term in the poem's remaining cantos and indeed one of the most important concepts in all of Shelley's work. In *Queen Mab* (1813), Necessity is described in general terms as the "Spirit of Nature," an "all-sufficing power" who is the "mother of the world" but without any "human sense" or "human mind" (6.197–98, 218–19). Like the wind who represents this same power in "Ode to the West Wind," Necessity treats human beings as "passive instruments," remaining wholly "impartial" to their interests (6.215–16). In "Ode to the West Wind," however, as in *Prometheus Unbound* and *Laon and Cythna,* Necessity takes on a political resonance and comes to mean something like the inexorable progressive movement of history, a movement that leads humanity toward a more equal and enlightened condition. *Prometheus Unbound,* for example, has Necessity working through the instrument of Demogorgon, the "people-monster" and allegory of the democratic will who brings down the tyrant Jupiter and ushers the world into a new, utopian state. In IX.xiv.123 below (p. 182), the term Necessity is appropriated by Othman's flunkies to undermine the principles and the goals of the revolution and to deny

And sympathy, fountains of hope and fear;
Justice, and truth, and time, and the world's natural sphere.

XXXII.

"And on the sand would I make signs to range
These woofs, as they were woven, of my thought;
Clear, elemental shapes, whose smallest change
A subtler language within language wrought:
The key of truths which once were dimly taught
In old Crotona;[1]—and sweet melodies
Of love, in that lone solitude I caught
From mine own voice in dream, when thy dear eyes
Shone thro' my sleep, and did that utterance harmonize.

XXXIII.

"Thy songs were winds whereon I fled at will,
As in a winged chariot, o'er the plain
Of crystal youth; and thou wert there to fill
My heart with joy, and there we sate again
On the grey margin of the glimmering main,[2]
Happy as then but wiser far, for we
Smiled on the flowery grave in which were lain
Fear, Faith, and Slavery; and mankind was free,
Equal, and pure and wise, in wisdom's prophecy.

XXXIV.

"For to my will my fancies were as slaves
To do their sweet and subtile ministries;
And oft from that bright fountain's shadowy waves
They would make human throngs gather and rise
To combat with my overflowing eyes,
And voice made deep with passion—thus I grew
Familiar with the shock and the surprise
And war of earthly minds, from which I drew
The power which has been mine to frame their thoughts anew.

---

altogether the possibility of improving the human social condition; it will be redeemed, however, and aligned with its more conventionally Shelleyan meaning, in IX.xxvii.24 (p. 186).

1 Crotone, a city on the southeastern coast of Italy, on the Ionian Sea, where Pythagoras founded his philosophical school.

2 I.e., the shore of the open sea.

XXXV.

"And thus my prison was the populous earth—
Where I saw—even as misery dreams of morn
Before the east has given its glory birth—
Religion's pomp made desolate by the scorn
Of Wisdom's faintest smile, and thrones uptorn,
And dwellings of mild people interspersed
With undivided fields of ripening corn,
And love made free,—a hope which we have nurst
Even with our blood and tears,—until its glory burst.

XXXVI.

"All is not lost! There is some recompense° *reward, result*
For hope whose fountain can be thus profound,° *deep*
Even throned Evil's splendid impotence,
Girt by its hell of power, the secret sound
Of hymns to truth and freedom—the dread bound° *limit, edge*
Of life and death past fearlessly and well,
Dungeons wherein the high resolve is found,
Racks which degraded woman's greatness tell,
And what may else be good and irresistible.

XXXVII.

"Such are the thoughts which, like the fires that flare
In storm-encompassed isles, we cherish yet
In this dark ruin—such were mine even there;
As in its sleep some odorous violet,
While yet its leaves with nightly dews are wet,
Breathes in prophetic dreams of day's uprise,
Or, as ere Scythian[1] frost in fear has met
Spring's messengers descending from the skies,
The buds foreknow their life—this hope must ever rise.

XXXVIII.

"So years had past, when sudden earthquake rent
The depth of ocean, and the cavern crackt
With sound, as if the world's wide continent
Had fallen in universal ruin wrackt;° *wracked, convulsing*
And thro' the cleft streamed in one cataract,
The stifling waters:—when I woke, the flood

---

1 Scythia was a mountainous region in Central Asia, encompassing the Ukrainian steppes and the northern Caucasus.

Whose banded waves that crystal cave had sacked° *stored, pocketed*
Was ebbing round me, and my bright abode
Before me yawned—a chasm desert,° and bare, and broad. *barren, dry*

XXXIX.

"Above me was the sky, beneath the sea:
I stood upon a point of shattered stone,
And heard loose rocks rushing tumultuously
With splash and shock into the deep—anon
All ceased, and there was silence wide and lone.
I felt that I was free! the Ocean-spray
Quivered beneath my feet, the broad Heaven shone
Around, and in my hair the winds did play
Lingering as they pursued their unimpeded way.

XL.

"My spirit moved upon the sea like wind
Which round some thymy cape[1] will lag and hover,
Tho' it can wake the still cloud, and unbind
The strength of tempest: day was almost over,
When thro' the fading light I could discover
A ship approaching—its white sails were fed
With the north wind—its moving shade did cover
The twilight deep;—the mariners in dread
Cast anchor when they saw new rocks around them spread.

XLI.

"And when they saw one sitting on a crag,
They sent a boat to me;—the sailors rowed
In awe thro' many a new and fearful jag
Of overhanging rock, thro' which there flowed
The foam of streams that cannot make abode.[2]
They came and questioned me, but when they heard
My voice, they became silent, and they stood
And moved as men in whom new love had stirred
Deep thoughts: so to the ship we passed without a word.

---

1 A promontory covered with thyme.

2 I.e., cannot come to a standstill.

Canto Eighth.

I.

"I sate beside the steersman then, and gazing
Upon the west, cried, 'Spread the sails! behold!
The sinking moon is like a watch-tower blazing
Over the mountains yet;—the City of Gold
Yon Cape alone does from the sight withhold;
The stream is fleet—the north breathes steadily
Beneath the stars, they tremble with the cold!
Ye cannot rest upon the dreary sea!—
Haste, haste to the warm home of happier destiny!'

II.

"The Mariners obeyed—the Captain stood
Aloof, and whispering to the Pilot, said,
'Alas, alas! I fear we are pursued
By wicked ghosts: a Phantom of the Dead,
The night before we sailed, came to my bed
In dream, like that!'—The Pilot then replied,
'It cannot be—she is a human Maid—
Her low voice makes you weep—she is some bride,
Or daughter of high birth—she can be nought beside.'[1]

III.

"We past the islets, borne by wind and stream,
And as we sailed, the Mariners came near
And thronged around to listen;—in the gleam
Of the pale moon I stood, as one whom fear
May not attaint,° and my calm voice did rear;[2] *touch, affect*
Ye are all human—yon broad moon gives light
To millions who the self-same likeness wear,
Even while I speak—beneath this very night,
Their thoughts flow on like ours, in sadness or delight.

IV.

"What dream ye? Your own hands have built an home,
Even for yourselves on a beloved shore:
For some, fond eyes are pining till they come,

1 Nothing more, i.e., not a supernatural creature.

2 For most of lines 24–243, Cythna is speaking aloud to the ship's company; in 200–27, she is quoting to Laon the speech of "a Youth" who is part of her audience.

How they will greet him when his toils are o'er,
And laughing babes rush from the well-known door!
Is this your care? ye toil for your own good—
Ye feel and think—has some immortal power
Such purposes? or in a human mood,
Dream ye that God[1] thus builds for man in solitude?

V.

"What then is God?[2] ye mock yourselves, and give
A human heart to what ye cannot know:
As if the cause of life could think and live!
'Twere as if man's own works should feel, and shew
The hopes, and fears, and thoughts from which they flow,
And he be like to them.[3] Lo! Plague is free
To waste, Blight, Poison, Earthquake, Hail, and Snow,
Disease, and Want, and worse Necessity[4]
Of hate and ill, and Pride, and Fear, and Tyranny.

VI.

"What then is God?[5] Some moon-struck sophist[6] stood
Watching the shade from his own soul upthrown
Fill Heaven and darken Earth, and in such mood
The Form he saw and worshipped was his own,
His likeness in the world's vast mirror shewn;
And 'twere an innocent dream, but that a faith
Nursed by fear's dew of poison, grows thereon,
And that men say, God has appointed Death
On all who scorn his will[7] to wreak immortal wrath.

VII.

"Men say they have seen God, and heard from God,
Or known from others who have known such things,

---

1 I.e., some God, as if he had a mind and personality like a human being's. Instead of "that God," *RoI* has "some Power."

2 *RoI* has "What is that power."

3 Cythna means that the assumption that God has feelings and intentions comparable to our own is as nonsensical as proposing that artifacts made by human beings share our features, or that we are like them. The suggestion is not so much that man has created God in his own image, but that the relationship between creator and created cannot be one of identity or reflection. Cf. Lucretius, *De Rerum Natura*, 6.50–79.

4 On Necessity, see p. 164, note 3.

5 *RoI* has "What is that power."

6 See Shelley's preface, p. 47, note 4.

7 *RoI* has "that Power has chosen Death / On all who scorn its laws."

And that his will is all our law, a rod
To scourge us into slaves[1]—that Priests and Kings,
Custom, domestic sway, aye, all that brings
Man's free-born soul beneath the oppressor's heel,
Are his strong ministers, and that the stings
Of death will make the wise his vengeance feel,
Tho' truth and virtue arm their hearts with tenfold steel.

VIII.

"And it is said that God[2] will punish wrong;
Yes, add despair to crime, and pain to pain!
And his red hell's undying snakes among,[3]
Will bind the wretch on whom is fixed a stain,
Which, like a plague, a burthen, and a bane,
Clung to him while he lived;—for, love and hate,
Virtue and vice, they say, are difference vain—
The will of strength is right[4]—this human state
Tyrants that they may rule, with lies thus desolate.

IX.

"Alas, what strength? opinion is more frail
Than yon dim cloud now fading on the moon
Even while we gaze, tho' it awhile avail[5]
To hide the orb of truth—and every throne
Of Earth or Heaven, tho' shadow, rests thereon,
One shape of many names:—for this ye plough
The barren waves of ocean, hence each one
Is slave or tyrant; all betray and bow,
Command, or kill, or fear, or wreak,° or suffer woe. *punish*

---

1 *RoI* has:
Men say that they themselves have heard and seen,
Or known from others who have known such things,
A Shade, a Form, which Earth and Heaven between
Wields an invisible rod[.]

2 *RoI* has "this Power."

3 *RoI* has "And deepest hell, and deathless snakes among[.]"

4 The difference between love and hate, or virtue and vice, is negligible or "vain" since, as it is currently practiced, religion does not give people the means to separate right from wrong, nor does it discriminate between them. Instead, it throws its own weight behind the "strength" of tyrants, aligning itself with whichever earthly power seems the mightiest.

5 Manages for a time.

X.

"Its names are each a sign which maketh holy
All power—ay, the ghost, the dream, the shade[1]
Of power—lust, falsehood, hate, and pride, and folly;
The pattern whence all fraud and wrong is made,
A law to which mankind has been betrayed;
And human love, is as the name well known
Of a dear mother, whom the murderer laid
In bloody grave, and, into darkness thrown,
Gathered her wildered babes around him as his own.

XI.

"O love! who to the hearts of wandering men
Art as the calm to Ocean's weary waves!
Justice, or truth, or[2] joy! those[3] only can
From slavery and religion's labyrinth caves
Guide us, as one clear star the seaman saves.
To give to all an equal share of good,
To track the steps of freedom tho' thro' graves
She pass, to suffer all in patient mood,
To weep for crime tho' stained with thy friend's dearest blood,

XII.

"To feel the peace of self-contentment's lot,
To own° all sympathies, and outrage none, *acknowledge, honor*
And in the inmost bowers of sense and thought,
Until life's sunny day is quite gone down,
To sit and smile with Joy, or, not alone,
To kiss salt tears from the worn cheek of Woe;
To live as if to love and live were one,—
This is not faith or law, nor those who bow
To thrones on Heaven or Earth, such destiny may know.

XIII.

"But children near their parents tremble now,
Because they must obey—one rules another,
For it is said God[4] rules both high and low,
And[5] man is made the captive of his brother,

---

1 Originally "the shade, the dream"; corrected from Shelley's list of errata.

2 Originally "and"; corrected from Shelley's list of errata.

3 Originally "these"; corrected from Shelley's list of errata.

4 *RoI* has "And, as one Power[.]"

5 *RoI* has "So[.]"

And Hate is throned on high with Fear her mother,
Above the Highest—and those fountain-cells,° *freshwater pools*
Whence love yet flowed when faith had choked all other,
Are darkened—Woman, as the bond-slave, dwells
Of man, a slave; and life is poisoned in its wells.

XIV.

"Man seeks for gold in mines, that he may weave
A lasting chain for his own slavery;—
In fear and restless care that he may live
He toils for others, who must ever be
The joyless thralls of like captivity;
He murders, for his chiefs delight in ruin;
He builds the altar, that its idol's fee
May be his very blood; he is pursuing
O, blind and willing wretch! his own obscure° undoing. *dark, dismal*

XV.

"Woman!—she is his slave, she has become
A thing I weep to speak—the child of scorn,
The outcast of a desolated home,
Falsehood, and fear, and toil, like waves have worn
Channels upon her cheek, which smiles adorn,
As calm decks° the false Ocean:—well ye know *adorns*
What Woman is, for none of Woman born,
Can choose but drain the bitter dregs of woe,
Which ever from the oppressed to the oppressors flow.

XVI.

"This need not be; ye might arise, and will
That gold should lose its power, and thrones their glory;
That love, which none may bind, be free to fill
The world, like light; and evil faith, grown hoary
With crime, be quenched and die.—Yon promontory
Even now eclipses the descending moon!—
Dungeons and palaces are transitory—
High temples fade like vapour—Man alone
Remains, whose will has power when all beside is gone.

XVII.

"Let all be free and equal!—from your hearts
I feel an echo; thro' my inmost frame
Like sweetest sound, seeking its mate, it darts—

Whence come ye, friends? alas, I cannot name
All that I read of sorrow, toil, and shame,
On your worn faces; as in legends old
Which make immortal the disastrous fame
Of conquerors and impostors false and bold,
The discord of your hearts, I in your looks behold.

XVIII.

"Whence come ye, friends? from pouring human blood
Forth on the earth?[1] or bring ye steel and gold,
That Kings may dupe and slay the multitude?
Or from the famished poor, pale, weak, and cold,
Bear ye the earnings of their toil? unfold!
Speak! are your hands in slaughter's sanguine hue
Stained freshly? have your hearts in guile grown old?
Know yourselves thus![2] ye shall be pure as dew,
And I will be a friend and sister unto you.

XIX.

"Disguise it not—we have one human heart—
All mortal thoughts confess° a common home: *disclose, reveal*
Blush not for what may to thyself impart
Stains of inevitable crime: the doom
Is this, which has, or may, or must, become
Thine, and all humankind's. Ye are the spoil
Which Time thus marks for the devouring tomb,
Thou and thy thoughts and they, and all the toil
Wherewith ye twine the rings of life's perpetual coil.

XX.

"Disguise it not—ye blush for what ye hate,
And Enmity is sister unto Shame;
Look on your mind—it is the book of fate—
Ah! it is dark with many a blazoned° name *painted*
Of misery—all are mirrors of the same;
But the dark fiend who with his iron pen,
Dipped in scorn's fiery poison, makes his fame
Enduring there, would o'er the heads of men
Pass harmless, if they scorned to make their hearts his den.

---

1 Cf. Job 2:2: "And the Lord said unto Satan, From whence comest thou? And Satan answered the Lord, and said, From going to and fro in the earth, and from walking up and down in it."

2 The phrase "know thyself"—the most famous of the Delphic maxims—was inscribed in stone at the Temple of Apollo at Delphi.

XXI.

"Yes, it is Hate, that shapeless fiendly thing
Of many names, all evil, some divine,
Whom self-contempt arms with a mortal sting;
Which, when the heart it[s] snaky folds intwine,
Is wasted quite, and when it doth repine
To gorge such bitter prey, on all beside
It turns with ninefold rage, as with its twine
When Amphisbæna[1] some fair bird has tied,
Soon o'er the putrid mass he threats° on every side. *menaces*

XXII.

"Reproach not thine own soul, but know thyself,
Nor hate another's crime, nor loathe thine own.
It is the dark idolatry of self,
Which, when our thoughts and actions once are gone,
Demands that man should weep, and bleed, and groan;
O vacant expiation![2] be at rest.—
The past is Death's, the future is thine own;
And love and joy can make the foulest breast
A paradise of flowers, where peace might build her nest.[3]

XXIII.

"Speak thou! whence come ye?"—A Youth made reply,[4]
"Wearily, wearily o'er the boundless deep
We sail;—thou readest well the misery
Told in these faded eyes, but much doth sleep
Within, which there the poor heart loves to keep,
Or dare not write on the dishonoured brow;
Even from our childhood have we learned to steep° *soak*
The bread of slavery in the tears of woe,
And never dreamed of hope or refuge until now.

XXIV.

"Yes—I must speak—my secret should have perished
Even with the heart it wasted, as a brand
Fades in the dying flame whose life it cherished,
But that no human bosom can withstand

---

1 A mythological lizard or serpent with a head at both ends of its body.

2 Useless repentance or self-punishment.

3 See p. 156, note 2.

4 Cythna now reports the Youth's speech.

Thee, wondrous Lady, and the mild command
Of thy keen eyes:—yes, we are wretched slaves,
Who from their wonted° loves and native land *accustomed, familiar*
Are reft,° and bear o'er the dividing waves *torn*
The unregarded prey of calm and happy graves.

XXV.

"We drag afar from pastoral° vales the fairest, *rural, idyllic*
Among the daughters of those mountains lone,[1]
We drag them there, where all things best and rarest
Are stained and trampled:—years have come and gone
Since, like the ship which bears me, I have known
No thought;—but now the eyes of one dear Maid
On mine with light of mutual love have shone—
She is my life,—I am but as the shade
Of her,[2]—a smoke sent up from ashes, soon to fade.

XXVI.

"For she must perish in the tyrant's hall—
Alas, alas!"—He ceased, and by the sail
Sate cowering—but his sobs were heard by all,
And still before the ocean and the gale
The ship fled fast 'till the stars 'gan to fail,
And round me gathered with mute countenance,
The Seamen gazed, the Pilot, worn and pale
With toil, the Captain with grey locks,[3] whose glance
Met mine in restless awe—they stood as in a trance.

XXVII.

"Recede not! pause not now! thou art grown old,
But Hope will make thee young, for Hope and Youth
Are children of one mother, even Love—behold![4]
The eternal stars gaze on us!—is the truth

---

1 Probably women from Circassia (the North Caucasus), who were said to be the loveliest in the world. In his *Lettres philosophiques*, translated into English and published in 1733 as *Letters Concerning the English Nation*, Voltaire (1694–1778) writes: "The *Circassians* are poor, and their Daughters are beautiful, and indeed 'tis in them they chiefly trade. They furnish with Beauties, the Seraglios of the *Turkish* Sultan, of the *Persian* Sophy, and of all of those who are wealthy enough to purchase and maintain such precious *Merchandize*" (75).

2 The Youth's description of the woman he loves recalls Laon's description of his reflection in IV.xxx.270 (p. 114).

3 Originally "looks"; corrected from Shelley's list of errata.

4 This line could be a third stray alexandrine, if "mother" and (more controversially) "even" are taken to have two syllables each.

Within your soul? care for your own,[1] or ruth
For other[s'][2] sufferings? do ye thirst to bear
A heart which not the serpent custom's tooth
May violate?—be free! and even here,
Swear to be firm till death!—they cried, 'We swear! we swear!'

XXVIII.

"The very darkness shook, as with a blast
Of subterranean thunder at the cry;
The hollow shore its thousand echoes cast
Into the night, as if the sea, and sky,
And earth, rejoiced with new-born liberty,
For in that name they swore! Bolts were undrawn,[3]
And on the deck with unaccustomed eye
The captives gazing stood, and every one
Shrank as the inconstant torch upon her countenance shone.

XXIX.

"They were earth's purest children, young and fair,
With eyes the shrines of unawakened thought,
And brows as bright as spring or morning, ere
Dark time had there its evil legend° wrought *symbol, trademark*
In characters of cloud which wither not.—
The change was like a dream to them; but soon
They knew the glory of their altered lot,
In the bright wisdom of youth's breathless noon,
Sweet talk, and smiles, and sighs, all bosoms did attune.° *harmonize*

XXX.

"But one was mute, her cheeks and lips most fair,
Changing their hue like lilies newly blown,° *bloomed*
Beneath a bright acacia's shadowy hair,
Waved by the wind amid the sunny noon,
Shewed that her soul was quivering; and full soon
That Youth arose, and breathlessly did look
On her and me, as for some speechless boon:
I smiled, and both their hands in mine I took,
And felt a soft delight from what[4] their spirits shook.

---

1 Originally "care for own"; corrected from Shelley's list of errata.

2 The emendation of "other's" to a plural possessive follows the suggestion of previous editions.

3 I.e., the enslaved women are released from the ship's hold.

4 From which; alternatively, Cythna means that whatever "shook" the young couple affected her as well.

Canto Ninth

I.

"THAT night we anchored in a woody bay,
And sleep no more around us dared to hover
Than, when all doubt and fear has passed away,
It shades the couch of some unresting lover,
Whose heart is now at rest: thus night past over
In mutual joy:—around, a forest grew
Of poplars and dark oaks, whose shade did cover
The waning stars prankt° in the waters blue, *dressed*
And trembled in the wind which from the morning flew.

II.

"The joyous mariners and each free maiden,
Now brought from the deep forest many a bough,
With woodland spoil most innocently laden;
Soon wreathes of budding foliage seemed to flow
Over the mast and sails, the stern and prow
Were canopied with blooming boughs,[1]—the while
On the slant sun's path o'er the waves we go
Rejoicing, like the dwellers of an isle
Doomed to pursue those waves that cannot cease to smile.

III.

"The many ships spotting the dark blue deep
With snowy sails, fled fast as our[s] came nigh,
In fear and wonder; and on every steep
Thousands did gaze, they heard the startling cry,
Like earth's own voice lifted unconquerably
To all her children, the unbounded mirth,
The glorious joy of thy name—Liberty!
They heard!—As o'er the mountains of the earth
From peak to peak leap on the beams of morning's birth:

IV.

"So from that cry over the boundless hills,
Sudden was caught one universal sound,
Like a volcano's voice, whose thunder fills

1 Cf. Spenser's *The Faerie Queene*, whose second book describes a boat or "litle Gondelay, bedecked trim / With boughes and arbours woven cunningly, / That like a litle forrest seemed outwardly" (II.vi.2).

Remotest skies,—such glorious madness found
A path thro' human hearts with stream which drowned
Its struggling fears and cares, dark custom's brood,[1]
They knew not whence it came, but felt around
A wide contagion poured—they called aloud
On Liberty—that name lived on the sunny flood.

V.

"We reached the port—alas! from many spirits
The wisdom which had waked that cry, was fled,
Like the brief glory which dark Heaven inherits
From the false dawn,[2] which fades e'er° it is spread, *before*
Upon the night's devouring darkness shed:
Yet soon bright day will burst—even like a chasm
Of fire, to burn the shrouds outworn and dead,
Which wrap the world; a wide enthusiasm,
To cleanse the fevered world as with an earthquake's spasm!

VI.

"I walked thro' the great City then, but free
From shame or fear; those toil-worn Mariners
And happy Maidens did encompass me;
And like a subterranean wind that stirs
Some forest among caves, the hopes and fears
From every human soul, a murmur strange
Made as I past; and many wept, with tears
Of joy and awe, and winged thoughts did range,
And half-extinguished words, which prophesied of change.

VII.

"For, with strong speech I tore the veil that hid
Nature, and Truth, and Liberty, and Love,—
As one who from some mountain's pyramid,
Points to the unrisen sun!—the shades approve
His truth, and flee from every stream and grove.
Thus, gentle thoughts did many a bosom fill,—
Wisdom, the mail of tried[3] affections wove
For many a heart, and tameless scorn of ill,
Thrice steeped in molten steel the unconquerable will.

---

1 Cf. I.xxxiii.293 (p. 70).

2 The Zodiacal light, a white glow sometimes visible in the night sky, and which seems to emanate from the direction of the sun's rising or setting.

3 Tested, reliable. Shelley means something like "steadfast," as in the expression "tried and true."

VIII.

"Some said I was a maniac wild and lost;
Some, that I scarce had risen from the grave
The Prophet's[1] virgin bride, a heavenly ghost:—
Some said I was a fiend from my weird° cave, *supernatural*
Who had stolen human shape, and o'er the wave,
The forest, and the mountain came;—some said
I was the child of God, sent down to save
Woman from bonds and death, and on my head
The burthen of their sins would frightfully be laid.

IX.

"But soon my human words found sympathy
In human hearts: the purest and the best,
As friend with friend, made common cause with me,
And they were few, but resolute;—the rest,
Ere yet success the enterprise had blest,
Leagued with me in their hearts;—their meals, their slumber,
Their hourly occupations, were possest
By hopes which I had arm'd to overnumber[2]
Those hosts of meaner cares, which life's strong wings encumber.

X.

"But chiefly women, whom my voice did waken
From their cold, careless,[3] willing slavery,
Sought me: one truth their dreary prison has shaken,—
They looked around, and lo! they became free!
Their many tyrants, sitting desolately
In slave-deserted halls, could none restrain;
For wrath's red fire had withered in the eye,
Whose lightning once was death,—nor fear nor gain
Could tempt one captive now to lock another's chain.

XI.

"Those who were sent to bind me, wept, and felt
Their minds outsoar the bonds which clasped them round,
Even as a waxen shape may waste and melt
In the white furnace; and a visioned swound,° *trance*

1 I.e., the Prophet Muhammad.

2 The original text has a comma after "overnumber," which confuses Shelley's meaning. I follow Reiman, Fraistat, and Crook, who follow the Bodleian manuscript, in omitting it here.

3 Unconcerned, passive; alternatively, without affection.

A pause of hope and awe the City bound,
Which, like the silence of a tempest's birth,
When in its awful shadow it has wound[1]
The sun, the wind, the ocean, and the earth,
Hung terrible, ere yet the lightnings have leapt forth.

XII.

"Like clouds inwoven in the silent sky,
By winds from distant regions meeting there,
In the high name of truth and liberty,
Around the City millions gathered were,
By hopes which sprang from many a hidden lair;
Words, which the lore of truth in hues of grace
Arrayed, thine own wild songs which in the air
Like homeless[2] odours floated, and the name
Of thee,[3] and many a tongue which thou hadst dipped in flame.

XIII.

"The Tyrant knew his power was gone, but Fear,
The nurse of Vengeance, bade him wait the event—
That perfidy° and custom, gold and prayer, *treachery*
And whatsoe'er, when force is impotent,
To fraud the scepter of the world has lent,
Might, as he judged, confirm his failing sway.
Therefore throughout the streets, the Priests he sent
To curse the rebels.—To their gods did they
For Earthquake, Plague, and Want, kneel in the public way.

XIV.

"And grave and hoary men were bribed to tell,
From seats w[h]ere law is made the slave of wrong,
How glorious Athens in her splendour fell,
Because her sons were free,—and that among
Mankind, the many to the few belong,
By Heaven, and Nature, and Necessity.[4]
They said, that age was truth, and that the young
Marred with wild hopes the peace of slavery,
With which old times and men had quelled the vain and free.

---

1 Originally "bound"; corrected from Shelley's list of errata.

2 Of uncertain origin or source.

3 I.e., Laon.

4 See p. 164, note 3. Necessity is usually a positive term for Shelley, one that stands in for the inevitably progressive movement of history. Here, however, it is appropriated by "grave and hoary men" to naturalize socioeconomic inequality, in a manner arguably similar to that of Malthus in his *Essay on Population*. On Malthus, see Shelley's preface, p. 44, note 1; and p. 44, note 2.

XV.[1]

"And with the falsehood of their poisonous lips
They breathed on the enduring memory
Of sages and of bards a brief eclipse;
There was one teacher, and must ever be,
They said, even God, who, the necessity
Of rule and wrong had armed against mankind,
His slave and his avenger aye to be;
That we were weak and sinful, frail and blind,
And that the will of one[2] was peace, and we
Should seek for nought on earth but toil and misery.

XVI.

"'For thus we might avoid the hell hereafter.'
So spake the hypocrites, who cursed and lied;
Alas, their sway was past, and tears and laughter
Clung to their hoary hair, withering the pride
Which in their hollow hearts dared still abide;
And yet obscener slaves with smoother brow,
And sneers on their strait lips, thin, blue and wide,
Said, that the rule of men was over now,
And hence, the subject world to woman's will must bow;

XVII.

"And gold was scattered through the streets, and wine
Flowed at a hundred feasts within the wall.
In vain! the steady towers in Heaven did shine
As they were wont, nor at the priestly call,
Left Plague her banquet in the Æthiop's hall,[3]
Nor Famine from the rich man's portal came,
Where at her ease she ever preys on all
Who throng to kneel for food: nor fear, nor shame,
Nor faith, nor discord, dimmed hope's newly kindled flame.

XVIII.

"For gold was as a God whose faith began
To fade, so that its worshippers were few,

---

1 This stanza runs to ten rather than nine lines. In *RoI*, Shelley amended his violation of the Spenserian form by rewriting the section of the stanza that begins "There was" and ends with "to be" as follows: "There was one teacher, who, necessity / Had armed, with strength and wrong against mankind, / His slave and his avenger aye to be."

2 I.e., autocracy, the rule of one person over all others.

3 Thucydides claims that the plague came to Athens from Ethiopia (2.48).

And Hell and Awe, which in the heart of man
Is God itself; the Priests its downfall knew,
As day by day their altars lonelier grew,
Till they were left alone within the fane;[1]
The shafts of falsehood unpolluting flew,
And the cold sneers of calumny° were vain *slander, misrepresentation*
The union of the free with discord's brand[2] to stain.

XIX.

"The rest thou knowest—Lo![3] we two are here—
We have survived a ruin wide and deep—
Strange thoughts are mine.—I cannot grieve or fear,
Sitting with thee upon this lonely steep
I smile, tho' human love should make me weep.
We have survived a joy that knows no sorrow,
And I do feel a mighty calmness creep
Over my heart, which can no longer borrow
Its hues from chance or change, dark children of to-morrow.

XX.

"We know not what will come—yet Laon, dearest,
Cythna shall be the prophetess of love,
Her lips shall rob thee of the grace thou wearest,
To hide thy heart, and clothe the shapes which rove
Within the homeless future's wintry grove;
For I now, sitting thus beside thee, seem
Even with thy breath and blood to live and move,
And violence and wrong are as a dream
Which rolls from stedfast truth an unreturning stream.

XXI.[4]

"The blasts of autumn drive the winged seeds
Over the earth,—next come the snows, and rain,

---

1 In *RoI*, lines 157–60 read:
    And Faith itself, which in the heart of man
    Gives shape, voice, name, to spectral Terror, knew
    Its downfall, as the altars lonelier grew,
    Till the Priests stood alone within the fane[.]
2 A hot iron used to mark, usually in ownership, the flesh of an animal or person.
3 Cythna has finished her tale, and the poem now returns to the time after the revolution's defeat.
4 Stanzas xxi–xxv are effectively rewritten in "Ode to the West Wind," the first twelve lines of which are as follows:
    O Wild West Wind, thou breath of Autumn's being
      Thou from whose unseen presence the leaves dead
    Are driven like ghosts from an enchanter fleeing,

And frosts, and storms, which dreary winter leads
Out of his Scythian cave, a savage train;
Behold! Spring sweeps over the world again,
Shedding soft dews from her æthereal wings;
Flowers on the mountains, fruits over the plain,
And music on the waves and woods she flings,
And love on all that lives, and calm on lifeless things.

XXII.

"O Spring, of hope, and love, and youth, and gladness
Wind-winged emblem! brightest, best and fairest!
Whence comest thou, when, with dark winter's sadness
The tears that fade in sunny smiles thou sharest;
Sister of joy, thou art the child who wearest[1]
Thy mother's dying smile, tender and sweet;
Thy mother Autumn, for whose grave thou bearest
Fresh flowers, and beams like flowers, with gentle feet,
Disturbing not the leaves which are her winding-sheet.° *burial shroud*

XXIII.

"Virtue, and Hope, and Love, like light and Heaven,
Surround the world.—We are their chosen slaves.
Has not the whirlwind of our spirit driven
Truth's deathless germs° to thought's remotest caves? *seeds*
Lo, Winter comes!—the grief of many graves,
The frost of death, the tempest of the sword,
The flood of tyranny, whose sanguine waves
Stagnate like ice at Faith, the inchanter's word,
And bind all human hearts in its repose abhorred.

Yellow, and black, and pale, and hectic red,
Pestilence-stricken multitudes! O thou
Who chariotest to their dark wintry bed

The wingèd seeds, where they lie cold and low,
Each like a corpse within its grave, until
Thine azure sister of the Spring shall blow

Her clarion o'er the dreaming earth, and fill
(Driving sweet buds like flocks to feed in air)
With living hues and odours plain and hill[.]

See "Ode to the West Wind," in *Shelley's Poetry and Prose* 1.1–12.

1 Originally "bearest"; corrected from Shelley's list of errata.

XXIV.

"The seeds are sleeping in the soil: meanwhile
The tyrant peoples dungeons with his prey,
Pale victims on the guarded scaffold smile
Because they cannot speak; and, day by day,
The moon of wasting° Science wanes away *neglected*
Among her stars, and in that darkness vast
The sons of earth to their foul idols pray,
And grey Priests triumph, and like blight or blast
A shade of selfish care° o'er human looks is cast. *concern, preoccupation*

XXV.

"This is the winter of the world;—and here
We die, even as the winds of Autumn fade,
Expiring in the frore° and foggy air.— *frozen*
Behold! Spring comes, tho' we must pass, who made
The promise of its birth,—even as the shade
Which from our death, as from a mountain, flings
The future, a broad sunrise; thus arrayed
As with the plumes of overshadowing wings,
From its dark gulph of chains, Earth like an eagle springs.

XXVI.

"O dearest love! we shall be dead and cold
Before this morn may on the world arise;
Wouldst thou the glory of its dawn behold?
Alas! gaze not on me, but turn thine eyes
On thine own heart—it is a paradise
Which everlasting spring has made its own,
And while drear Winter fills the naked skies,
Sweet streams of sunny thought, and flowers fresh blown,
Are there, and weave their sounds and odours into one.

XXVII.

"In their own hearts the earnest[1] of the hope
Which made them great, the good will ever find;
And tho' some envious shade may interlope
Between the effect and it, one comes behind,
Who aye the future to the past will bind—
Necessity,[2] whose sightless strength forever

---

1 Passion, seriousness of intention.

2 Necessity is reclaimed from abuse by the "grave and hoary men" of stanza xiv, and takes on its more standard meaning for Shelley: the inevitably progressive movement of humankind toward its historical and moral destiny.

Evil with evil, good with good, must wind
In bands of union, which no power may sever:[1]
They must bring forth their kind, and be divided never!

XXVIII.

"The good and mighty of departed ages
Are in their graves, the innocent and free,
Heroes, and Poets, and prevailing Sages,
Who leave the vesture° of their majesty *clothing, garb*
To adorn and clothe this naked world;—and we
Are like to them—such perish, but they leave
All hope, or love, or truth, or liberty,
Whose forms their mighty spirits could conceive
To be a rule and law to ages that survive.

XXIX.

"So be the turf heaped over our remains
Even in our happy youth, and that strange lot,
Whate'er it be, when in these mingling veins
The blood is still, be ours; let sense and thought
Pass from our being, or be numbered not
Among the things that are; let those who come
Behind, for whom our steadfast will has bought
A calm inheritance, a glorious doom,° *destiny*
Insult with careless tread, our undivided tomb.

XXX.

"Our many thoughts and deeds, our life and love,
Our happiness, and all that we have been,
Immortally must live, and burn and move,
When we shall be no more;—the world has seen
A type of peace; and as some most serene
And lovely spot to a poor maniac's eye,
After long years, some sweet and moving scene
Of youthful hope returning suddenly,
Quells his long madness—thus man shall remember thee.

XXXI.

"And Calumny meanwhile shall feed on us,
As worms devour the dead, and near the throne
And at the altar, most accepted thus

1 Cf. *Ahrimanes,* I.xvii (Appendix F6, p. 283).

Shall sneers and curses be—what we have done
None shall dare vouch,° tho' it be truly known; *affirm, support*
That record shall remain, when they must pass
Who built their pride on its oblivion;
And fame, in human hope which sculptured was,
Survive the perished scrolls of unenduring brass.[1]

XXXII.

"The while we two, beloved, must depart,
And Sense and Reason, those inchanters fair,
Whose wand of power is hope, would bid the heart
That gazed beyond the wormy grave despair:
These eyes, these lips, this blood, seems darkly there
To fade in hideous ruin; no calm sleep
Peopling with golden dreams the stagnant air,
Seems our obscure and rotting eyes to steep
In joy;—but senseless° death—a ruin *non-sentient, without feeling*
   dark and deep!

XXXIII.

"These are blind fancies—reason cannot know
What sense can neither feel, nor thought conceive;[2]
There is delusion in the world—and woe,
And fear, and pain—we know not whence we live,
Or why, or how, or what mute Power may give
Their being to each plant, and star, and beast,
Or even these thoughts:—Come near me! I do weave
A chain I cannot break—I am possest
With thoughts too swift and strong for one lone human breast.

XXXIV.

"Yes, yes—thy kiss is sweet, thy lips are warm[3]—
O! willingly beloved, would these eyes,

---

1 In other words, Laon and Cythna's history may be recorded wrongly by their enemies on the corruptible material of brass, but it remains "sculptured" or given form in the durable material of human hope.

2 Reacting to her own description of death in stanza xxxii above, Cythna states that we have no idea what death is like, and could not "conceive" it if we tried. Consequently, it is nothing to be afraid of. The philosophy behind this conclusion is associated with Epicureanism, which, as indicated by the poem's preface, attracted Shelley throughout his life; Cythna's language here and in following stanzas recalls passages from Book 3 of Lucretius' *De Rerum Natura,* which focuses on the impossibility of feeling and consciousness after death. See especially Lucretius, 3.417–831.

3 "Thy lips are warm!" exclaims Juliet of Shakespeare's *Romeo and Juliet*, kissing the lifeless Romeo's lips just before she stabs herself with his dagger (5.3.167).

Might they no more drink being from thy form,
Even as to sleep whence we again arise,
Close their faint orbs in death: I fear nor prize
Aught that can now betide,[1] unshared by thee—
Yes, Love when wisdom fails makes Cythna wise:
Darkness and death, if death be true, must be
Dearer than life and hope, if unenjoyed with thee.

XXXV.

"Alas, our thoughts flow on with stream,° whose waters *with the current*
Return not to their fountain—Earth and Heaven,
The Ocean and the Sun, the clouds their daughters,
Winter, and Spring, and Morn, and Noon, and Even,
All that we are or know, is darkly° driven *mysteriously*
Towards one gulph—Lo! what a change is come
Since I first spake—but time shall be forgiven,
Tho' it change all but thee!"—She ceased, night's gloom
Meanwhile had fallen on earth from the sky's sunless dome.

XXXVI.

Tho' she had ceased, her countenance uplifted
To Heaven, still spake, with solemn glory bright;
Her dark deep eyes, her lips, whose motions gifted
The air they breathed with love, her locks undight;° *undone*
"Fair star of life and love," I cried, "my soul's delight,[2]
Why lookest thou on the crystalline skies?
O, that my spirit were yon Heaven of night,
Which gazes on thee with its thousand eyes!"[3]
She turned to me and smiled—that smile was Paradise!

---

1 Anything that can happen now.

2 The second of the stray alexandrines mentioned in Shelley's preface (see p. 46).

3 These lines are a loose translation of an epigram attributed to Plato. They crop up too, in slightly modified form, in a document known as the *Smaller Silsbee Account Book* (now held in the Houghton Library at Harvard University, but printed in the third volume of *The Complete Poetry of Percy Bysshe Shelley*), where they appear to have been transcribed by Mary Shelley. Coleridge took a turn with Plato's epigram as well in his much-revised and retitled "Absence: A Poem," which contains the lines: "Or soar aloft to be the spangled skies / And gaze upon her with a thousand eyes!" (*Poetical Works* 69–70).

Canto Tenth.

I.

WAS there a human spirit in the steed,
That thus with his proud voice, ere night was gone,
He broke our linked rest? or do indeed
All living things a common nature own,
And thought erect an universal throne,
Where many shapes one tribute ever bear?
And Earth, their mutual mother, does she groan
To see her sons contend?° and makes she bare *fight*
Her breast, that all in peace its drainless stores may share?[1]

II.

I have heard friendly sounds from many a tongue,
Which was not human—the lone Nightingale[2]
Has answered me with her most soothing song,
Out of her ivy bower, when I sate pale
With grief, and sighed beneath; from many a dale
The Antelopes who flocked for food have spoken
With happy sounds, and motions, that avail
Like man's own speech; and such was now the token
Of waning night, whose calm by that proud neigh was broken.

III.

Each night, that mighty steed bore me abroad,
And I returned with food to our retreat,
And dark intelligence;° the blood which flowed *information, reports*
Over the fields, had stained the courser's feet;—
Soon the dust drinks that bitter dew,—then meet
The vulture, and the wild-dog, and the snake,
The wolf, and the hyæna grey, and eat
The dead in horrid truce: their throngs did make
Behind the steed, a chasm like waves in a ship's wake.

---

1 Earth is implicitly compared to the female pelican who, according to legend, uses her beak to cut open her own chest and let her young feed on her blood. Unlike the pelican's blood, however, Earth's resources ("stores") are said to be "drainless," unlimited.

2 Ovid's *Metamorphoses* recounts the tale of Philomela, a young woman who is raped by her sister's husband, Tereus, who then cuts out her tongue so she cannot accuse him. After avenging herself upon Tereus, Philomela is turned into a nightingale, whose subsequent association with sexual violence aligns her with Cythna, a woman of "soothing song" with whom Laon shares an "ivy bower" (6.422–674).

IV.

For, from the utmost realms of earth, came pouring
The banded slaves whom every despot sent
At that thron'd traitor's summons; like the roaring
Of fire, whose floods the wild deer circumvent° *maneuver around*
In the scorched pastures of the South; so bent
The armies of the leagued kings around
Their files of steel and flame;—the continent
Trembled, as with a zone of ruin bound,
Beneath their feet, the sea shook with their Navies' sound.

V.

From every nation of the earth they came,
The multitude of moving heartless things,
Whom slaves call men: obediently they came,
Like sheep whom from the fold the shepherd brings
To the stall, red with blood; their many kings
Led them, thus erring, from their native land;[1]
Tartar and Frank,[2] and millions whom the wings
Of Indian breezes lull, and many a band
The Arctic Anarch[3] sent, and Idumea's[4] sand,

VI.

Fertile in prodigies° and lies;—so there *monsters*
Strange natures made a brotherhood of ill.
The desart savage ceased to grasp in fear
His Asian shield and bow, when, at the will
Of Europe's subtler° son, the bolt would kill *trickier, wilier*
Some shepherd sitting on a rock secure;
But smiles of wondering joy his face would fill,
And savage sympathy: those slaves impure,
Each one the other thus from ill to ill did lure.

---

1 Originally "home." This mistake survived into *RoI*, but Shelley's draft shows he intended "land," which keeps to the rhyme scheme of the stanza.

2 French or, more broadly, Western European.

3 Russian tsar. Shelley may be thinking of both Catherine the Great (1729–96), whose anxiety over the French Revolution led her to quell rebellions in Poland and the Ukraine, and Alexander I (1777–1825), who led Russia as part of the Sixth Coalition against Napoleon. Although Shelley was wary of Napoleon, his defeat represented to many English radicals the final death knell of the revolutionary process begun in France in 1789.

4 Idumea, or Edom, was an ancient Semitic kingdom spanning present-day Israel and Jordan. It was the land given to Esau following his accidental abdication of his birthright (Genesis 36:6–9).

VII.

For traitorously did that foul Tyrant robe
His countenance in lies,—even at the hour
When he was snatched from death, then o'er the globe,
With secret signs from many a mountain tower,
With smoke by day, and fire by night,[1] the power
Of kings and priests, those dark conspirators
He called:—they knew his cause their own, and swore
Like wolves[2] and serpents to their mutual wars
Strange truce, with many a rite which Earth and Heaven abhors.

VIII.

Myriads had come—millions were on their way;
The Tyrant past, surrounded by the steel
Of hired assassins, thro' the public way,° *road*
Choked with his country's dead:—his footsteps reel[3]
On the fresh blood—he smiles, "Ay, now I feel
I am a King in truth!" he said, and took
His royal seat, and bade the torturing wheel[4]
Be brought, and fire, and pincers, and the hook,
And scorpions; that his soul on its revenge might look.

IX.

"But first, go slay the rebels—why return
The victor bands[?]"[5] he said, "millions yet live,
Of whom the weakest with one word might turn
The scales of victory yet;—let none survive
But those within the walls—each fifth shall give
The expiation for his brethren here.—
Go forth, and waste and kill!"—"O king, forgive
My speech," a soldier answered, "but we fear
The spirits of the night, and morn is drawing near;

---

1 Cf. Exodus 13:21: "And the Lord went before them by day in a pillar of a cloud, to lead them the way; and by night in a pillar of fire, to give them light; to go by day and night"; and Exodus 40:38: "So the cloud of the Lord was over the tabernacle by day, and fire was in the cloud by night, in the sight of all the Israelites during all their travels."

2 The original text has a comma here that editions since 1834 sensibly omit.

3 Slip, spin; alternatively, dance.

4 I.e., a Catherine's wheel, an instrument of capital punishment in the Middle Ages and used as a torture device long after. A body would be tied to the wheel and, through a variety of means, its bones would be broken and crushed until the victim died, usually from shock or else from internal bleeding.

5 All printed editions of the poem since 1829 substitute a question mark for Shelley's original comma.

X.

"For we were slaying still without remorse,
And now that dreadful chief[1] beneath my hand
Defenceless lay, when on a hell-black horse,
An Angel bright as day, waving a brand
Which flashed among the stars, past."—"Dost thou stand
Parleying° with me, thou wretch?" the king replied; *negotiating*
"Slaves, bind him to the wheel; and of this band
Whoso will drag that woman to his side
That scared him thus, may burn his dearest foe beside;

XI.

"And gold and glory shall be his.—Go forth!"
They rushed into the plain.—Loud was the roar
Of their career: the horsemen shook the earth;
The wheeled artillery's[2] speed the pavement tore;
The infantry, file after file did pour
Their clouds on the utmost hills. Five days they slew
Among the wasted fields: the sixth saw gore
Stream thro' the city; on the seventh, the dew
Of slaughter[3] became stiff, and there was peace anew:

XII.

Peace in the desart fields and villages,
Between the glutted beasts and mangled dead!
Peace in the silent streets! save when the cries
Of victims to their fiery judgment led,
Made pale their voiceless lips who seemed to dread
Even in their dearest kindred, lest some tongue
Be faithless to the fear yet unbetrayed;[4]
Peace in the Tyrant's palace, where the throng
Waste the triumphal hours in festival and song!

---

1 I.e., Laon.

2 I.e., the cannons'.

3 I.e., blood.

4 This language of surveillance gestures not only to life in France under the Terror, during which all persons were subject (according to the 1793 Law of Suspects) to be brought before a tribunal if their loyalty to the Revolution was in question, but also to life in England during the same period, when progressive political activists, writers, and publishers were routinely imprisoned, tried, and sometimes deported.

XIII.

Day after day the burning Sun rolled on
Over the death-polluted land—it came
Out of the east like fire, and fiercely shone
A lamp of Autumn, ripening with its flame
The few lone ears of corn;—the sky became
Stagnate° with heat, so that each cloud and blast *motionless*
Languished and died,—the thirsting air did claim
All moisture, and a rotting vapour past
From the unburied dead, invisible and fast.

XIV.

First Want, then Plague came on the beasts; their food
Failed, and they drew the breath of its decay.
Millions on millions, whom the scent of blood
Had lured, or who, from regions far away
Had tracked the hosts in festival array,[1]
From their dark desarts; gaunt and wasting now,
Stalked like fell shades among their perished prey;
In their green eyes a strange disease did glow,
They sank in hideous spasm, or pains severe and slow.[2]

XV.

The fish were poisoned in the streams; the birds
In the green woods perished; the insect race
Was withered up; the scattered flocks and herds
Who had survived the wild beasts' hungry chace
Died moaning, each upon the other's face
In helpless agony gazing; round the City
All night, the lean hyænas their sad case
Like starving infants wailed; a woful ditty!
And many a mother wept, pierced with unnatural[3] pity.

XVI.

Amid the aërial minarets on high,
The Æthiopian vultures fluttering fell
From their long line of brethren in the sky,
Startling the concourse of mankind.—Too well

1 Predatory animals had followed the various armies.

2 Cf. Thucydides 2.47–52, as well as Lucretius' versification of Thucydides' account of the plague in *De Rerum Natura*, 6.1138–1246.

3 I.e., insofar as their pity is directed at creatures that do not belong to their own species.

These signs the coming mischief did foretell:—
Strange panic first, a deep and sickening dread
Within each heart, like ice, did sink and dwell,
A voiceless thought of evil, which did spread
With the quick glance of eyes, like withering lightnings shed.

XVII.

Day after day, when the year wanes, the frosts
Strip its green crown of leaves, till all is bare;
So on those strange and congregated hosts
Came Famine, a swift shadow, and the air
Groaned with the burthen of a new despair;
Famine, than whom Misrule no deadlier daughter
Feeds from her thousand breasts, tho' sleeping there
With lidless eyes, lie Faith, and Plague, and Slaughter,
A ghastly brood; conceived of Lethe's sullen water.[1]

XVIII.

There was no food, the corn was trampled down,
The flocks and herds had perished; on the shore
The dead and putrid fish were ever thrown;
The deeps were foodless, and the winds no more
Creaked with the weight of birds, but as before
Those winged things sprang forth, were void of shade;
The vines and orchards, Autumn's golden store,
Were burned;—so that the meanest food was weighed
With gold, and avarice died before the god it made.

XIX.

There was no corn—in the wide market-place
All loathliest things, even human flesh, was sold;
They weighed it in small scales—and many a face
Was fixed in eager horror then: his gold
The miser brought, the tender maid, grown bold
Thro' hunger, bared her scorned charms in vain;
The mother brought her eldest born, controuled° *driven, compelled*
By instinct blind as love, but turned again
And bade her infant suck, and died in silent pain.

XX.

Then fell blue Plague upon the race of man.
"Oh, for the sheathed steel, so late which gave

---

1 Cf. V.xlii.370–71 (p. 128).

Oblivion to the dead, when the streets ran
With brothers' blood! O, that the earthquake[']s grave
Would gape, or Ocean lift its stifling wave!"
Vain cries—throughout the streets thousands pursued
Each by his fiery torture howl and rave,
Or sit, in frenzy's unimagined° mood, *unimaginable*
Upon fresh heaps of dead; a ghastly multitude.

XXI.

It was not hunger now, but thirst. Each well
Was choked with rotting corpses, and became
A cauldron of green mist made visible
At sunrise. Thither still the myriads came,
Seeking to quench the agony of the flame,
Which raged like poison thro' their bursting veins;
Naked they were from torture, without shame,
Spotted with nameless scars and lurid blains,° *sores, blisters*
Childhood, and youth, and age, writhing in savage pains.

XXII.

It was not thirst but madness! Many saw
Their own lean image every where, it went
A ghastlier self beside them, till the awe
Of that dread sight to self-destruction sent
Those shrieking victims; some, ere life was spent,
Sought, with a horrid sympathy, to shed
Contagion on the sound; and others rent
Their matted hair, and cried aloud, "We tread
On fire! Almighty God[1] his hell on earth has spread."

XXIII.

Sometimes the living by the dead were hid.
Near the great fountain in the public square,
Where corpses made a crumbling pyramid[2]
Under the sun, was heard one stifled prayer
For life, in the hot silence of the air;
And strange 'twas, amid that hideous heap to see
Some shrouded in their long and golden hair,
As if not dead, but slumbering quietly,
Like forms which sculptors carve, then love to agony.[3]

---

1 *RoI* has "the avenging Power."

2 Cf. the pyramid built by the revolutionaries, p. 128, V.xl.354–58.

3 An allusion to the story of Pygmalion, a sculptor who fell in love with his own statue. Shelley omits the happy ending, where the statue is brought to life by Venus, goddess of love. See Ovid, *Metamorphoses* 10.238–97.

XXIV.

Famine had spared the palace of the king:—
He rioted° in festival the while, *indulged*
He and his guards and priests; but Plague did fling
One shadow upon all. Famine can smile
On him who brings it food and pass, with guile
Of thankful falsehood, like a courtier grey,
The house-dog of the throne; but many a mile
Comes Plague, a winged wolf, who loathes alway
The garbage and the scum that strangers make her prey.[1]

XXV.

So, near the throne, amid the gorgeous feast,
Sheathed in resplendent arms;° or loosely dight *weapons*
To luxury,[2] ere the mockery yet had ceased
That lingered on his lips, the warrior's might
Was loosened, and a new and ghastlier night
In dreams of frenzy lapped his eyes; he fell
Headlong, or with stiff eyeballs sate upright
Among the guests, or raving mad, did tell
Strange truths; a dying seer of dark oppression's hell.

XXVI.

The Princes and the Priests were pale with terror;
That monstrous faith wherewith they ruled mankind,
Fell, like a shaft loosed by the bowman's error,
On their own hearts: they sought and they could find
No refuge—'twas the blind who led the blind![3]
So, thro' the desolate streets to the high fane,
Of their Almighty God, the armies wind[4]
In sad procession: each among the train
To his own Idol lifts his supplications vain.

XXVII.

"O God!" they cried, "we know our secret pride
Has scorned thee, and thy worship, and thy name;
Secure in human power we have defied

---

1 Unlike obsequious Famine, who appears grateful for every meal, Plague despises the refuse that she is forced to eat.

2 Disheveled, in disarray, in this case from an excess of hedonistic behavior.

3 Cf. Matthew 15:14: "Let them alone: they be blind leaders of the blind. And if the blind lead the blind, both shall fall into the ditch." See also Luke 6:39.

4 *RoI* has "the many-tongued and endless armies wind."

Thy fearful might; we bend in fear and shame
Before thy presence; with the dust we claim
Kindred; be merciful, O King of Heaven!
Most justly have we suffered for thy fame
Made dim, but be at length our sins forgiven,
Ere to despair and death thy worshippers be driven!

XXVIII.

"O God Almighty![1] thou alone hast power!
Who can resist thy will? who can restrain
Thy wrath, when on the guilty thou dost shower
The shafts of thy revenge, a blistering rain?
Greatest and best, be merciful again!
Have we not stabbed thine enemies, and made
The Earth an altar, and the Heavens a fane,
Where thou wert worshipped with their blood, and laid
Those hearts in dust which would thy searchless[2] works have weighed?

XXIX.

"Well didst thou loosen on this impious City
Thine angels of revenge: recall them now;
Thy worshippers abased, here kneel for pity,
And bind their souls by an immortal vow:
We swear by thee! and to our oath do thou
Give sanction, from thine hell of fiends and flame,
That we will kill with fire and torments slow,
The last of those who mocked thy holy name,
And scorned the sacred laws thy prophets did proclaim."

XXX.

Thus they with trembling limbs and pallid lips
Worshipped their own hearts' image,[3] dim and vast,
Scared by the shade wherewith they would eclipse
The light of other minds;—troubled they passed
From the great Temple;—fiercely still and fast
The arrows of the plague among them fell,
And they on one another gazed aghast,
And thro' the hosts contention wild befell,
As each of his own god the wondrous works did tell.

---

1 *RoI* has "O King of Glory!"

2 Inscrutable, mysterious.

3 Cf. VIII.v.39–42 (p. 170) and VIII.vi.48–50 (p. 170).

XXXI.

And Oromaze, and Christ,[1] and Mahomet,
Moses, and Buddh, Zerdusht, and Brahm, and Foh,[2]
A tumult of strange names, which never met
Before, as watchwords of a single woe,
Arose; each raging votary 'gan to throw
Aloft his armed hands, and each did howl
"Our God alone is God!" and slaughter now
Would have gone forth, when from beneath a cowl
A voice came forth, which pierced like ice thro' every soul.

XXXII.

He was a Christian[3] Priest from whom it came,
A zealous man, who led the legioned west
With words which faith and pride had steeped in flame,
To quell the rebel Atheists;[4] a dire guest
Even to his friends was he, for in his breast
Did hate and guile lie watchful, intertwined,
Twin serpents in one deep and winding nest;[5]
He loathed all faith beside his own, and pined
To wreak his fear of Heaven in vengeance on mankind.

XXXIII.

But more he loathed and hated the clear light
Of wisdom and free thought, and more did fear,
Lest, kindled once, its beams might pierce the night,
Even where his Idol stood; for far and near
Did many a heart in Europe leap to hear
That faith and tyranny were trampled down;

---

1 *RoI* has "Joshua" (meaning Yeshua, or Jesus).

2 The gods, principal deities, or founders of Zoroastrianism (Ahura Mazda, or "Oromaze," and "Zerdusht," Zoroaster himself), Christianity, Judaism, Buddhism ("Buddh" and "Foh," the Chinese name for Buddha), and Hinduism.

3 *RoI* has "'Twas an Iberian," i.e., from Iberia or Spain—in other words, a Catholic priest. In that instance, Shelley focuses on Spanish Catholicism for its associations with religious extremism, imperial depredation, and the regime of torture that was the Spanish Inquisition. The influence of Sydney Owenson's *The Missionary* (Appendix F4) shows in this revision, since in that novel it is likewise the Inquisition that menaces the two protagonists.

4 *RoI* has "unbelievers." Again, the term "atheist" for Shelley connotes not someone who does not believe in God, but someone who does not subscribe to any extant religion's account of the deity or to its pertinent concepts (e.g., sin, the afterlife, and so on).

5 Cf. the two sea serpents that strangle Laocoön and his sons in the *Aeneid* 2.40–198.

Many a pale victim, doomed for truth to share
The murderer's cell, or see, with helpless groan
The priests his children drag for slaves to serve their own.

XXXIV.

He dared not kill the infidels with fire
Or steel, in Europe: the slow agonies
Of legal torture mocked his keen desire:
So he made truce with those who did despise
His cradled Idol, and the sacrifice
Of God to God's own wrath,—that Islam's creed[1]
Might crush for him those deadlier[2] enemies;
For fear of God did in his bosom breed
A jealous hate of man, an unreposing° need. *restless, unquenchable*

XXXV.

"Peace! Peace!" he cried, "when we are dead, the Day
Of Judgment comes, and all shall surely know
Whose God is God, each fearfully shall pay
The errors of his faith in endless woe!
But there is sent a mortal vengeance now
On earth, because an impious race had spurned
Him whom we all adore,—a subtile° foe, *devious*
By whom for ye this dread reward was earned,
And kingly thrones, which rest on faith, nigh° overturned. *almost*

XXXVI.

"Think ye, because ye weep, and kneel, and pray,
That God will lull the pestilence? it rose
Even from beneath his throne, where, many a day
His mercy soothed it to a dark repose:
It walks upon the earth to judge his foes,
And what art thou and I, that he should deign
To curb his ghastly minister, or close
The gates of death, ere they receive the twain
Who shook with mortal spells his undefended[3] reign?

---

1 *RoI* has: "The expiation, and the sacrifice, / That, though detested, Islam's kindred creed [...]."

2 In other words, the priest identifies his true enemies not as proponents or followers of other faiths, but of free thought in general.

3 Abandoned, i.e., by those who have left him to join Laon and Cythna's revolution or by those who sat by while the revolution happened.

XXXVII.

"Ay, there is famine in the gulph of hell,
Its giant worms of fire for ever yawn,—
Their lurid eyes are on us![1] those who fell
By the swift shafts of pestilence ere dawn
Are in their jaws! they hunger for the spawn
Of Satan, their own brethren, who were sent
To make our souls their spoil. See, see! they fawn
Like dogs, and they will sleep with luxury spent,
When those detested hearts their iron fangs have rent!

XXXVIII.

"Our God may then lull Pestilence to sleep:—
Pile high the pyre of expiation now![2]
A forest's spoil of boughs, and on the heap
Pour venomous gums, which sullenly and slow,
When touched by flame, shall burn, and melt, and flow,
A stream of clinging fire,—and fix on high
A net of iron, and spread forth below
A couch of snakes, and scorpions, and the fry° *spawn*
Of centipedes and worms, earth's hellish progeny!

XXXIX.

"Let Laon and Laone on that pyre,
Linked tight with burning brass, perish!—then pray
That, with this sacrifice the withering ire
Of God[3] may be appeased." He ceased, and they
A space stood silent, as far, far away
The echoes of his voice among them died;
And he knelt down upon the dust, alway
Muttering the curses of his speechless° pride, *unutterable, inexpressible*
Whilst shame, and fear, and awe, the armies did divide.

XL.

His voice was like a blast that burst the portal
Of fabled hell; and as he spake, each one
Saw gape beneath the chasms of fire immortal,
And Heaven above seemed cloven, where, on a throne

---

1 Cf. VIII.viii.64–66 (p. 171).

2 Cf. Isaiah 30:33: "For Tophet is ordained of old; yea, for the king it is prepared; he hath made it deep and large: the pile thereof is fire and much wood; the breath of the Lord, like a stream of brimstone, doth kindle it."

3 *RoI* has "Heaven."

With storms and shadows girt, sate God, alone,[1]
Their King and Judge—fear killed in every breast
All natural pity then, a fear unknown
Before, and with an inward fire possest,
They raged like homeless beasts whom burning woods invest.[2]

XLI.

'Twas morn—at noon the public crier went forth,
Proclaiming thro' the living and the dead,
"The Monarch saith that his great Empire's worth
Is set on Laon and Laone's head:
He who but one yet living here can lead,
Or who the life from both their hearts can wring,
Shall be the kingdom's heir, a glorious meed!° *reward*
But he who both alive can hither bring
The Princess shall espouse,° and reign an equal King." *marry*

XLII.

Ere night the pyre was piled, the net of iron
Was spread above, the fearful couch below,
It overtopped the towers that did environ
That spacious square; for Fear is never slow
To build the thrones of Hate, her mate and foe,
So, she scourged forth the maniac multitude
To rear this pyramid[3]—tottering and slow,
Plague-stricken, foodless, like lean herds pursued
By gad-flies, they have piled the heath, and gums, and wood.

XLIII.

Night came, a starless and a moonless gloom.
Until the dawn, those hosts° of many a nation *crowds*
Stood round that pile, as near one lover's tomb
Two gentle sisters mourn their desolation;[4]
And in the silence of that expectation,
Was heard on high the reptiles['] hiss and crawl—
It was so deep, save when the devastation
Of the swift pest with fearful interval,
Marking its path with shrieks, among the crowd would fall.

---

1 *RoI* has "Girt round with storms and shadows, sate alone [...]."

2 Cover, surround.

3 Cf. V.xl.354–58 (p. 128) and X.xxiii.201 (p. 197).

4 An image perhaps inspired by Shelley's relationships with his wife Mary and her stepsister Claire.

XLIV.

Morn came,—among those sleepless multitudes,
Madness, and Fear, and Plague, and Famine still
Heaped corpse on corpse, as in autumnal woods
The frosts of many a wind with dead leaves fill
Earth's cold and sullen brooks; in silence, still
The pale survivors stood; ere noon, the fear
Of Hell became a panic, which did kill
Like hunger or disease, with whispers drear,
As "hush! hark! Come they yet? God, God,[1] thine hour is near!"

XLV.

And Priests rushed thro' their ranks, some counterfeiting° *simulating, faking*
The rage they did inspire, some mad indeed
With their own lies; they said their god was waiting
To see his enemies writhe, and burn, and bleed,—
And that, till then, the snakes of hell had need
Of human souls:—three hundred furnaces
Soon blazed thro' the wide City, where, with speed,
Men brought their infidel kindred to appease
God's wrath, and while they burned, knelt round on quivering knees.

XLVI.

The noontide sun was darkened with that smoke,
The winds of eve dispersed those ashes gray,
The madness which these rites had lulled, awoke
Again at sunset.—Who shall dare to say
The deeds which night and fear brought forth, or weigh
In balance just the good and evil there?
He might man's deep and searchless° heart display, *unfathomable*
And cast a light on those dim labyrinths, where
Hope, near imagined chasms, is struggling with despair.

XLVII.

'Tis said a mother dragged three children then,
To those fierce flames which roast the eyes in the head,
And laughed, and died; and that unholy men,
Feasting like fiends upon the infidel dead,
Looked from their meal, and saw an Angel tread
The threshold of God's throne,[2] and it was she!

---

1 *RoI* has "Just Heaven!"

2 *RoI* has "the visible floor of Heaven."

And, on that night, one without doubt or dread
Came to the fire, and said, "Stop, I am he!
Kill me!"—They burned them both[1] with hellish mockery.

XLVIII.

And, one by one, that night, young maidens came,
Beauteous and calm, like shapes of living stone
Clothed in the light of dreams, and by the flame,
Which shrank as overgorged, they laid them down,
And sung a low sweet song, of which alone
One word was heard, and that was Liberty;[2]
And that some kist their marble feet, with moan
Like love, and died, and then that they did die
With happy smiles, which sunk in white tranquillity.

---

1 William Michael Rossetti (1829–1919) and Shelley's subsequent editors have suggested that Shelley meant to have two people "without doubt or dread" approach the pyre, a conjecture backed up to some extent by Shelley's notes. It's also worth considering the possibility that "both" in 423 might include the "one" of 421 and the "Angel" of 419, since this female figure is perceived to be supernatural only by those "unholy men" and might rather be a living person; the men, on this reading, would have confused the "mother" of 415 with someone else, whom they mistakenly take to be her apparition. In any case, the confusion that hangs over this stanza is appropriate to the states of delirium it describes.

2 Cf. Owenson, *The Missionary* (Appendix F4, p. 275.)

Canto Eleventh.

I.

SHE saw me not—she heard me not—alone
Upon the mountain's dizzy brink she stood;
She spake not, breathed not, moved not—there was thrown
Over her look, the shadow of a mood
Which only clothes the heart in solitude,
A thought of voiceless° depth;—she stood alone, *unspeakable*
Above, the Heavens were spread;—below, the flood
Was murmuring in its caves;—the wind had blown
Her hair apart, thro' which her eyes and forehead shone.

II.

A cloud was hanging o'er the western mountains;
Before its blue and moveless depth were flying
Grey mists poured forth from the unresting fountains
Of darkness in the North:—the day was dying:—
Sudden, the sun shone forth, its beams were lying
Like boiling gold on Ocean, strange to see,
And on the shattered vapours,° which defying *mists, fog*
The power of light in vain, tossed restlessly
In the red Heaven, like wrecks in a tempestuous sea.

III.

It was a stream of living beams, whose bank
On either side by the cloud's cleft was made;
And where its chasms that flood of glory drank,
Its waves gushed forth like fire, and as if swayed
By some mute tempest, rolled on *her*; the shade
Of her bright image floated on the river
Of liquid light, which then did end and fade—
Her radiant shape upon its verge did shiver;
Aloft, her flowing hair like strings of flame did quiver.

IV.

I stood beside her, but she saw me not—
She looked upon the sea, and skies, and earth;
Rapture, and love, and admiration wrought
A passion deeper far than tears, or mirth,
Or speech, or gesture, or whate'er has birth
From common joy; which, with the speechless feeling
That led her there united, and shot forth

From her far eyes, a light of deep revealing,
All but her dearest self from my regard concealing.

V.

Her lips were parted, and the measured breath
Was now heard there;—her dark and intricate[1] eyes
Orb within orb, deeper than sleep or death,
Absorbed the glories of the burning skies,
Which, mingling with her heart's deep ecstacies,
Burst from her looks and gestures;—and a light
Of liquid tenderness like love, did rise
From her whole frame, an atmosphere which quite
Arrayed[2] her in its beams, tremulous and soft and bright.

VI.

She would have clasped me to her glowing frame;
Those warm and odorous° lips might soon have shed *fragrant, scented*
On mine the fragrance and the invisible flame
Which now the cold winds stole;—she would have laid
Upon my languid heart her dearest head;
I might have heard her voice, tender and sweet;
Her eyes mingling with mine, might soon have fed
My soul with their own joy.—One moment yet
I gazed—we parted then, never again to meet!

VII.

Never but once to meet on Earth again!
She heard me as I fled—her eager tone
Sunk on my heart, and almost wove a chain
Around my will to link it with her own,
So that my stern resolve was almost gone.
"I cannot reach thee! whither dost thou fly?
My steps are faint°—Come back, thou dearest one— *flagging*
Return, ah me! return"—the wind past by
On which those accents died, faint, far, and lingeringly.

VIII.

Woe! woe! that moonless midnight—Want and Pest° *Famine and Plague*
Were horrible, but one more fell doth rear,
As in a hydra's swarming lair,[3] its crest

---

1 Perplexing, mysterious, hard to read.

2 Outfitted, attired, especially in martial dress.

3 Cf. I.xxxiii.293 (p. 70).

Eminent among those victims—even the Fear
Of Hell: each girt by the hot atmosphere
Of his blind agony, like a scorpion stung
By his own rage upon his burning bier
Of circling coals of fire; but still there clung
One hope, like a keen sword on starting° threads uphung: *disintegrating, precarious*

IX.

Not death—death was no more refuge or rest;
Not life—it was despair to be!—not sleep,
For fiends and chasms of fire[1] had dispossest
All natural dreams: to wake was not to weep,
But to gaze mad and pallid, at the leap
To which the Future, like a snaky scourge,
Or like some tyrant's eye, which aye doth keep
Its withering beam upon his slaves, did urge
Their steps; they heard the roar of Hell's sulphureous[2] surge.

X.

Each of that multitude alone, and lost
To sense of outward things, one hope yet knew;
As on a foam-girt crag some seaman tost,
Stares at the rising tide, or like the crew
Whilst now the ship is splitting thro' and thro';
Each, if the tramp of a far steed was heard,
Started from sick despair, or if there flew
One murmur on the wind, or if some word
Which none can gather yet, the distant crowd has stirred.

XI.

Why became cheeks wan with the kiss of death,
Paler from hope? they had sustained despair.
Why watched those myriads with suspended breath
Sleepless a second night? they are not here
The victims, and hour by hour, a vision drear,° *depressing, frightening*
Warm corpses fall upon the clay cold dead;
And even in death their lips are wreathed with fear.—

---

1 I.e., images of hell.

2 Made of sulfur. In the King James Bible, sulfur is referred to as "brimstone," as in Revelation 14:10: "[H]e shall be tormented with fire and brimstone in the presence of the holy angels, and in the presence of the Lamb."

The crowd is mute and moveless—overhead
Silent Arcturus[1] shines—ha! hear'st thou not the tread

XII.

Of rushing feet? laughter? the shout, the scream,
Of triumph not to be contained? see! hark!
They come, they come, give way! alas, ye deem
Falsely—'tis but a crowd of maniacs stark
Driven, like a troop of spectres, thro' the dark,
From the choked well, whence a bright death-fire sprung,
A lurid earth-star, which dropped many a spark
From its blue train, and spreading widely, clung
To their wild hair, like mist the topmost pines among.

XIII.

And many, from the crowd collected there,
Joined that strange dance in fearful sympathies;
There was the silence of a long despair,
When the last echo of those terrible cries
Came from a distant street, like agonies
Stifled afar.—Before the Tyrant's throne
All night his aged Senate sate, their eyes
In stony expectation fixed; when one
Sudden before them stood, a Stranger and alone.

XIV.

Dark Priests and haughty Warriors gazed on him
With baffled wonder, for a hermit's vest[2]
Concealed his face; but when he spake, his tone,
Ere yet the matter did their thoughts arrest,[3]
Earnest, benignant, calm, as from a breast
Void of all hate or terror, made them start;
For as with gentle accents° he addressed *rhythms*
His speech to them, on each unwilling heart
Unusual awe did fall—a spirit-quelling dart.

XV.

"Ye Princes of the Earth, ye sit aghast
Amid the ruin which yourselves have made,
Yes, desolation heard your trumpet's blast,

---

1 The fourth brightest star in the night sky.

2 Garment, in this case probably a hooded robe.

3 I.e., before the senators could understand what he was saying.

And sprang from sleep!—dark Terror has obeyed
Your bidding—O, that I whom ye have made
Your foe, could set my dearest enemy free
From pain and fear! but evil casts a shade,
Which cannot pass so soon, and Hate must be
The nurse and parent still of an ill progeny.

XVI.

"Ye turn to Heaven for aid in your distress;
Alas, that ye, th[e][1] mighty and the wise,
Who, if ye dared, might not aspire to less
Than ye conceive of power, should fear the lies
Which thou, and thou, didst frame for° mysteries *pass off as*
To blind your slaves:—consider your own thought,
An empty and a cruel sacrifice
Ye now prepare, for a vain idol wrought
Out of the fears and hate which vain desires have brought.

XVII.

"Ye seek for happiness—alas, the day!
Ye find it not in luxury nor in gold,
Nor in the fame, nor in the envied sway
For which, O willing slaves to Custom old,
Severe task mistress! ye your hearts have sold.
Ye seek for peace, and when ye die, to dream
No evil dreams: all mortal things are cold
And senseless then; if aught survive, I deem
It must be love and joy, for they immortal seem.

XVIII.

"Fear not the future, weep not for the past.
O, could I win your ears to dare be now
Glorious, and great, and calm! that ye would cast
Into the dust those symbols of your woe,
Purple, and gold, and steel![2] that ye would go
Proclaiming to the nations whence ye came,
That Want, and Plague, and Fear, from slavery flow;
And that mankind is free, and that the shame
Of royalty and faith is lost in freedom's fame!

1 Both the original text and *RoI* have "tho'." The substitution of "the" is standard, even if the line makes sense, though rather awkwardly, without it.

2 I.e., kingship, money, and military power.

XIX.

"If thus 'tis well—if not, I come to say
That Laon"—while the Stranger spoke, among
The Council sudden tumult and affray° *conflict, fighting*
Arose, for many of those warriors young,
Had on his eloquent accents fed and hung
Like bees on mountain flowers; they knew the truth,
And from their thrones° in vindication sprung; *seats*
The men of faith and law then without ruth° *remorse, compunction*
Drew forth their secret steel, and stabbed each ardent youth.

XX.

They stabbed them in the back and sneered—a slave,
Who stood behind the throne, those corpses drew
Each to its bloody, dark, and secret grave;
And one more daring raised his steel anew
To pierce the Stranger: "What hast thou to do
With me, poor wretch?"—Calm, solemn, and severe,
That voice unstrung his sinews,[1] and he threw
His dagger on the ground, and pale with fear,
Sate silently—his voice then did the Stranger rear.° *raise*

XXI.

"It doth avail not[2] that I weep for ye—
Ye cannot change, since ye are old and grey,
And ye have chosen your lot—your fame must be
A book of blood, whence in a milder day
Men shall learn truth, when ye are wrapt in clay:
Now ye shall triumph. I am Laon's friend,
And him to your revenge will I betray,
So ye concede one easy boon.° Attend! *favor*
For now I speak of things which ye can apprehend.

XXII.

"There is a People mighty in its youth,
A land beyond the Oceans of the West,[3]
Where, tho' with rudest rites, Freedom and Truth
Are worshipped; from a glorious Mother's[4] breast,

---

1 I.e., made him go limp.

2 I.e., it's no use, it has no effect.

3 I.e., the United States of America, former colonies of Britain.

4 The "Mother" is England.

Who, since high Athens fell, among the rest
Sate like the Queen of Nations, but in woe,
By inbred° monsters outraged and oppressed, *native, produced within*
Turns to her chainless child for succour now,
It draws the milk of Power in Wisdom's fullest flow.

XXIII.

"That land is like an Eagle,[1] whose young gaze
Feeds on the noontide beam, whose golden plume
Floats moveless on the storm, and in the blaze
Of sun-rise gleams when Earth is wrapt in gloom;
An epitaph of glory for the tomb
Of murdered Europe may thy fame be made,
Great People: as the sands shalt thou become;
Thy growth is swift as morn, when night must fade;
The multitudinous Earth shall sleep beneath thy shade.

XXIV.

"Yes, in the desart there is built a home
For Freedom. Genius is made strong to rear
The monuments of man beneath the dome
Of a new Heaven; myriads assemble there,
Whom the proud lords of man, in rage or fear,
Drive from their wasted homes: the boon I pray
Is this,—that Cythna shall be conveyed there—
Nay, start not at the name—America!
And then to you this night Laon will I betray.[2]

XXV.

"With me do what ye will. I am your foe!"
The light of such a joy as makes the stare
Of hungry snakes like living emeralds glow,
Shone in a hundred human eyes—"Where, where
Is Laon?—haste! fly! drag him swiftly here!
We grant thy boon."—"I put no trust in ye,
Swear by your dreadful God."[3]—"We swear, we swear!"
The Stranger threw his vest back suddenly,
And smiled in gentle pride, and said, "Lo! I am he!"

---

1 Once more, Shelley inverts the allegorical logic of Canto First.

2 Cf. Matthew 26:31: "Then saith Jesus unto them, All ye shall be offended because of me this night: for it is written, I will smite the shepherd, and the sheep of the flock shall be scattered abroad." Like Christ, Laon suggests that he will betray and thus destroy a person who turns out to be himself.

3 *RoI* has "the Power ye dread."

Canto Twelfth

I.

THE transport° of a fierce and monstrous gladness *frenzy*
Spread thro' the multitudinous streets, fast flying
Upon the winds of fear; from his dull madness
The starveling° waked, and died in joy; the dying, *starving person*
Among the corpses in stark agony lying,
Just heard the happy tidings, and in hope
Closed their faint eyes; from house to house replying
With loud acclaim, the living shook Heaven's cope,° *vault*
And filled the startled Earth with echoes: morn did ope° *open*

II.

Its pale eyes then; and lo! the long array
Of guards in golden arms, and priests beside,
Singing their bloody hymns, whose garbs betray
The blackness of the faith it seems to hide;
And see, the Tyrant's gem-wrought chariot glide
Among the gloomy cowls and glittering spears—
A Shape of light is sitting by his side,
A child most beautiful. I'the midst appears
Laon,—exempt alone from mortal hopes and fears.

III.

His head and feet are bare, his hands are bound
Behind with heavy chains, yet none do wreak
Their scoffs on him, tho' myriads throng around;
There are no sneers upon his lip which speak
That scorn or hate has made him bold; his cheek
Resolve has not turned pale, his eyes are mild
And calm, and like the morn about to break,
Smile on mankind—his heart seems reconciled
To all things and itself, like a reposing child.

IV.

Tumult was in the soul of all beside,[1]
Ill joy, or doubt, or fear; but those who saw
Their tranquil victim pass, felt wonder glide
Into their brain, and became calm with awe.—
See, the slow pageant near the pile doth draw.

---

1 Everyone nearby; alternatively, everyone else (besides Laon).

A thousand torches in the spacious square,
Borne by the ready slaves of ruthless law,
Await the signal round: the morning fair
Is changed to a dim night by that unnatural glare.

V.

And see! beneath a sun-bright canopy,
Upon a platform level with the pile,
The anxious Tyrant sit, enthroned on high,
Girt by the chieftains of the host;[1] all smile
In expectation, but one child: the while
I, Laon, led by mutes, ascend my bier
Of fire, and look around; each distant isle
Is dark in the bright dawn; towers far and near,
Pierce like reposing flames the tremulous atmosphere.

VI.

There was such silence through the host, as when
An earthquake trampling on some populous town,
Has crushed ten thousand with one tread, and men
Expect the second; all were mute but one,
That fairest child, who, bold with love, alone
Stood up before the King, without avail,
Pleading for Laon's life—her stifled groan
Was heard—she trembled like one aspen pale
Among the gloomy pines of a Norwegian vale.

VII.

What were his thoughts linked in the morning sun,
Among those reptiles, stingless with delay,[2]
Even like a tyrant's wrath?—the signal gun
Roared—hark, again! in that dread pause he lay
As in a quiet dream—the slaves obey—
A thousand torches drop,—and hark, the last
Bursts on that awful silence; far away
Millions, with hearts that beat both loud and fast,
Watch for the springing flame expectant and aghast.

VIII.

They fly—the torches fall—a cry of fear
Has startled the triumphant!—they recede!

1 I.e., leaders of the foreign armies.

2 The reptiles gathered on the pyre have been waiting so long they've lost their venom, or "sting."

For, ere the cannon's roar has died, they hear
The tramp of hoofs like earthquake, and a steed
Dark and gigantic, with the tempest's speed,
Bursts thro' their ranks: a woman sits thereon,
Fairer it seems than aught that earth can breed,
Calm, radiant, like the phantom of the dawn,
A spirit from the caves of day-light wandering gone.[1]

IX.

All thought it was God's Angel come to sweep
The lingering guilty to their fiery grave;
The tyrant from his throne in dread did leap,—
Her innocence his child from fear did save;
Scared by the faith they feigned, each priestly slave
Knelt for his mercy whom they served with blood,
And, like the refluence° of a mighty wave *reflux, pulling backwards*
Sucked into the loud sea, the multitude
With crushing panic, fled in terror's altered mood.

X.

They pause, they blush, they gaze,—a gathering shout
Bursts like one sound from the ten thousand streams[2]
Of a tempestuous sea:—that sudden rout
One checked, who, never in his mildest dreams
Felt awe from grace or loveliness, the seams
Of his rent heart so hard and cold a creed
Had seared with blistering ice—but he misdeems
That he is wise, whose wounds do only bleed
Inly for self, thus thought the Christian[3] Priest indeed,

XI.

And others too, thought he was wise to see,
In pain, and fear, and hate, something divine,
In love and beauty—no divinity.—
Now with a bitter smile, whose light did shine
Like a fiend's hope upon his lips and eyne,° *eyes*
He said, and the persuasion of that sneer
Rallied his trembling comrades—"Is it mine
To stand alone, when kings and soldiers fear
A woman? Heaven has sent its other victim here."

---

1 Cf. VI.xix.163–69 (p. 142).

2 Originally "waves"; corrected from Shelley's list of errata.

3 *RoI* has "Iberian."

XII.

"Were it not impious," said the King, "to break
Our holy oath?"—"Impious to keep it, say!"
Shrieked the exulting Priest—"Slaves, to the stake
Bind her, and on my head the burthen lay
Of her just torments:—at the Judgment Day
Will I stand up before God's golden throne,
And cry, O Lord, to thee did I betray
An Atheist;[1] but for me she would have known
Another moment's joy! the glory be thine own."

XIII.

They trembled, but replied not, nor obeyed,
Pausing in breathless silence. Cythna sprung
From her gigantic steed, who, like a shade
Chased by the winds, those vacant streets among
Fled tameless, as the brazen rein she flung
Upon his neck, and kissed his mooned brow.
A piteous sight, that one so fair and young,
The clasp of such a fearful death should woo
With smiles of tender joy as beamed from Cythna now.

XIV.

The warm tears burst in spite of faith and fear,
From many a tremulous eye, but like soft dews
Which feed spring's earliest buds, hung gathered there,
Frozen by doubt,—alas, they could not chuse,
But weep;[2] for, when her faint limbs did refuse
To climb the pyre, upon the mutes she smiled;
And with her eloquent gestures, and the hues
Of her quick lips, even as a weary child
Wins sleep from some fond nurse with its caresses mild,

---

1 In *RoI*, the lines read thus:
Will I stand up before God's golden throne
Of Heaven, and cry, to thee did I betray
An Infidel[.]

2 Cf. Ophelia's "I cannot choose but weep, to think they should lay him i' the cold ground." Shakespeare, *Hamlet* 4.5.69–70.

XV.

She won them, tho' unwilling, her to bind
Near me, among the snakes. When the[se][1] had fled
One soft reproach that was most thrilling kind,
She smiled on me, and nothing then we said,
But each upon the other's countenance fed
Looks of insatiate° love; the mighty veil *insatiable*
Which doth divide the living and the dead
Was almost rent, the world grew dim and pale,—
All light in Heaven or Earth beside our love did fail.—

XVI.

Yet,—yet—one brief relapse, like the last beam
Of dying flames, the stainless° air around *clear, clean*
Hung silent and serene—a blood-red gleam
Burst upwards, hurling fiercely from the ground
The globed smoke,—I heard the mighty sound
Of its uprise, like a tempestuous ocean;
And, thro' its chasms I saw, as in a swound,
The tyrant's child fall without life or motion
Before his throne, subdued by some unseen emotion.

XVII.

And is this death? the pyre has disappeared,
The Pestilence, the Tyrant, and the throng;
The flames grow silent—slowly there is heard
The music of a breath-suspending° song, *breathtaking*
Which, like the kiss of love when life is young,
Steeps the faint eyes in darkness sweet and deep;
With ever changing notes it floats along,
Till on my passive soul there seemed to creep
A melody, like waves on wrinkled sands that leap.

XVIII.

The warm touch of a soft and tremulous hand
Wakened me then; lo, Cythna sate reclined
Beside me, on the waved and golden sand

1 In both *RoI* and the original text of *Laon and Cythna*, "then." There is some editorial controversy about how to render this word. I follow Reiman, Fraistat, and Crook, who follow C.D. Locock's 1911 edition of *The Poems of Percy Bysshe Shelley*, in choosing "these," which would refer in this instance to the "mutes" who bind Cythna to the stake. The sense of lines 128–30 is that after the mutes leave Laon and Cythna alone on the pyre, Cythna smiles a "soft reproach" or gentle rebuke "on" or at Laon for his plan to sacrifice his life for hers.

Of a clear pool, upon a bank o'ertwined
With strange and star-bright flowers, which to the wind
Breathed divine odour; high above, was spread
The emerald heaven of trees of unknown kind,
Whose moonlike blooms and bright fruit overhead
A shadow, which was light, upon the waters shed.

XIX.

And round about sloped many a lawny mountain
With incense-bearing forests,[1] and vast caves
Of marble radiance, to that mighty fountain;
And where the flood its own bright margin laves,° *washes*
Their echoes talk with its eternal waves,
Which, from the depths whose jagged caverns breed
Their unreposing strife, it lifts and heaves,—
Till thro' a chasm of hills they roll, and feed
A river deep, which flies with smooth but arrowy speed.

XX.

As we sate gazing in a trance of wonder,
A boat approached, borne by the musical air
Along the waves which sung and sparkled under
Its rapid keel—a winged shape sate there,
A child with silver-shining wings, so fair
That, as her bark did thro' the waters glide,
The shadow of the lingering waves did wear
Light, as from starry beams; from side to side,
While veering to the wind her plumes the bark did guide.[2]

XXI.

The boat was one curved shell of hollow pearl,[3]
Almost translucent with the light divine
Of her within; the prow and stern did curl,
Horned on high, like the young moon supine,[4]
When o'er dim twilight mountains dark with pine,
It floats upon the sunset's sea of beams,
Whose golden waves in many a purple line

---

1 Cf. the "incense-bearing tree[s]" of Coleridge's "Kubla Khan."

2 The child's wings ("plumes") operate as the boat's sails, guiding its course.

3 Rather like Venus herself, the child is carried upon the waves by a shell, an image that enhances her identification with Love and recalls the violence of her origins: according to myth, Venus is born when the Titan Saturn cuts off the genitals of his father Uranus and throws them into the sea.

4 Reclining, lying on its back.

Fade fast, till borne on sunlight's ebbing streams,
Dilating, on earth's verge the sunken meteor gleams.

XXII.

Its keel has struck the sands beside our feet;—
Then Cythna turned to me, and from her eyes
Which swam with unshed tears, a look more sweet
Than happy love, a wild and glad surprise,
Glanced as she spake; "Ay, this is Paradise
And not a dream, and we are all united!
Lo, that is mine own child, who in the guise
Of madness came, like day to one benighted
In lonesome woods: my heart is now too well requited!"

XXIII.

And then she wept aloud, and in her arms
Clasped that bright Shape, less marvellously fair
Than her own human hues and living charms;
Which, as she leaned in passion's silence there,
Breathed warmth on the cold bosom of the air,
Which seemed to blush and tremble with delight;
The glossy darkness of her streaming hair
Fell o'er that snowy child, and wrapt from sight
The fond and long embrace which did their hearts unite.

XXIV.

Then the bright child, the plumed Seraph° came, *angel*
And fixed its blue and beaming eyes on mine,
And said, "I was disturbed by tremulous shame
When once we met, yet knew that I was thine
From the same hour in which thy lips divine
Kindled a clinging dream within my brain,[1]
Which ever waked when I might sleep, to twine
Thine image with *her* memory dear—again
We meet; exempted now from mortal fear or pain.

XXV.

"When the consuming flames had wrapt ye round,
The hope which I had cherished went away;
I fell in agony on the senseless ground,
And hid mine eyes in dust, and far astray

---

1 The sense of this passage seems to be that Laon is the child's spiritual and intellectual father, if not her biological one, and has been so since the moment she heard his songs

My mind was gone, when bright, like dawning day,
The Spectre of the Plague before me flew,
And breathed upon my lips, and seemed to say,
'They wait for thee beloved';—then I knew
The death-mark on my breast, and became calm anew.

XXVI.

"It was the calm of love—for I was dying.
I saw the black and half-extinguished pyre
In its own gray and shrunken ashes lying;
The pitchy° smoke of the departed fire *black or wicked*
Still hung in many a hollow dome and spire
Above the towers like night; beneath whose shade
Awed by the ending of their own desire
The armies stood; a vacancy° was made *vacuum, emptiness*
In expectation's depth, and so they stood dismayed.

XXVII.

"The frightful silence of that altered mood
The tortures of the dying clove alone,
Till one uprose among the multitude,
And said—'The flood of time is rolling on,
We stand upon its brink, whilst *they* are gone
To glide in peace down death's mysterious stream.
Have ye done well? they moulder° flesh and bone, *rot*
Who might have made this life's envenomed° dream *poisoned*
A sweeter draught° than ye will ever taste, I deem.° *drink; think, suspect*

XXVIII.

"'These perish as the good and great of yore
Have perished, and their murderers will repent,
Yes, vain and barren tears shall flow before
Yon smoke has faded from the firmament
Even for this cause, that ye who must lament
The death of those that made this world so fair,
Cannot recall them now; but then is lent
To man the wisdom of a high despair,
When such can die, and he live on and linger here.

XXIX.

"'Ay, ye may fear not now the Pestilence,
From fabled hell as by a charm withdrawn,
All power and faith must pass, since calmly hence

In pain and fire have Atheists[1] gone;
And ye must sadly turn away, and moan[2]
In secret, to his home each one returning,
And to long ages shall this hour be known;
And slowly shall its memory, ever burning,
Fill this dark night of things with an eternal morning.

XXX.

"'For me that world is grown too void and cold,
Since hope pursues immortal destiny
With steps thus slow—therefore shall ye behold
How Atheists and Republicans can die[3]—
Tell to your children this!' then suddenly
He sheathed a dagger in his heart and fell;
My brain grew dark in death, and yet to me
There came a murmur from the crowd, to tell
Of deep and mighty change which suddenly befell.

XXXI.

"Then suddenly I stood a winged Thought,
Before the immortal Senate, and the seat
Of that star-shining spirit, whence is wrought
The strength of its dominion, good and great,
The better Genius of this world's estate.
His realm around one mighty Fane is spread,
Elysian[4] islands bright and fortunate,
Calm dwellings of the free and happy dead,
Where I am sent to lead!" These winged words she said,

XXXII.

And with the silence of her eloquent smile,
Bade us embark in her divine canoe;
Then at the helm we took our seat, the while
Above her head those plumes of dazzling hue
Into the winds' invisible stream she threw,
Sitting beside the prow: like gossamer,[5]
On the swift breath of morn, the vessel flew
O'er the bright whirlpools of that fountain fair,
Whose shores receded fast, while we seemed lingering there;

---

1 *RoI* has "unbelievers."

2 Originally "mourn"; corrected from Shelley's list of errata.

3 *RoI* has "How those who love, yet fear not, dare to die."

4 Blissful, paradisical. In the classical tradition, Elysium is a realm in the afterlife.

5 A light and filmy substance spun by spiders.

XXXIII.

Till down that mighty stream dark, calm, and fleet,
Between a chasm of cedarn mountains riven,[1]
Chased by the thronging winds whose viewless° feet, *invisible*
As swift as twinkling beams, had, under Heaven,
From woods and waves wild sounds and odours driven,
The boat fled visibly—three nights and days,
Borne like a cloud thro' morn, and noon, and even,
We sailed along the winding watery ways
Of the vast stream, a long and labyrinthine maze.

XXXIV.

A scene of joy and wonder to behold
That river's shapes and shadows changing ever,
Where the broad sunrise, filled with deepening gold,
Its whirlpools, where all hues did spread and quiver,
And where melodious falls did burst and shiver
Among rocks clad with flowers, the foam and spray
Sparkled like stars upon the sunny river,
Or, when the moonlight poured a holier day,
One vast and glittering lake around green islands lay.

XXXV.

Morn, noon, and even, that boat of pearl outran
The streams which bore it, like the arrowy cloud
Of tempest, or the speedier thought of man,
Which flieth forth and cannot make abode,° *cannot stop*
Sometimes thro' forests, deep like night, we glode,
Between the walls of mighty mountains crowned
With Cyclopean piles,[2] whose turrets proud,
The homes of the departed, dimly frowned
O'er the bright waves which girt their dark foundations round.

XXXVI.

Sometimes between the wide and flowering meadows,
Mile after mile we sailed, and 'twas delight
To see far off the sunbeams chase the shadows

---

1 I.e., in a canyon cut through cedar-covered mountains.

2 According to ancient sources including Hesiod and Homer, the Cyclopes were a race of one-eyed giants, one of whom memorably terrorizes Odysseus and his men in Book IX of Homer's *Odyssey*. Shelley uses the adjective "Cyclopean" to suggest that these "piles" or ruins are so large as to have been made by the Cyclopes.

Over the grass; sometimes beneath the night
Of wide and vaulted caves, whose roofs were bright
With starry gems, we fled, whilst from their deep
And dark-green chasms, shades beautiful and white,
Amid sweet sounds across our path would sweep,
Like swift and lovely dreams that walk the waves of sleep.

XXXVII.

And ever as we sailed, our minds were full
Of love and wisdom, which would overflow
In converse wild, and sweet, and wonderful;
And in quick smiles whose light would come and go,
Like music o'er wide waves, and in the flow
Of sudden tears, and in the mute caress—
For a deep shade was cleft,[1] and we did know,
That virtue, tho' obscured on Earth, not less
Survives all mortal change in lasting loveliness.

XXXVIII.

Three days and nights we sailed, as thought and feeling
Number delightful hours—for thro' the sky
The sphered lamps of day and night, revealing
New changes and new glories, rolled on high,
Sun, Moon, and moonlike lamps, the progeny
Of a diviner Heaven, serene and fair:
On the fourth day, wild as a wind-wrought sea
The stream became, and fast and faster bare° *bore*
The spirit-winged boat, steadily speeding there.

XXXIX.

Steady and swift, where the waves rolled like mountains
Within the vast ravine, whose rifts did pour
Tumultuous floods from their ten thousand fountains,
The thunder of whose earth-uplifting roar
Made the air sweep in whirlwinds from the shore,
Calm as a shade,° the boat of that fair child *ghost, spirit*
Securely fled, that rapid stress before,
Amid the topmost spray, and sunbows[2] wild,
Wreathed in the silver mist: in joy and pride we smiled.

---

1 I.e., something hitherto obscure had become clear.

2 Rainbow-colored arched or circular shapes created by sunlight shining through mist.

XL.

The torrent of that wide and raging river
Is past, and our aërial speed suspended.
We look behind; a golden mist did quiver
When its wild surges with the lake were blended:
Our bark hung there, as on a line[1] suspended
Between two heavens, that windless waveless lake;
Which four great cataracts from four vales, attended
By mists, aye feed; from rocks and clouds they break,
And of that azure sea a silent refuge make.

XLI.

Motionless resting on the lake awhile,
I saw its marge° of snow-bright mountains rear *margin, border*
Their peaks aloft, I saw each radiant isle,
And in the midst, afar, even like a sphere
Hung in one hollow sky, did there appear
The Temple of the Spirit; on the sound
Which issued thence, drawn nearer and more near,
Like the swift moon this glorious earth around,
The charmed boat approached, and there its haven found.

Finis.

---

1 Starting with Rossetti's 1870 edition of *The Poetical Works of Percy Bysshe Shelley*, some editors adopt "on a line" in place of "one line." The image of the boat "suspended / Between two heavens" is certainly made clearer by this emendation, and the line's meter is preserved.

Appendix A: Shelley's Political and Philosophical Prose

1. From *A Vindication of Natural Diet* (London: J. Callow, 1813), 9–11, 15–18, 20–21

[Originally composed as one of Shelley's long notes to *Queen Mab*, this essay on the benefits of vegetarianism anticipates the politicization of meat-eating in *Laon and Cythna*. Contrary to what one might expect, the revolutionaries' vegetarian feast in Canto Fifth (pp. 135–36) is not intended to invoke a return to Paradise, in which human beings were said to have eschewed animal flesh, but rather a nascent world order in which our species lives cooperatively with others. As Shelley makes clear in what follows, "crime" or moral failure expresses the violence of the spirit, and political absolutism is among the greatest crimes of all. Taking up a plant-based diet is a political and ethical gesture as well as a health-conscious one: it makes us better people, capable of building a better and more just world for all of earth's inhabitants. Interestingly, Shelley's argument about land use, and how the globalization of meat-based diets creates a dangerous economic dependency on farm-raised animals, also anticipates contemporary debates on factory farming, sustainable agriculture, and food security.]

In no cases has a return to vegetable diet produced the slightest injury; in most it has been attended with changes undeniably beneficial. Should ever a physician be born with the genius of Locke, I am persuaded that he might trace all bodily and mental derangements to our unnatural habits, as clearly as that philosopher has traced all knowledge to sensation.[1] What prolific sources of disease are not those mineral and vegetable poisons that have been introduced for its extirpation?[2] How many thousands have become murderers and robbers, bigots and domestic tyrants, dissolute and abandoned adventurers, from the use of fermented liquors; who had they slaked their thirst only at the mountain stream, would have lived but to diffuse the happiness of their own unperverted feelings. How many groundless opinions and absurd institutions have not received a general sanction from the sottishness[3] and intemperance of individuals? Who will assert, that had the populace of Paris drank at the pure source of the Seine, and satisfied their hunger at the ever-furnished table of vegetable nature that they would have lent their brutal suffrage to the pro-

1 In his *Essay Concerning Human Understanding* (1689), the English philosopher John Locke (1632–1704) claimed that human beings are born without innate ideas or mental content and acquire knowledge only through their experiences and perceptions of the world.

2 Eradication.

3 Drunkenness.

scription-list of Robespierre?[1] Could a set of men, whose passions were not perverted by unnatural stimuli, look with coolness on an *auto da fé*?[2] Is it to be believed that a being of gentle feelings, rising from his meal of roots, would take delight in sports of blood?

[...]

There is no disease, bodily or mental, which adoption of vegetable diet and pure water has not infallibly mitigated, wherever the experiment has been fairly tried. Debility is gradually converted into strength, disease into healthfulness: madness, in all its hideous variety, from the ravings of the fettered maniac, to the unaccountable irrationalities of ill temper, that make a hell of domestic life, into a calm and considerate evenness of temper, that alone might offer a certain pledge of the future moral reformation of society. On a natural system of diet, old age would be our last and our only malady; the term of our existence would be protracted; we should enjoy life, and no longer preclude others from the enjoyment of it; all sensational delights would be infinitely more exquisite and perfect; the very sense of being would then be a continued pleasure, such as we now feel it in some few and favoured moments of our youth. By all that is sacred in our hopes for the human race, I conjure those who love happiness and truth, to give a fair trial to the vegetable system. Reasoning is surely superfluous on a subject, whose merits an experience of six months would set for ever at rest. But it is only among the enlightened and benevolent, that so great a sacrifice of appetite and prejudice can be expected, even though its ultimate excellence should not admit of dispute.

[...]

[W]hen a thousand persons can be produced, living on vegetables and distilled water, who have to dread no disease but old age, the world will be compelled to regard animal flesh and fermented liquors as slow but certain poisons. The change which would be produced by simpler habits on political economy is sufficiently remarkable. The monopolizing eater of animal flesh would no longer destroy his constitution by devouring an acre at a meal, and many loaves of bread would cease to contribute to gout, madness and apoplexy,[3] in the shape of a pint of porter, or a dram[4] of gin, when appeasing the long-protracted famine of the hard-working peasant's hungry babes. The quantity of nutritious vegetable matter, consumed in fattening the carcase of

---

1 Shelley implies that the French Revolution would not have succumbed to the so-called Reign of Terror, largely orchestrated by Maximilien de Robespierre (1758–94), if the people of France had adopted vegetable diets, eschewed alcohol, and drunk instead from the river Seine.

2 An "auto-da-fé," literally "act of faith" in Portuguese, refers to the burning of heretics by the Spanish Inquisition, which began in 1478.

3 Stroke.

4 A pour, a drink.

an ox, would afford ten times the sustenance, undepraving indeed, and incapable of generating disease, if gathered immediately from the bosom of the earth.

The most fertile districts of the habitable globe are now actually cultivated by men for animals, at a delay and waste of aliment[1] absolutely incapable of calculation. It is only the wealthy that can, to any great degree, even now, indulge the unnatural craving for dead flesh, and they pay for the greater licence of the privilege by subjection to supernumerary diseases. Again, the spirit of the nation that should take lead in this great reform would insensibly[2] become agricultural; commerce, with all its vice, selfishness and corruption, would gradually decline; more natural habits would produce gentler manners, and the excessive complication of political relations would be so far simplified that every individual might feel and understand why he loved his country, and took a personal interest in its welfare. How would England, for example, depend on the caprices of foreign rulers, if she contained within herself all the necessaries, and despised whatever they possessed of the luxuries of life? How could they starve her into compliance with their views? Of what consequence would it be that they refused to take her woollen manufactures, when large and fertile tracts of the island ceased to be allotted to the waste of pasturage? On a natural system of diet, we should require no spices from India; no wines from Portugal, Spain, France, or Madeira; none of those multitudinous articles of luxury, for which every corner of the globe is rifled, and which are the causes of so much individual rivalship, such calamitous and sanguinary national disputes.

In the history of modern times, the avarice of commercial monopoly, no less than the ambition of weak and wicked chiefs, seems to have fomented the universal discord, to have added stubbornness to the mistakes of cabinets, and indocility to the infatuation of the people. Let it ever be remembered that it is the direct influence of commerce to make the interval between the richest and the poorest man wider and more unconquerable. Let it be remembered, that it is a foe to every thing of real worth and excellence in the human character. The odious and disgusting aristocracy of wealth, is built upon the ruins of all that is good in chivalry or republicanism; and luxury is the forerunner of a barbarism scarce capable of cure. Is it impossible to realize a state of society, where all the energies of man shall be directed to the production of his solid happiness?

2. From "On Love," ed. Mary Shelley, *Keepsake for 1829* (1818; London: Hurst, Chance, & Co., 1828), 47–49

[This prose fragment was first published posthumously in the 1829 edition of the literary annual *The Keepsake*. The text was prepared and edited by Mary Shelley, who, in her preface to Shelley's *Essays, Letters from Abroad, Translations and Fragments* (1840), describes "On Love" as revealing "the secrets of the most impassioned, and yet the purest and softest heart that ever yearned for sympathy, and was ready to give its own, in lavish measure, in return" (I.8).

1 Food, nourishment.

2 Without realizing it, i.e., little by little.

Like many of Shelley's essays, this one displays a strong Platonic streak that marries some of the ideas about love set out in Plato's *Symposium*—which Shelley began translating in the summer of 1818—with Shelley's own metaphysical speculations and autobiographical asides. In the *Symposium*, Plato (through the character of the female philosopher Diotima) argues that love for another person ultimately leads to a love of the beautiful itself, which Plato effectively identifies with the good, the just, and the divine. The emphasis on love's transformative properties is borne out repeatedly in the dynamic between Laon and Cythna, who are frequently cast both as mirror images and "antitypes," or symbols, of each other (see, for example, p. 113, IV.xxix–xxx).

Later editions of "On Love" tend to alter some of the punctuation Mary Shelley gives here; as noted below, Shelley's line "from the instant we live and move thirsts" is misprinted in the *Keepsake* as "from the instant we live more and more thirsts."]

What is Love?—Ask him who lives what is life; ask him who adores what is God.

[...]

Thou demandest what is Love. It is that powerful attraction towards all that we conceive, or fear, or hope beyond ourselves, when we find within our own thoughts the chasm of an insufficient void, and seek to awaken in all things that are, a community with what we experience within ourselves. If we reason, we would be understood; if we imagine, we would that the airy children of our brain were born anew within another's; if we feel, we would that another's nerves should vibrate to our own, that the beams of their eyes should kindle at once and mix and melt into our own, that lips of motionless ice should not reply to lips quivering and burning with the heart's best blood:—this is Love. This is the bond and the sanction which connects not only man with man, but with every thing which exists. We are born into the world, and there is something within us which from the instant that we live [and move][1] thirsts after its likeness. It is probably in correspondence with this law that the infant drains milk from the bosom of its mother; this propensity developes [sic] itself with the developement of our nature. We dimly see within our intellectual nature, a miniature as it were of our entire self, yet deprived of all that we condemn or despise, the ideal prototype of every thing excellent and lovely that we are capable of conceiving as belonging to the nature of man. Not only the portrait of our external being, but an assemblage of the minutest particles of which our nature is composed:[2] a mirror whose surface reflects only the forms of purity and brightness: a soul within our soul that describes a circle around its proper Paradise, which pain and sorrow and evil dare not overleap. To this we eagerly refer all sensations, thirsting that they should resemble or correspond with it.

1 *The Keepsake* has "more and more."

2 [Shelley's note in his draft:] These words are inefficient and metaphorical—Most words so—No help—. [In *The Keepsake*, Mary Shelley provides a slightly altered version.]

The discovery of its antitype; the meeting with an understanding capable of clearly estimating the deductions of our own; an imagination which should enter into and seize upon the subtle and delicate peculiarities which we have delighted to cherish and unfold in secret, with a frame, whose nerves, like the chords of two exquisite lyres, strung to the accompaniment of one delightful voice, vibrate with the vibrations of our own; and of a combination of all these in such proportion as the type within demands: this is the invisible and unattainable point to which Love tends; and to attain which, it urges forth the powers of man to arrest the faintest shadow of that, without the possession of which, there is no rest nor respite to the heart over which it rules. Hence in solitude, or in that deserted state when we are surrounded by human beings and yet they sympathize not with us, we love the flowers, the grass, the waters, and the sky. In the motion of the very leaves of spring, in the blue air there is then found a secret correspondence with our heart. There is eloquence in the tongueless wind, and a melody in the flowing brooks and the rustling of the reeds beside them, which by their inconceivable relation to something within the soul awaken the spirits to a dance of breathless rapture, and bring tears of mysterious tenderness to the eyes like the enthusiasm of patriotic success, or the voice of one beloved singing to you alone. Sterne says that if he were in a desert he would love some cypress.[1] So soon as this want or power is dead, man becomes the living sepulchre of himself, and what yet survives is the mere husk of what once he was.

3. From *A Philosophical View of Reform*, ed. T.W. Rolleston (1819–20; Oxford: Oxford UP, 1920), 43–50, 88–91

[Published a century after it was composed, *A Philosophical View of Reform* represents Shelley's most concrete expression of his political principles, revealed here to be considerably more pragmatic than his reputation as a dreamer might suggest. In a letter to Leigh Hunt dated 26 May 1820, Shelley himself described the essay as "intended for a kind of standard book for the philosophical reformers"—a remark that shows the extent to which Shelley aspired to be taken seriously as both an imaginative writer and a political philosopher, not unlike his mother-in-law Mary Wollstonecraft and his father-in-law William Godwin.[2] About 200 pages long in manuscript, *A Philosophical View of Reform* lays out a plan for the reform of England's political system. Along the way, it

1 "I pity the man who can travel from *Dan* to *Beersheba*, and cry, 'Tis all barren—and so it is; and so is all the world to him who will not cultivate the fruits it offers. I declare, said I, clapping my hands chearily together, that was I in a desart, I would find out wherewith in it to call forth my affections—If I could not do better, I would fasten them upon some sweet myrtle, or seek some melancholy cypress to connect myself to—I would court their shade, and greet them kindly for their protection—I would cut my name upon them, and swear they were the loveliest trees throughout the desert: if their leaves wither'd, I would teach myself to mourn, and when they rejoiced, I would rejoice along with them." Laurence Sterne (1713–68), *A Sentimental Journey* 85–86.

2 In *Complete Works*, ed. Roger Ingpen and Walter E. Peck (New York: Gordian P, 1965), 10.172.

touches upon topics such as European history and the rise of modern despotism, Enlightenment philosophy, imperialism, the evils of paper currency and the national debt, the legitimacy (or lack thereof) of Parliament, Malthusian demographics, just and unjust forms of property, female suffrage, and the Peterloo Massacre. The following excerpts—from Chapters II and III, respectively—address the emergence of what Shelley calls "the new aristocracy" produced by capitalism and the virtues of non-violent resistance.]

Chapter II, "On the Sentiment of the Necessity of Change"

Mankind seem to acquiesce, as in a necessary condition of the imbecility of their own will and reason, in the existence of an aristocracy. With reference to this imbecility, it has doubtless been the instrument of great social advantage, although that advantage would have been greater which might have been produced according to the forms of a just distribution of the goods and evils of life. The object therefore of all enlightened legislation, and administration, is to enclose within the narrowest practicable limits this order of drones.[1] The effect of the financial impostures of the modern rulers of England has been to increase the number of the drones. Instead of one aristocracy, the condition *to* which, in the present state of human affairs, the friends of virtue and liberty are willing to subscribe as to an inevitable evil, they have supplied us with two aristocracies. The one, consisting in great land proprietors, and wealthy merchants who receive and interchange the produce of this country with the produce of other countries: in this, because all other great communities have as yet acquiesced in it, we acquiesce. Connected with the members of it is a certain generosity and refinement of manners and opinion which, although neither philosophy nor virtue, has been that acknowledged substitute for them which at least is a religion which makes respected those venerable names. The other aristocracy is one of attornies and excisemen[2] and directors[3] and government pensioners, usurers, stockjobbers,[4] country[5] bankers, with their dependents and descendants. These are a set of pelting[6] wretches in whose employment there is nothing to exercise even to their distortion the more majestic faculties of the soul. Though at the bottom it is all trick, there is something frank and magnificent in the chivalrous disdain of infamy connected with a gentleman. There is something to which—until you see through the base falsehood upon which all inequality is founded—it is difficult for the imagination to refuse its respect, in the faithful and direct dealings of the substantial merchant. But in the habits and lives of this new aristocracy created out of an increase in public calamities, and whose existence must be determined by their

1 Male honey bees who must be fed by the worker bees. As a pejorative term, the word "drone" is used to describe lazy, useless, and parasitic persons.

2 Tax collectors.

3 Members of the board of a commercial corporation or company.

4 Stockbrokers.

5 Small-time.

6 Petty, insignificant, worthless.

termination, there is nothing to qualify our disapprobation. They eat and drink and sleep, and in the intervals of these things performed with most vexatious ceremony and accompaniments they cringe and lie. They poison the literature of the age in which they live by requiring either the antitype of their own mediocrity in books, or such stupid and distorted and inharmonious idealisms as alone have the power to stir their torpid imaginations. Their hopes and fears are of the narrowest description. Their domestic affections are feeble, and they have no others. They think of any commerce with their species but as a means, never as an end, and as a means to the basest forms of personal advantage.

If this aristocracy had arisen from a false and depreciated currency to the exclusion of the other, its existence would have been a moral calamity and disgrace, but it would not have constituted an oppression. But the hereditary aristocracy who had the political administration of affairs took the measures which created this other for purposes peculiarly its own. Those measures were so contrived as in no manner to diminish the wealth and power of the contrivers. The lord does not spare himself one luxury, but the peasant and artizan[1] are assured of many *necessary* things. To support the system of social order according to its supposed unavoidable constitution, those from whose labour all those external accommodations which distinguish a civilized being from a savage arise, worked, before the institution of this double aristocracy, light hours. And of these only the healthy were compelled to labour, the efforts of the old, the sick and the immature being dispensed with, and they maintained by the labour of the sane,[2] for such is the plain English of the poor-rates.[3] That labour procured a competent share of the decencies of life, and society seemed to extend the benefits of its institution even to its most unvalued instrument. Although deprived of those resources of sentiment and knowledge which might have been their lot could the wisdom of the institutions of social forms have established a system of strict justice, yet they earned by their labour a competency in those external materials of life which, and not the loss of moral and intellectual excellence, is supposed to be the legitimate object of the desires and murmurs of the poor. Since the institution of this double aristocracy, however, they have often worked not ten but twenty hours a day. Not that the poor have rigidly worked twenty hours, but that the worth of the labour of twenty hours now, in food and clothing, is equivalent to the worth of ten hours then. And because twenty hours cannot, from the nature of the human frame, be exacted from those who before performed ten, the aged and the sickly are compelled either to work or starve. Children who were exempted from labour are put in requisition, and the vigorous promise of the coming generation blighted by premature exertion. For fourteen hours' labour, which they do perforce,[4] they receive—no matter in what nominal amount—the price of seven. They eat less bread, wear worse clothes, are more ignorant, immoral, miserable

1 Artisan, skilled worker.

2 Healthy, from the Latin *sanus*.

3 Property taxes levied on parishes in England and Wales, and used to provide relief to the poor of each parish.

4 By necessity.

and desperate. This then is the condition of the lowest and largest class, from whose labour the whole materials of life are wrought, of which the others are only the receivers or the consumers. They are more superstitious, for misery on earth begets a diseased expectation and panic-stricken faith in miseries beyond the grave. "God," they argue, "rules this world as well as that; and assuredly since his nature is immutable, and his powerful will unchangeable, he rules them by the same laws." The gleams of hope which speak of Paradise seem like the flames in Milton's hell only to make darkness visible,[1] and all things take their colour from what surrounds them. They become revengeful....

From Chapter III, "Probable Means"

The last resort of resistance is undoubtedly insurrection. The right of insurrection is derived from the employment of armed force to counteract the will of the nation. Let the government disband the standing army, and the purpose of resistance would be sufficiently fulfilled by the incessant agitation of the points of dispute before the courts of common law, and by an unwarlike display of the irresistible number and union of the people.

Before we enter into a consideration of the measures which might terminate in civil war, let us for a moment consider the nature and the consequences of war. This is the alternative which the unprincipled cunning of the tyrants has presented to us, and which we must not shun. There is secret sympathy between Destruction and Power, between Monarchy and War; and the long experience of all the history of all recorded time teaches us with what success they have played into each other's hands. War is a kind of superstition; the pageantry of arms and badges corrupts the imagination of men. How far more appropriate would be the symbols of an inconsolable grief—muffled drums, and melancholy music, and arms reversed, and the livery of sorrow rather than of blood. When men mourn at funerals for what do they mourn in comparison with the calamities which they hasten with every circumstance of festivity to suffer and to inflict! Visit in imagination the scene of a field of battle or a city taken by assault, collect into one group the groans and the distortions of the innumerable dying, the inconsolable grief and horror of their surviving friends, the hellish exultation and unnatural drunkenness of destruction of the conquerors, the burning of the harvests and the obliteration of the traces of cultivation—to this, in a civil war, is to be added the sudden disruption of the bonds of social life, and "father against son."

If there had never been war, there could never have been tyranny in the world; tyrants take advantage of the mechanical organization of armies to establish and defend their encroachments. It is thus that the mighty advantages of the French Revolution have been almost compensated by a succession of tyrants (for demagogues, oligarchies, usurpers and legitimate kings are merely varieties of the same class) from Robespierre to Louis XVIII.[2] War, waged from

1 See *Paradise Lost*, I.63–64.

2 Robespierre became the face of the Terror, a time of state surveillance and mass beheadings of people accused of being disloyal to the French Revolution, before being

whatever motive, extinguishes the sentiment of reason and justice in the mind. The motive is forgotten, or only adverted[1] to in a mechanical and habitual manner. A sentiment of confidence in brute force and in a contempt of death and danger is considered the highest virtue, when in truth, and however indispensable, they are merely the means and the instrument, highly capable of being perverted to destroy the cause they were assumed to promote. It is a foppery the most intolerable to an amiable and philosophical mind. It is like what some reasoners have observed of religious faith; no fallacious and indirect motive to action can subsist in the mind without weakening the effect of those which are genuine and true. The person who thinks it virtuous to believe, will think a less degree of virtue attaches to good actions than if he had considered it as indifferent. The person who has been accustomed to subdue men by force will be less inclined to the trouble of convincing or persuading them.

These brief considerations suffice to show that the true friend of mankind and of his country would hesitate before he recommended measures which tend to bring down so heavy a calamity as war.

---

executed himself in 1794. Louis XVIII (1755–1824) was King of France from 1814 to 1824 (with a hiatus for Napoleon's return during the so-called Hundred Days in 1815), and began the Restoration of the Bourbon monarchy.

1 Attended.

Appendix B: Correspondence about Laon and Cythna

[Excerpts are taken from Volume I of *The Letters of Percy Bysshe Shelley*, ed. Frederick L. Jones (Oxford: Clarendon, 1964).]

1. Shelley to an unknown publisher, likely a member of the company Longman, Hurst, Rees, Orme and Brown, 13 October 1817

[In this letter, Shelley tries to pique the interest of an unknown publisher by sending him some of *Laon and Cythna*. Critics suspect that the publisher in question was a member of Longman, Hurst, Rees, Orme and Brown, the firm that had published Thomas Moore's best-selling *Lalla Rookh* in 1817. Since *Lalla Rookh*, like *Laon and Cythna*, is set in an eastern country, Shelley may have thought his poem would be a good fit for the publisher's list, and that Longman and partners would jump at the chance to publish a work with a similar setting if not exactly similar themes.]

Sir,

I send you the first 4 sheets of my poem entitled "Laon & Cythna, or the Revolution of the Golden City."

I believe this commencement affords a sufficient specimen of the work. I am conscious indeed that some of the concluding cantos, when "the plot thickens" & human passions are brought into more critical situations of development, are written with more energy & clearness, & that to see a work of which *unity* is one of the qualifications aimed at by the author, in a disjointed state, is in a certain degree, unfavourable to the general impression. If, however, you submit it to Mr. Moore's[1] judgment, he will make due allowance for these circumstances.

The whole poem, with the exception of the first canto & part of the last is a mere human story without the smallest intermixture of supernatural interference. The first Canto is indeed, in some measure a distinct poem, tho' very necessary to the wholeness of the work. I say this, because if it were all written in the manner of the first Canto, I could not expect that it would be interesting to any great number of people—

I have attempted in the progress of my work to speak to the common & elementary emotions of the human heart, so that, tho it is the story of violence & revolution, it is relieved by milder pictures of friendship & love & natural affection.

The scene is supposed to be laid in Constantinople & modern Greece, but without much attempt at minute delineation of Mahometan[2] manners. It is in fact a tale illustrative of such a Revolution as might be supposed to take place

1 Thomas Moore (1779–1852), Irish poet and novelist.

2 Muslim.

in an European nation, acted upon by the opinions of what has been called (erroneously, as I think) the modern philosophy, & contending with antient notions & the supposed advantage derived from them to those who support them. It is a Revolution of this kind, that is, the *beau ideal*[1] as it were of the French Revolution, but produced by the influence of individual genius, & out of general knowledge. The authors of it are supposed to be my hero & heroine whose names appear in the title.

My private friends have expressed to me a very high, & therefore I do not doubt a very erroneous judgment of my work. However of this I can determine neither way. I have resolved to give it a fair chance, & my wish therefore is first, to know whether you would purchase *my* interest in the copyright, an arrangement which if there be any truth in the opinions of my friends Lord Byron & Mr. Leigh Hunt[2] of my powers cannot be disadvantageous to you, & in the second place how far you are willing to be the publisher of it on my own account,[3] if such an arrangement, which I should infinitely prefer, cannot be made.—

I rely however on your having the goodness at least to send the sheets to Mr. Moore & ask his opinion of their merits.

Sir

I have the honour to be
Your very obed. Ser—[4]
Percy B. Shelley

2. From Shelley to Charles Ollier, 3 December 1817

[*Laon and Cythna* was published jointly by the firms of Charles and James Ollier and Sherwood, Neely, and Jones, but the poem ran into trouble when the Olliers' printer, Buchanan McMillan, took issue with its more controversial passages. The list of errata Shelley refers to below would accompany the second issue of the poem's first edition.]

Dear Sir,

That McMillan is an obstinate old dog as troublesome as he is impudent. 'Tis a mercy as the old women say that I got him thro' the poem at all—let him print the errata, & say at top if he likes, that it was all the Author's fault, & that he is as immaculate as the Lamb of God. Only let him do it directly, or if he won[']t, let some one else.

[...]

---

1 Literally "ideal beauty," though Shelley seems to mean "beautiful ideal."

2 George Gordon, Lord Byron, poet (1788–1824) and Leigh Hunt, poet and journalist (1784–1859).

3 Shelley proposes to fund the publication of the volume himself if the publisher is not interested in purchasing the copyright from him.

4 I.e., "obedient servant." Shelley abbreviates this customary sign-off in various ways in his letters.

I should be glad to hear any news that is authentic & that would mark the feeling of people public or private respecting the Poem—I am tolerably indifferent to whether it be good or bad—

[…]

Dear Sir,
Your obliged Servant,
Percy B Shelley

3. From Shelley to William Godwin, 11 December 1817

[In a letter that typifies his increasingly frosty but still deferential relationship to his father-in-law, Shelley defends *Laon and Cythna* to Godwin, who evidently thought it wasn't as good as Shelley's other writing, including a document he had produced for the Court of Chancery while suing for custody of his two children with Harriet Westbrook, and a review of Godwin's 1817 novel *Mandeville.*]

My dear Godwin,

[…]

I have read & considered all that you say about my general powers, & the particular instance of the Poem in which I have attempted to develope them. Nothing can be more satisfactory to me than the interest which your admonitions express. But I think you are mistaken in some points with regard to the peculiar nature of my powers, whatever be their amount. I listened with deference & self suspicion to your censures of "Laon and Cythna"; but the productions of mine which you commend hold a very low place in my own esteem; & this reassured me, in some degree at least. The Poem was produced by a series of thoughts which filled my mind with unbounded & sustained enthusiasm. I felt the precariousness of my life, & I engaged in this task resolved to leave some record of myself. Much of what the volume contains was written with the same feeling, as real, though not so prophetic, as the communications of a dying man. I never presumed, indeed, to consider it anything approaching to faultless, but when I considered the contemporary productions of the same apparent pretensions, I will own that I was filled with confidence. I felt that it was in many respects a genuine picture of my own mind. I felt that the sentiments were true, not assumed. And in this have I long believed that my power consists: in sympathy & that part of imagination which relates to sentiment and contemplation.—I am formed,—if for any thing not in common with the herd of mankind—to apprehend minute & remote distinctions of feeling whether relative to external nature, or the living beings which surround us, & to communicate the conceptions which result from considering either the moral or the material universe as a whole. Of course I believe these faculties, which perhaps comprehend all that is sublime in man, to exist very imperfectly in my own mind. But when you advert to my Chancery paper,—a cold, forced, unimpassioned, & insignificant piece of cramped & cautious argument; & to the little scrap about Mandeville,[1] which expressed my feelings indeed, but cost scarcely two minutes thought to express, as specimens of my powers, more favourable than that which grew as it were from "the agony & blood sweat"[2] of intellectual travail—surely I must feel that in some manner, either I am mistaken in believing that I have any talent at all, or you in the selection of specimens of it.

Yet after all, I cannot but be conscious in much of what I write of an absence of that tranquillity which is the attribute and accompaniment of power. This feeling alone would make your most kind & wise admonitions on the subject of the economy of intellectual force, valuable to me. And if I live, or if I see any trust in coming years, doubt not but that I shall do something whatever it might be, which a serious & earnest es[ti]mate of my powers will suggest to me, & which will be in every respect accommodated to their utmost limits....

My dear Godwin

Most affectionately yours

P.B.S.

4. Shelley to Charles Ollier, 11 December 1817

[The Olliers decided not to proceed with *Laon and Cythna*, much to Shelley's outrage. In this letter, Shelley exhorts them to persist in publishing the poem as a way of striking a blow for freedom of the press, which had been severely compromised in Britain in the decades following the French Revolution. He alludes specifically to the case of Leigh Hunt and his brother John (1775–1848), who were found guilty of seditious libel and imprisoned for a period of two years after publishing a negative account of the Prince Regent in *The Examiner*, and suggests—somewhat confusingly—that if the Olliers show weakness in shelving the poem, the government will likely give them the same treatment.]

Dear Sir,

It is to be regretted that you did not consult your own safety and advantage,[3] if you consider it connected with the non-publication of my book, before your declining the publication, after having accepted it, would have operated to so extensive and serious an injury to my views as now.[4] The instances of

---

1 See *The Prose Works of Percy Bysshe Shelley* 277.

2 The reference is to the Litany from the Book of Common Prayer: "By thine Agony and bloody sweat; by thy Cross and Passion; by thy precious Death and Burial; by thy glorious Resurrection and Ascension; and by the coming of the Holy Ghost, Good Lord, deliver us." These lines build on Luke 22:44: "And being in an agony [Jesus] prayed more earnestly: and his sweat was as it were great drops of blood falling down to the ground."

3 Good or superior position; alternatively, best interests.

4 Shelley seems to have two points here: first, that Ollier should have thought twice before publishing the poem if he thought that doing so would pose such a risk to him and his firm; and second, that by pulling the book Ollier has also damaged his relationship with Shelley.

abuse and menace which you cite were such as you expected, and were, as I conceived, prepared for. If not, it would have been just to me to have given them their due weight and consideration before. You foresaw, you foreknew, all that these people would say. You do your best to condemn my book before it is given forth, because you publish it, and then withdraw, so that no other bookseller will publish it, because one has already rejected it. You must be aware of the great injury which you prepare for me. If I had never consulted your advantage, my book would have had a fair hearing. But now it is first published, and then the publisher, as if the author had deceived him as to the contents of the work, and as if the inevitable consequence of its publication would be ignominy and punishment, and as if none should dare to touch it or look at it, retracts, at a period when nothing but the most extraordinary and unforeseen circumstances can justify his retraction.

I beseech you to reconsider the matter, for your sake no less than for my own. Assume the high and the secure ground of courage. The people who visit your shop, and the wretched bigot who gave his worthless custom to some other bookseller, are not the public. The public respect talent, and a large portion of them are already undeceived with regard to the prejudices which my book attacks. You would lose some customers, but you would gain others. Your trade would be diverted into a channel more consistent with your own principles. Not to say that a publisher is in no wise[1] pledged to all the opinions of his publications, or to any; and that he may enter his protest with each copy sold, either against the truth or the discretion of the principles of the books he sells. But there is a much more important consideration in the case. You are, and have been to a certain extent, the publisher. I don't believe that if the book was quietly and regularly published the Government would touch anything of a character so refined and so remote from the conceptions of the vulgar. They would hesitate before they invaded[2] a member of the higher circles of the republic of letters. But if they see us tremble, they will make no distinctions; they will feel their strength. You might bring the arm of the law down on us by flinching now. Directly these scoundrels see that people are afraid of them, they seize upon them and hold them up to mankind as criminals already convicted by their own fears. You lay yourself prostrate and they trample on you. How glad they would be to seize on any connection of Hunt's[3] by this most powerful of all their arms—the terrors and self-condemnation of their victim! Read all the *ex officio* cases[4] and see what reward booksellers and printers have received for their submission.

If, contrary to common sense and justice, you resolve to give me up, you shall receive no detriment from a connexion with me in small matters, though you determine to inflict so serious a one on me in great. You shall not be at a farthing's expense. I shall still, so far as my powers extend, do my best to

1 In no way.

2 Harassed, came after.

3 Leigh Hunt, Shelley's friend and frequent advocate in the pages of *The Examiner*.

4 Shelley means cases like the Hunts', in which publishers were tried and in some cases imprisoned for distributing controversial material.

promote your interest. On the contrary supposition, even admitting you derive no benefit from the book itself—and it should be my care that you shall do so—I hold myself ready to make ample indemnity for any loss you may sustain.

There is one compromise you might make, though that would be still injurious to me. Sherwood and Neely[1] wished to be the principal publishers—call on them and say that it was through a mistake that you undertook the principal direction of the book, as it was *my wish* that it should be theirs, and that I have written to you to that effect. This, if it would be advantageous to you, would be detrimental to, but not utterly destructive of, my views. To withdraw your name entirely, would be to inflict on me a bitter and undeserved injury.

Let me hear from you by return of post. I hope that you will be influenced to fulfil your engagement with me, and proceed with the publication, as justice to me, and indeed a well-understood estimate of your own interest and character, demand. I do hope that you will have too much regard to the well-chosen motto of your seal[2] to permit the murmurs of a few bigots to outweigh the serious and permanent considerations presented in this letter. To their remonstrances you have only to reply, "I did not write the book; I am not responsible; here is the author's address; state your objections to him; I do no more than sell it to those who inquire for it, and if they are not pleased with their bargain, the author empowers me to receive the book and to return the money." As to the interference of Government, nothing is more improbable [than] that in any case it would be attempted; but if it should, it would be owing entirely to your perseverance in the groundless apprehensions which dictated your communication received this day, and conscious terror would be perverted into an argument of guilt.

I have just received a most kind and encouraging letter from Mr. Moore[3] on the subject of my poem. I have the fairest chance of the public approaching my work with unbiassed and unperverted feeling; the fruit of reputation (and you know for *what purposes* I value it) is within my reach. It is for you, now you have been once named as publisher and have me in your power, to blast all this, and to hold up my literary character in the eye of mankind as that of a proscribed and rejected outcast. And for no evil that I have ever done you, but in return for a preference which, although you falsely now esteem [it] injurious to you, was solicited by Hunt, and conferred by me, as a source and a proof of nothing but kind intentions.

Dear Sir,

I remain your sincere well-wisher,

Percy B. Shelley

5. From Shelley to Thomas Moore, 16 December 1817

[Here Shelley, who as we have seen thought *Laon and Cythna* shared some affinities with Moore's *Lalla Rookh*, explains the circumstances under which

---

1 Sherwood, Neely, and Jones, co-publishers with the Olliers of *Laon and Cythna*.

2 The Olliers' motto was "in omnibus libertas," meaning "liberty in all things."

3 See above, p. 237.

his poem has been withdrawn from the public. He also claims that he had no idea the incest between Laon and Cythna would prove so offensive, and describes how, in *The Revolt of Islam,* he has altered the nature of their relationship to suit the public's sensibilities.]

Dear Sir,

The present edition of "Laon and Cythna" is to be suppressed, & it will be republished in about a fortnight under the title of "The Revolt of Islam," with some alterations which consist in little else than the substitution of the words *friend* or *lover* for that of *brother* & *sister*. The truth is, that the seclusion of my habits has confined me so much within the circle of my own thoughts, that I have formed to myself a very different measure of approbation or disapprobation for actions than that which is in use among mankind; and the result of that peculiarity, contrary to my intention, revolts & shocks many who might be inclined to sympathise with me in my general views.—

As soon as I discovered that this effect was produced by the circumstance alluded to, I hastened to cancel it—not from any personal feeling of terror, or repentance, but from the sincere desire of doing all the good & conferring all the pleasure which might flow from so obscure a person as myself. I don[']t know why I trouble you with these words, but your kind approbation of the opening of the Poem has emboldened me to believe that this account of my motives might interest you....

Dear Sir,

Y{ou} very obliged

& sin{cere},

Per{cy B. Shelley}

6. From Shelley to Charles Ollier, 22 January 1818

[After a painful editing process, *Laon and Cythna* is published by the Olliers as *The Revolt of Islam*.]

Dear Sir,

[...]

Don't relax in the advertising—I suppose at present that it[1] scarcely sells at all.—If you see any reviews of [or] notices of it in any periodical paper pray send it me,—it is part of my reward—the amusement of hearing the abuse of the bigots—

Dear Sir,

Your very obliged Sert.

Percy B. Shelley

1 I.e., *The Revolt of Islam*.

Appendix C: Contemporary Reviews of The Revolt of Islam

1. From Leigh Hunt, "Literary Notices, No. 39," *The Examiner* 527 (1 February 1818): 75

[Although his name is now seldom mentioned alongside Shelley, Byron, or Keats, Leigh Hunt (1784–1859) was a central figure in the Romantic movement. His left-leaning paper, *The Examiner*, was engaged in a public battle against the Tory (or conservative) periodical press, led by *The Quarterly Review* and *Blackwood's Edinburgh Magazine*, on cultural as well as political grounds: *The Examiner* favored younger, more radical writers while *The Quarterly* and its ilk promoted the work of Walter Scott (1771–1832) and the Poet Laureate Robert Southey (1774–1843). In this and subsequent essays on *The Revolt of Islam* (the revised version of *Laon and Cythna*), Hunt shows clearly how, in the early nineteenth century, the politics and character of an author could not be separated from the politics and character of his work. To defend Shelley and his poetry was also to defend the causes for which he stood, while to criticize them was to reveal one's collusion with the most repressive aspects of the British government.]

This[1] is an extraordinary production. The ignorant will not understand it; the idle will not take the pains to get acquainted with it; even the intelligent will be startled at first with its air of mysticism and wildness; the livelier man of the world will shake his head at it good naturedly; the sulkier one will cry out against it; the bigot will be shocked, terrified, and enraged, and fall to proving all that is said against himself; the negatively virtuous will resent the little quarter that is given to mere custom; the slaves of bad customs or base passions of any sort will either seize their weapons against it, trembling with rage or conscious worthlessness, or hope to let it quietly pass by, as an enthusiasm that must end in air; finally, the hopeless, if they are ill-tempered, will envy it's [*sic*] hopefulness.—if good tempered, will sorrowfully anticipate it's [*sic*] disappointment.—both from self-love, though of two different sorts;—but we will venture to say, that the intelligent and the good, who are yet healthy-minded, and who have not been so far blinded by fear and self-love as to confound superstition with desert,[2] anger and hatred with firmness, or despondency with knowledge, will find themselves amply repaid by breaking through the outer shell of this production, even if it be with the single reflection, that so much ardour for the happy virtues, and so much power to recommend them, have united in the same person. To will them with hope indeed is to create them; and to extend that will is the object of the writer before us.

1 I.e., *The Revolt of Islam*.

2 Merit.

2. From Leigh Hunt, "Literary Notices, No. 41," *The Examiner* 531 (1 March 1818): 139–41[1]

[Continuing in his defense of Shelley's poem, Hunt both clarifies Shelley's political objectives and concedes that *The Revolt of Islam* may not be his best work.]

Mr. Shelley is of opinion with many others that the world is a very beautiful one externally, but wants a good deal of mending with respect to its minds and habits; and for this purpose he would quash as many cold and selfish passions as possible, and rouse up the general element of Love, till it set our earth rolling more harmoniously. The answer made to a writer, who sets out with endeavours like these, is that he is idly aiming at perfection; but Mr. Shelley has no such aim, neither have nine hundred and ninety-nine out of a thousand of the persons who have ever been taunted with it. Such a charge, in truth, is only the first answer which egotism makes to any one who thinks he can go beyond its own ideas of the possible. If this however be done away, the next answer is, that you are attempting something wild and romantic,—that you will get disliked for it as well as lose your trouble,—and that you had better coquet,[2] or rather play the prude, with things as they are....

[...]

Mr. Shelley's defects are obscurity, inartificial and yet not natural economy, violation of costume,[3] and too great a sameness and gratituitousness of image and metaphor, and of image and metaphor too drawn from the elements, particularly the sea. The book is full of humanity; and yet it certainly does not go the best way to work of appealing to it, because it does not appeal to it through the medium of its common knowledges. It is for this reason that we must say something, which we would willingly leave unsaid, both from admiration of Mr. Shelley's genius and love of his benevolence; and this is, that the work cannot possibly become popular. It may set others thinking and writing, and we have no doubt will do so; and those who can understand and relish it, will relish it exceedingly; but the author must forget his metaphysics and sea-sides a little more in his future works, and give full effect to that nice[4] knowledge of men and things which he otherwise really possesses to an extraordinary degree. We have no doubt he is destined to be one of the leading spirits of his age, and indeed has already fallen into his place as such; but however resolute as to his object, he will only be doing it justice to take the most effectual means in his power to forward it.

---

1 Hunt published an intervening "Literary Notice" on *The Revolt of Islam* between the two reprinted here. It consists mainly of an extended quotation from Shelley's "Preface" to the poem, and a few critical remarks on the elder generation of Romantic poets, who have become "as dogmatic in their despair as they used to be in their hope." See Hunt, "Literary Notices, No. 40," *The Examiner* 530 (22 February 1818).

2 Flirt, be coy.

3 I.e., anachronism.

4 Detailed.

3. From [John Gibson Lockhart,] "Observations on *The Revolt of Islam*," *Blackwood's Edinburgh Magazine* 4.22 (January 1819): 475–82

[Son-in-law to Walter Scott, John Gibson Lockhart (1794–1854) is best known as the anonymous author of a series of articles viciously attacking what he called "The Cockney School of Poetry," which included Hunt, John Keats (1795–1821), and William Hazlitt (1778–1830). As an aristocrat, Shelley was exempt from the "Cockney" label and its suggestion of lower-middle-class origins, but his politics nonetheless made him a favorite target of the Tory press. Here, Lockhart openly acknowledges his disparate treatment of Shelley, the "gentleman" or person of high social class, and Keats, who was the son of a stable manager, and encourages Shelley to dissociate himself from Cockney company.]

We forbear from making any comments on this strange narrative; because we could not do so without entering upon other points which we have already professed our intention of wa[i]ving for the present. It will easily be seen, indeed, that neither the main interest nor the main merit of the poet at all consists in the conception of his plot or in the arrangement of his incidents. His praise is, in our judgment, that of having poured over his narrative a very rare strength and abundance of poetic imagery and feeling—of having steeped every word in the essence of his inspiration. The Revolt of Islam contains no detached passages at all comparable with some which our readers recollect in the works of the great poets our contemporaries; but neither does it contain any such intermixture of prosaic materials as disfigure even the greatest of them. Mr. Shelly [*sic*] has displayed his possession of a mind intensely poetical, and of an exuberance of poetic language, perpetually strong and perpetually varied. In spite, moreover, of a certain perversion in all his modes of thinking, which, unless he gets rid of it, will ever prevent him from being acceptable to any considerable or respectable body of readers, he has displayed many glimpses of right understanding and generous feeling, which must save him from the unmingled condemnation even of the most rigorous judges. His destiny is entirely in his own hands; if he acts wisely, it cannot fail to be a glorious one; if he continues to pervert his talents, by making them the instruments of a base sophistry, their splendour will only contribute to render his disgrace the more conspicuous. Mr. Shelly, whatever his errors may have been, is a scholar, a gentleman, and a poet; and he must therefore despise from his soul the only eulogies to which he has hitherto been accustomed—paragraphs from the Examiner, and sonnets from Johnny Keats. He has it in his power to select better companions; and if he does so, he may very securely promise himself abundance of better praise.

4. From [John Taylor Coleridge,] "Shelley's *Revolt of Islam*," *The Quarterly Review* 21.42 (April 1819): 460–71

[John Taylor Coleridge (1790–1876) was Samuel Taylor Coleridge's nephew, and he shared his uncle's increasingly reactionary views. His long review of *The Revolt of Islam* makes vivid the extent to which the poem was seen as genuinely subversive and even dangerous, and how difficult it was for any reviewer to treat the poem's aesthetic merits as distinct from its content.]

Mr. Shelley is a philosopher by the courtesy of the age,[1] and has a theory of course respecting the government of the world; we will state in as few words as we can the general outlines of that theory, the manner in which he demonstrates it, and the practical consequences, which he proposes to deduce from it. It is to the second of these divisions that we would beg his attention; we despair of convincing him directly that he has taken up false and pernicious notions; but if he pays any deference to the common laws of reasoning, we hope to shew him that, let the goodness of his cause be what it may, his manner of advocating it is false and unsound. This may be mortifying to a teacher of mankind; but a philosopher seeks the truth, and has no vanity to be mortified.

The existence of evil, physical and moral, is the grand problem of all philosophy; the humble find it a trial, the proud make it a stumbling-block; Mr. Shelley refers it to the faults of those civil institutions and religious creeds which are designed to regulate the conduct of man here, and his hopes in a hereafter. In these he seems to make no distinction, but considers them all as bottomed upon principles pernicious to man and unworthy of God, carried into details the most cruel, and upheld only by the stupidity of the many on the one hand, and the selfish conspiracy of the few on the other. According to him the earth is a boon[2] garden needing little care or cultivation, but pouring forth spontaneously and inexhaustibly all innocent delights and luxuries to her innumerable children; the seasons have no inclemencies, the air no pestilences for man in his proper state of wisdom and liberty; his business here is to enjoy himself, to abstain from no gratification, to repent of no sin, hate no crime, but be wise, happy and free, with plenty of "lawless love."[3] This is man's natural state, the state to which Mr. Shelley will bring us, if we will but break up the "crust of our outworn opinions,"[4] as he calls them, and put them into his magic cauldron. But kings have introduced war, legislators crime, priests sin; the dreadful consequences have been that the earth has lost her fertility, the seasons their mildness, the air its salubrity, man his freedom and happiness. We have become a foul-feeding carnivorous race, are foolish enough to feel uncomfortable after the commission of sin; some of us even go so far as to consider vice odious; and we all groan under a multiplied burthen of crimes merely

1 I.e., according to contemporary standards.

2 Blessed.

3 From Cythna's hymn, p. 134, V.5.512.

4 See Shelley's preface, p. 49 above.

conventional; among which Mr. Shelley specifies with great sang froid[1] the commission of incest![2]

[...]

... We have examined Mr. Shelley's system slightly, but, we hope, dispassionately; there will be those, who will say that we have done so coldly. He has indeed, to the best of his ability, wounded us in the tenderest part.—As far as in him lay, he has loosened the hold of our protecting laws, and sapped the principles of our venerable polity; he has invaded the purity and chilled the unsuspecting ardour of our fireside[3] intimacies; he has slandered, ridiculed and blasphemed our holy religion; yet these are all too sacred objects to be defended bitterly or unfairly. We have learned too, though not in Mr. Shelley's school, to discriminate between a man and his opinions, and while we shew no mercy to the sin, we can regard the sinner with allowance and pity. It is in this spirit, that we conclude with a few lines, which may serve for a warning to others, and for reproof, admonition, and even if he so pleases of encouragement to himself. We have already said what we think of his powers as a poet, and doubtless, with those powers, he might have risen to respectability in any honourable path, which he had chosen to pursue, if to his talents he had added industry, subordination, and good principles. But of Mr. Shelley much may be said with truth, which we not long since said of his friend and leader Mr. Hunt: he has not, indeed, all that is odious and contemptible in the character of that person; so far as we have seen he has never exhibited the bustling vulgarity, the ludicrous affectation, the factious flippancy, or the selfish heartlessness, which it is hard for our feelings to treat with the mere contempt they merit. Like him, however, Mr. Shelley is a very vain man; and like most very vain men, he is but half instructed in knowledge, and less than half-disciplined in his reasoning powers; his vanity, wanting[4] the controul of the faith which he derides, has been his ruin; it has made him too impatient of applause and distinction to earn them in the fair course of labour; like a speculator in trade, he would be rich without capital and without delay, and, as might have been anticipated, his speculations have ended only in disappointments. They both began, his speculations and his disappointments, in early childhood, and even from that period he has carried about with him a soured and discontented spirit—unteachable in boyhood, unamiable in youth, querulous and unmanly in manhood,—singularly unhappy in all three. He speaks[5] of his school as "a world of woes," of his masters "as tyrants," of his school-fellows as "enemies,"—alas! what is this, but to bear evidence against himself? every one who knows what a public school ordinarily must be, will only trace in these lines the language of an insubordinate, a vain, a mortified spirit.

1 Literally, cold blood; figuratively, nonchalance, detachment.

2 Coleridge ignores the fact that, in *The Revolt of Islam,* the references to incest that proved so problematic for *Laon and Cythna* have been removed.

3 I.e., domestic.

4 Lacking.

5 I.e., in his Preface.

We would venture to hope that the past may suffice for the speculations in which Mr. Shelley has hitherto engaged; they have brought him neither honour abroad nor peace at home, and after so fair a trial it seems but common prudence to change them for some new venture. He is still a young man, and though his account be assuredly black and heavy, he may yet hope to redeem his time, and wipe it out. He may and he should retain all the love for his fellow-creatures, all the zeal for their improvement in virtue and happiness which he now professes, but let that zeal be armed with knowledge and regulated by judgment. Let him not be offended at our freedom,[1] but he is really too young, too ignorant, too inexperienced, and too vicious to undertake the task of reforming any world, but the little world within his own breast; that task will be a good preparation for the difficulties which he is more anxious at once to encounter. There is a book[2] which will help him to this preparation, which has more poetry in it than Lucretius, more interest than Godwin, and far more philosophy than both. But it is a sealed book to a proud spirit; if he would read it with effect, he must be humble where he is now vain, he must examine and doubt himself where now he boldly condemns others, and instead of relying on his own powers, he must feel and acknowledge his weakness, and pray for strength from above.

5. From Leigh Hunt, "*The Quarterly Review* and *The Revolt of Islam*," *The Examiner* 615 (10 October 1819): 652–53

[Nearly two years after its publication, Hunt is still defending *The Revolt of Islam* against its detractors. In this case, he explicitly references the reviews by Lockhart and Coleridge, above, and excoriates Shelley's critics for attacking the poet on personal and moral grounds.]

Failing in the attempt to refute Mr. Shelley's philosophy,[3] the Reviewers attack his private life. What is the argument of this? or what right have they to know any thing of the private life of an author? or how would they like to have the same argument used against themselves? Mr. Shelley is now seven and twenty years of age. He entered life[4] about 17; and every body knows, and every candid person will allow, that a young man at that time of life, upon the very strength of a warm and trusting nature, especially with theories to which the world are not accustomed, may render himself liable to the misrepresentation of the worldly. But what have the Quarterly Reviewers to do with this? What is Mr. Shelley's private life to the Quarterly Review, any more than Mr. Gifford's,[5] or Mr. Croker's,[6] or any other Quarterly Reviewer's private life is to

1 Candor, frankness.

2 I.e., the Bible.

3 [Hunt's note:] There are some further observations on Christianity in our political article in this week, which will apply to the present subject.

4 I.e., public life.

5 William Gifford (1756–1826), editor of *The Quarterly Review*.

6 John Wilson Croker (1780–1857), frequent contributor to *The Quarterly Review*.

the Examiner, or the Morning Chronicle, or to the Edinburgh Review,—a work, by the bye, as superior to the Quarterly, in all the humanities of social intercourse, as in the liberality of it's [*sic*] opinions in general. The Reviewer talks of what he "now" knows of Mr. Shelley. What does this pretended judge and actual male-gossip, this willing listener to scandal, this minister to the petty wants of excitement, now know more than he ever knew, of an absent man, whose own side of whatever stories have been told him he has never heard? Suppose the opponents of the *Quarterly Review* were to listen to all the scandals that have been reported of writers in it, and to proclaim this man by name as a pimp, another as a scamp,[1] and another as a place or pulpit hunting slave[2] made out of a school-boy tyrant? If the use of private matters in public criticism is not to be incompatible with the decencies and charities of life, let it be proved so; and we know who would be the sufferers. We have experienced, in our own persons, what monstrous misrepresentations can be given of a man, even with regard to the most difficult and unselfish actions of his life, and solely because others just knew enough of delicacy, to avail themselves of the inflexible love of it in others.[3]

We shall therefore respect the silence hitherto observed publicly by Mr. Shelley respecting such matters, leaving him when he returns to England to take such notice or otherwise of his calumniators as may seem best to him. But we cannot resist the impulse to speak of one particular calumny of this Reviewer, the falshood [sic] of which is doubly impressed upon us in consequence of our own personal and repeated knowledge of the reverse. He says Mr. Shelley "is shamefully dissolute in his conduct." We laugh the scandal-monger to scorn.... We heard of similar assertions, when we resided in the same house with Mr. Shelley for nearly three months; and how was he living all that time? As much like Plato himself, as any of his theories resemble Plato,—or rather still more like a Pythagorean.[4] This was the round of his daily life:—He was up early; breakfasted sparingly; wrote this *Revolt of Islam* all the morning; went out in his boat or into the woods with some Greek author or the Bible in his hands; came home to a dinner of vegetables (for he took neither meat nor

1 A thief, a generally worthless person.

2 I.e., a social climber.

3 [Hunt's note:] The Reviewer in question, always true to his paltry trade, is pleased, in speaking of the Editor of this paper, to denounce his "bustling vulgarity, the ludicrous affectation, the factious flippancy, and the selfish heartlessness, which it is hard for the Reviewer's feelings to treat with the mere gentle contempt they merit." Indeed! The saying is a borrowed one, and much the worse for its shabby wear. Oh, good God! how applicable are all these charges but the political one, to some of those we could tell the world! Applied as they are, they have only excited a contemptuous mirth against the Reviewer among the companions of the Editor, who hereby, with a more than exemplary fairness of dealing, repays his mock-contempt with real. [The reviewer in question is John Taylor Coleridge; see Appendix C4.]

4 The followers of the philosopher and mathematician Pythagoras (c. 570–c. 495 BCE) engaged in ascetic practices, including vegetarianism.

wine); visited (if necessary) "the sick and the fatherless,"[1] whom others gave Bibles to and no help; wrote or studied again, or read to his wife and friends the whole evening; took a crust of bread or a glass of whey for his supper; and went early to bed. This is literally the whole of the life he led, or that we believe he now leads in Italy; nor have we ever known him, in spite of the malignant and ludicrous exaggerations on this point, deviate, notwithstanding his theories, even into a single action which those who differ from him might think blameable. We do not say, that he would always square his conduct by their opinions as a matter of principle: we only say, that he acted just as if he did so square them. We forbear, out of regard for the very bloom of their beauty, to touch upon numberless other charities and generosities which we have known him exercise; but this we must say is general, that we never lived with a man who gave so completely an idea of an ardent and principled aspirant in philosophy as Percy Shelley; and that we believe him, from the bottom of our hearts, to be one of the noblest hearts as well as heads which the world has seen for a long time....

1 Cf. James 1:27. The phrase "the sick and the fatherless" appears in one of the three prayers Jonathan Swift (1667–1745) wrote for his beloved Stella in 1727 (she died in 1728). Hunt—who christened his *Examiner* after an earlier Tory periodical of the same name, edited for a time by Swift—might well have had Swift's prayer in mind.

Appendix D: Revising the Romance

1. From Richard Hurd, *Letters on Chivalry and Romance* (London: A. Millar, 1762), 12–13, 17–19

[Richard Hurd (1720–1808) was bishop of Worcester as well as a writer and literary scholar. In his *Letters on Chivalry and Romance,* he was keen to show that the violent, militaristic, and deeply patriarchal culture of the Middle Ages had an unexpectedly positive effect on cultural representations of women. Here, he draws special attention to the number of romances that feature female warriors, and explains the chivalric deference to women by insisting that "violations of chastity" were thought, at this moment in history, to be the most serious of crimes.]

[O]ne of the strangest circumstances in those books, and which looks most like a mere extravagance of the imagination, is that of the *women-warriors,* with which they all abound. Butler in his Hudibras,[1] who saw it in this light, ridicules it, as a most unnatural idea, with great spirit. Yet in this representation they did but copy from the manners of the times. Anna Comena tells us, in the life of her father, that the wife of Robert the Norman fought side by side with her husband, in his battles;[2] that she would rally the flying soldiers, and lead them back to the charge: And Nicetas observes that, in the time of Manuel Comena, there were in one Crusade many women, armed like men, and on horseback.[3]

What think you now of Tasso's Clorinda,[4] whose prodigies[5] of valour I dare say you have often laughed at? Or, rather, what think you of that constant pair,

> Gildippe, & Odoardo amanti e sposi,
> In valor d'arme, e in lealtà famosi[.][6]

---

1 *Hudibras* (1684) is a mock-epic poem by Samuel Butler (1613–80). It includes many satirical elements that poke fun at the chivalric tradition, including, as Hurd says, the presence of a female knight (whom Butler names Trulla).

2 Anna Komnene (1083–1153) was the daughter of Emperor Alexios I Komnenos of Byzantium. She wrote an epic poem, the *Alexiad* (c. 1148), about her father's reign. In Book IV of the *Alexiad,* she describes how Gaïta, the wife of Alexios's enemy Robert the Norman, rallied her husband's failing troops at the Battle of Dyrrhachium in 1081.

3 Niketas Choniates (c. 1125–1215/16) was a Greek historian best known for his history of Constantinople during the time of the Crusades. Manuel I Komnenos was a Byzantine emperor who ruled 1143–80.

4 A character in Torquato Tasso's *Gerusalemme Liberata* (1580–81), Clorinda is a Muslim warrior-maiden who risks her life to save the Christian lovers Sofronia and Olindo from being burned at the stake. She is later killed in battle accidentally by the crusader Tancredi, who loves her and (at her request) baptizes her before she dies.

5 Wonders, freaks.

6 "Gildippe and Odoardo, lovers and spouses / Renowned for bravery and also for devotion." Tasso, *Gerusalemme Liberata,* III.40. Gildippe and Odoardo are minor characters in *Gerusalemme Liberata*; both are killed fighting against Solyman, Sultan of Nicea.

[...]

... The free commerce of the ladies, in those knots and circles of the great, would operate so far on the sturdiest knights as to give birth to the attentions of gallantry. But this gallantry would take a refined turn, not only from the necessity there was of maintaining the strict forms of decorum, amidst a promiscuous conversation under the eye of the Prince and in his own family; but also from the inflamed sense they must needs have of the frequent outrages committed, by their neighbouring clans of adversaries, on the honour of the Sex, when by chance of war they had fallen into their hands. Violations of chastity being the most atrocious crimes they had to charge on their enemies, they would pride themselves in the glory of being its protectors: And as this virtue was, of all others, the fairest and strongest claim of the sex itself to such protection, it is no wonder that the notions of it were, in time, carried to so platonic[1] an elevation.

2. From Edmund Burke, *Reflections on the Revolution in France, and on the Proceedings in Certain Societies in London Relative to That Event. In a Letter Intended to Have Been Sent to a Gentleman in Paris*, 1st ed. (London: J. Dodsley, 1790), 111–15, 117

[Edmund Burke (1729–97) was a politician, political theorist, and philosopher who had spoken in support of the American colonists and their grievances against the British Crown. The intensity of his reaction to the French Revolution therefore took many by surprise and inaugurated a pamphlet war that became known as the Revolution Controversy. His primary antagonist was Mary Wollstonecraft, who scorned Burke's admiration for chivalry—and his depiction of Marie Antoinette as the ultimate damsel in distress—as not only old-fashioned and politically retrograde but also effeminate. In this famous passage from his *Reflections*, Burke presents the Revolution as an act of sexual violence, one that will destroy the intimate and emotional bonds that hold civil society together better (he says) than the law itself.]

I hear, and I rejoice to hear, that the great lady ... has borne that day (one is interested that beings made for suffering should suffer well) and that she bears all the succeeding days, that she bears the imprisonment of her husband, and her own captivity, and the exile of her friends, and the insulting adulation of addresses, and the whole weight of her accumulated wrongs, with a serene patience, in a manner suited to her rank and race, and becoming the offspring of a sovereign[2] distinguished for her piety and her courage: that like her she has lofty sentiments; that she feels with the dignity of a Roman matron;[3] that in the

1 Idealized.

2 The Empress Maria Theresa (1717–80), Marie Antoinette's mother, was known for her piety.

3 The women of ancient Rome were associated with bravery and self-sacrifice, as well as with an unflinching sense of personal and civic honor. Burke is probably thinking here

last extremity she will save herself from the last disgrace, and that if she must fall, she will fall by no ignoble hand.[1]

It is now sixteen or seventeen years since I saw the queen of France,[2] then the dauphiness, at Versailles; and surely never lighted on this orb, which she hardly seemed to touch, a more delightful vision. I saw her just above the horizon, decorating and cheering the elevated sphere she just began to move in,—glittering like the morning-star, full of life, and splendour, and joy. Oh! what a revolution! and what [a] heart must I have, to contemplate without emotion that elevation and that fall! Little did I dream that, when she added titles of veneration to those of enthusiastic, distant, respectful love, that she should ever be obliged to carry the sharp antidote against disgrace concealed in that bosom;[3] little did I dream that I should have lived to see such disasters fallen upon her in a nation of gallant men, in a nation of men of honour and of cavaliers.[4] I thought ten thousand swords must have leaped from their scabbards to avenge even a look that threatened her with insult.—But the age of chivalry is gone.—That of sophisters,[5] economists, and calculators,[6] has succeeded; and the glory of Europe is extinguished for ever. Never, never more, shall we behold that generous loyalty to rank and sex, that proud submission, that dignified obedience, that subordination of the heart, which kept alive, even in servitude itself, the spirit of an exalted freedom. The unbought grace of life, the cheap defence of nations, the nurse of manly sentiment and heroic enterprise, is gone! It is gone, that sensibility of principle, that chastity of honour, which felt a stain like a wound, which inspired courage whilst it mitigated ferocity, which ennobled whatever it touched, and under which vice itself lost half its evil, by losing all its grossness.

This mixed system of opinion and sentiment had its origin in the antient chivalry; and the principle, though varied in its appearance by the varying state of human affairs, subsisted and influenced through a long succession of generations, even to the time we live in. If it should ever be totally extinguished, the loss I fear will be great. It is this which has given its character to modern Europe. It is this which has distinguished it under all its forms of government, and distinguished it to its advantage, from the states of Asia, and possibly from those states which flourished in the most brilliant periods of the antique world.

---

of the story of Lucretia, who killed herself after being raped by the son of the king. There is considerable irony here, since Lucretia's fate was said to have precipitated the revolution that led to the overthrow of the Regnum Romanum (i.e., the monarchy) and the establishment of the Roman Republic, whose founding is traditionally dated to 509 BCE.

1 I.e., she will commit suicide.

2 Marie Antoinette (1755–93) was queen of France and Navarre from 1774 to 1792. She was executed in 1793, after being found guilty of treason by France's Revolutionary Tribunal.

3 I.e., a small dagger with which to commit suicide if faced with the threat of sexual assault.

4 Knights.

5 Someone who makes compelling but ultimately unsound arguments.

6 I.e., someone who assigns financial value to seemingly priceless things.

It was this, which, without confounding[1] ranks, had produced a noble equality, and handed it down through all the gradations of social life. It was this opinion which mitigated kings into companions, and raised private men to be fellows with kings. Without force, or opposition, it subdued the fierceness of pride and power; it obliged sovereigns to submit to the soft collar of social esteem, compelled stern authority to submit to elegance, and gave a dominating vanquisher of laws to be subdued by manners.

But now all is to be changed. All the pleasing illusions, which made power gentle and obedience liberal,[2] which harmonized the different shades of life, and which, by a bland[3] assimilation, incorporated into politics the sentiments which beautify and soften private society, are to be dissolved by this new conquering empire of light and reason. All the decent drapery of life is to be rudely torn off. All the superadded[4] ideas, furnished from the wardrobe of a moral imagination, which the heart owns, and the understanding ratifies, as necessary to cover the defects of our naked shivering nature, and to raise it to dignity in our own estimation, are to be exploded as a ridiculous, absurd, and antiquated fashion.

3. From Helen Maria Williams, *Letters from France: Containing Many New Anecdotes Relative to the Revolution, and the Present State of French Manners* (London: G.G.J. and J. Robinson, 1792), 4–5

[Helen Maria Williams (1759–1827) was a poet, novelist, and translator who became one of the French Revolution's most vocal public supporters. Her eyewitness accounts of life in France during and after the Revolution are recorded in her multi-volume series of *Letters from France*, which are outstanding not only for their degree of detail but also for the optimism Williams always maintains about France's future—even after she was briefly imprisoned by Robespierre on suspicion of treason.]

[L]iving in France at present, appears to me somewhat like living in a region of romance. Events the most astonishing and marvellous are here the occurrences of the day, and every newspaper is filled with articles of intelligence that will form a new era in the history of mankind. The sentiments of the people also are elevated far above the pitch of common life. All the motives which most powerfully stimulate the mind in its ordinary state, seem repressed in consideration of the public good, and every selfish interest is sacrificed with fond alacrity at the altar of the country. For my part, when I contemplate these things, I sometimes think that the age of chivalry, instead of being past forever, is just returned; not indeed in its erroneous notions of loyalty, honour, and gallantry, which are as little "à l'ordre du jour"[5] as its dwarfs, giants, and impris-

1 Confusing, mixing up.

2 Free, as in "freely given."

3 Gentle, soothing.

4 I.e., higher-order.

5 [Williams's note:] The order of the day.

oned damsels; but in its noble contempt of sordid cares, its spirit of unsullied generosity, and its heroic zeal for the happiness of others.

4. From William Wordsworth, "The Female Vagrant," *Lyrical Ballads, with a Few Other Poems* (London: T.N. Longman, 1798), 71–75, lines 37–117

["The Female Vagrant" is the only poem in *Lyrical Ballads* written in Spenserian stanzas. Originally part of a longer poem called *Salisbury Plain*, it tells the story of rural tragedy and geopolitical conflict, as a young woman's life is upended first by poverty and then by her husband's decision to fight for Britain in the American Revolutionary War. Wordsworth's choice of the Spenserian form, coupled with the terrible but wholly ordinary suffering the poem recounts, gives the lie to the rhetoric of patriotism mobilized by the British government, first against America and, in the 1790s, against Revolutionary France. His poem emphasizes the human cost of war and its disproportionate impact on the poor.]

The suns of twenty summers danced along,—
Ah! little marked, how fast they rolled away:
Then rose a mansion proud our woods among,
And cottage after cottage owned its sway,
No joy to see a neighbouring house, or stray
Through pastures not his own, the master took;
My Father dared his greedy wish gainsay;[1]
He loved his old hereditary nook,
And ill could I the thought of such sad parting brook.

But, when he had refused the proffered gold,
To cruel injuries he became a prey,
Sore traversed in whate'er he bought and sold:
His troubles grew upon him day by day,
Till all his substance fell into decay.
His little range of water was denied;[2]
All but the bed where his old body lay,
All, all was seized, and weeping, side by side,
We sought a home where we uninjured might abide.

Can I forget that miserable hour,
When from the last hill-top, my sire surveyed,
Peering above the trees, the steeple tower,
That on his marriage-day sweet music made?
Till then he hoped his bones might there be laid,
Close by my mother in their native bowers:

1 Oppose.

2 [Wordsworth's note:] Several of the Lakes in the north of England are let out to different Fishermen, in parcels marked out by imaginary lines drawn from rock to rock.

Bidding me trust in God, he stood and prayed,—
I could not pray:—through tears that fell in showers,
Glimmer'd our dear-loved home, alas! no longer ours!

There was a youth whom I had loved so long,
That when I loved him not I cannot say.
'Mid the green mountains many and many a song
We two had sung, like little birds in May.
When we began to tire of childish play
We seemed still more and more to prize each other:
We talked of marriage and our marriage day;
And I in truth did love him like a brother,
For never could I hope to meet with such another.

His father said, that to a distant town
He must repair, to ply the artist's[1] trade.
What tears of bitter grief till then unknown!
What tender vows our last sad kiss delayed!
To him we turned:—we had no other aid.
Like one revived, upon his neck I wept,
And her whom he had loved in joy, he said
He well could love in grief: his faith he kept;
And in a quiet home once more my father slept.

Four years each day with daily bread was blest,
By constant toil and constant prayer supplied.
Three lovely infants lay upon my breast;
And often, viewing their sweet smiles, I sighed,
And knew not why. My happy father died
When sad distress reduced the children's meal:
Thrice happy! that from him the grave did hide
The empty loom, cold hearth, and silent wheel,[2]
And tears that flowed for ills which patience could not heal.

'Twas a hard change, an evil time was come;
We had no hope, and no relief could gain.
But soon, with proud parade, the noisy drum
Beat round, to sweep the streets of want and pain.
My husband's arms now only served to strain[3]
Me and his children hungering in his view:
In such dismay my prayers and tears were vain:
To join those miserable men he flew;
And now to the sea-coast, with numbers more, we drew.

---

1 Craftsman's.

2 I.e., spinning wheel.

3 Hold, clasp.

There foul neglect for months and months we bore,
Nor yet the crowded fleet its anchor stirred.
Green fields before us and our native shore,
By fever, from polluted air incurred,
Ravage was made, for which no knell was heard.
Fondly we wished, and wished away, nor knew,
'Mid that long sickness, and those hopes deferr'd,
That happier days we never more must view:
The parting signal streamed, at last the land withdrew,

But from delay the summer calms were past.
On as we drove, the equinoctial deep[1]
Ran mountains-high before the howling blast.
We gazed with terror on the gloomy sleep
Of them that perished in the whirlwind's sweep,
Untaught that soon such anguish must ensue,
Our hopes such harvest of affliction reap,
That we the mercy of the waves should rue.
We reached the western world, a poor, devoted crew.

5. From Lord Byron, Canto II of *Childe Harold's Pilgrimage*, in *Childe Harold's Pilgrimage, a Romaunt: And Other Poems*, 5th ed. (London: John Murray, 1812), 66–68, lines 82–135

[In an early draft of *Laon and Cythna*, Shelley wrote a note to himself that reads: "Is this an imitation of L[ord] Byron's poem? It is certainly written in the same metre." The poem in question is *Childe Harold's Pilgrimage*, the Spenserian travelogue that made Byron famous. In this excerpt, Byron contemplates the ruins of the Parthenon, recently divested of its architectural treasures by Lord Elgin (1766–1841), the Scottish diplomat responsible for ultimately removing about half of the temple's sculptures and decorative elements. Although Byron mentions the Ottoman occupation of Greece, he is intent on showing that Britain, presented here as a marauding naval power, is just as much a threat to that nation as Greece's more familiar and proximate enemy.]

X

Here let me sit upon this massy stone,
The marble column's yet unshaken base;
Here, son of Saturn![2] was thy fav'rite throne:[3]

---

1 I.e., the ocean during the autumn equinox.

2 I.e., Zeus, son of Kronos, whose Latin name was Saturn.

3 [Byron's note:] The temple of Jupiter Olympius, of which sixteen columns entirely of marble yet survive: originally there were 150. These columns, however, are by many supposed to have belonged to the Pantheon.

Mightiest of many such! Hence let me trace
The latent grandeur of thy dwelling place.
It may not be: nor ev'n can Fancy's eye
Restore what Time hath labour'd to deface.
Yet these proud pillars claim no passing sigh;
Unmov'd the Moslem[1] sits, the light[2] Greek carols[3] by.

XI

But who, of all the plunders of yon fane[4]
On high—where Pallas[5] linger'd, loth to flee[6]
The latest relic of her ancient reign—
The last, the worst, dull spoiler,[7] who was he?
Blush, Caledonia![8] such thy son could be!
England! I joy no child he was of thine:
Thy free-born men should spare what once was free;
Yet they could violate each saddening shrine,
And bear these altars o'er the long-reluctant brine.[9]

XII

But most the modern Pict's[10] ignoble boast,
To rive[11] what Goth,[12] and Turk, and Time hath spar'd:
Cold as the crags upon his native coast,
His mind as barren and his heart as hard,
Is he whose head conceiv'd, whose hand prepar'd,
Aught[13] to displace Athena's poor remains:
Her sons too weak the sacred shrine to guard,
Yet felt some portion of their mother's pains,[14]
And never knew, till then, the weight of Despot's chains.

---

1 Muslim.
2 Light-hearted, unconcerned, shallow.
3 Sings.
4 Temple.
5 Pallas Athena, daughter of Zeus, Greek goddess of war and wisdom.
6 Reluctant to abandon.
7 Thief. Byron is referring to Lord Elgin.
8 Scotland, birthplace of Lord Elgin.
9 [Byron's note:] The ship was wrecked in the Archipelago. ["Brine" means sea water.]
10 The Picts lived in eastern and northern Scotland during the Iron Age and early Middle Ages.
11 Split, tear apart.
12 The Goths were an East Germanic people who made several raids on the Roman Empire, including parts of Greece.
13 Anything.
14 A long note by Byron is omitted here.

XIII

What! shall it e'er be said by British tongue,
Albion[1] was happy in Athena's tears?
Though in thy name the slaves her bosom wrung,
Tell not the deed to blushing Europe's ears;
The ocean queen, the free Britannia[2] bears
The last poor plunder from a bleeding land:
Yes, she, whose gen'rous aid her name endears,
Tore down those remnants with a Harpy's[3] hand,
Which envious Eld[4] forbore, and tyrants left to stand.[5]

XIV

Where was thine Ægis,[6] Pallas! that appall'd[7]
Stern Alaric[8] and Havoc[9] on their way?[10]
Where Peleus'son?[11] whom Hell[12] in vain enthrall'd,
His shade from Hades upon that dread day
Bursting to light in terrible array!
What! could not Pluto[13] spare the chief once more,
To scare a second robber[14] from his prey?

---

1 Britain.

2 Britain is often personified as a goddess (Britannia) bearing a trident to symbolize the nation's naval power.

3 In Greek mythology, the harpies were winged monsters usually depicted as half-woman, half-bird.

4 Antiquity.

5 A long note by Byron is omitted here.

6 Shield.

7 Frightened, scared away.

8 Alaric I, king of the Visigoths, led the sack of Rome in 410.

9 A word probably of Germanic origin, "havoc" was apparently used as a signal to troops to begin seizing the spoils of war. Cf. Shakespeare, *Julius Caesar*: "Cry havoc and let slip the dogs of war" (3.1.273).

10 [Byron's note:] According to Zozimus, Minerva and Achilles frightened Alaric from the Acropolis; but others relate that the Gothic king was nearly as mischievous as the Scottish peer. [According to the Byzantine historian Zosimus (fl. c. 490–518), when Alaric (r. 395–410) was about to storm Athens he saw a vision of Athena walking along the city walls, and the celebrated Greek warrior Achilles ("Peleus's son" in the next line)—temporarily let out from "Hell," Hades, or the underworld—standing in front of them. Awed by this sight, Alaric called off his attack and instead offered terms of peace to Athens. See Zosimus, *Nova Historia* (c. 450–502), Book V. The "Scottish peer" is Elgin.]

11 I.e., Achilles, legendary Greek warrior.

12 Byron is using "Hell" either to refer to the king of Hades, i.e., the underworld, or interchangeably with "Hades" to avoid repetition.

13 King of the underworld and god of the dead.

14 I.e., Lord Elgin.

Idly he wander'd on the Stygian shore,
Nor now preserv'd the walls he loved to shield before.

XV

Cold is the heart, fair Greece! that looks on thee,
Nor feels as lovers o'er the dust they lov'd;
Dull is the eye that will not weep to see
Thy walls defac'd, thy mouldering shrines remov'd
By British hands, which it had best behov'd[1]
To guard those relics ne'er to be restor'd.
Curst be the hour when their isle they rov'd,
And once again thy hapless bosom gor'd,
And snatch'd thy shrinking Gods to northern climes abhorr'd!

1 Benefitted.

Appendix E: The Rights of Women

1. From Mary Wollstonecraft, *A Vindication of the Rights of Woman: with Strictures on Political and Moral Subjects*, 2nd ed. (London: J. Johnson, 1792), 88–93

[Shelley never knew his mother-in-law Mary Wollstonecraft (1759–97), who died shortly after giving birth to her daughter Mary, Shelley's future wife. He was nonetheless profoundly influenced by her political and social philosophy, and in particular by her pioneering feminist work *A Vindication of the Rights of Woman*. Modeled closely on Wollstonecraft's own *A Vindication of the Rights of Men* (1790), a response to Edmund Burke's 1790 attack on the French Revolution, her second *Vindication* applies the same egalitarian principles animating the Revolution to the condition of women in Britain and Europe near the turn of the century. Here Wollstonecraft suggests that, in a world divided between "voluptuous tyrants, and [their] cunning envious dependents," women are at once the oppressor and the oppressed. The only solution to this state of affairs, as she puts it in the excerpt from Chapter 3 below, is "to effect a revolution in female manners" by prioritizing women's education, and by giving them a life's purpose other than being pleasing to men.]

I once knew a weak woman of fashion, who was more than commonly proud of her delicacy and sensibility. She thought a distinguishing taste and puny appetite the height of all human perfection, and acted accordingly.—I have seen this weak sophisticated being neglect all the duties of life, yet recline with self-complacency on a sofa, and boast of her want of appetite as a proof of delicacy that extended to, or, perhaps, arose from, her exquisite sensibility: for it is difficult to render intelligible such ridiculous jargon.—Yet, at the moment, I have seen her insult a worthy old gentlewoman, whom unexpected misfortunes had made dependent on her ostentatious bounty, and who, in better days, had claims on her gratitude. Is it possible that a human creature should have become such a weak and depraved being, if, like the Sybarites,[1] dissolved in luxury, every thing like virtue had not been worn away, or never impressed by precept, a poor substitute it is true, for cultivation of mind, though it serves as a fence against vice?

Such a woman is not a more irrational monster than some of the Roman emperors, who were depraved by lawless power. Yet, since kings have been more under the restraint of law, and the curb, however weak, of honour, the records of history are not filled with such unnatural instances of folly and cruelty, nor does the despotism that kills virtue and genius in the bud, hover over Europe with that destructive blast which desolates Turkey, and renders the men, as well as the soil, unfruitful.

1 A reference to the people of the ancient Greek city of Sybaris, in southern Italy. Sybarites were reputed to be excessively pleasure-seeking, and to wallow in unseemly luxury.

Women are every where in this deplorable state; for, in order to preserve their innocence, as ignorance is courteously termed, truth is hidden from them, and they are made to assume an artificial character before their faculties have acquired any strength. Taught from their infancy that beauty is woman's sceptre, the mind shapes itself to the body, and, roaming round its gilt cage, only seeks to adorn its prison. Men have various employments and pursuits which engage their attention, and give a character to the opening mind; but women, confined to one, and having their thoughts constantly directed to the most insignificant part of themselves, seldom extend their views beyond the triumph of the hour. But was their understanding once emancipated from the slavery to which the pride and sensuality of man and their short-sighted desire, like that of dominion in tyrants, of present sway, has subjected them, we should probably read of their weaknesses with surprise. I must be allowed to pursue the argument a little farther.

Perhaps, if the existence of an evil being was allowed, who, in the allegorical language of scripture, went about seeking whom he should devour, he could not more effectually degrade the human character than by giving a man absolute power.

This argument branches into various ramifications.—Birth, riches, and every intrinsic advantage that exalt a man above his fellows, without any mental exertion, sink him in reality below them. In proportion to his weakness, he is played upon by designing men, till the bloated monster has lost all traces of humanity. And that tribes of men, like flocks of sheep, should quietly follow such a leader, is a solecism[1] that only a desire of present enjoyment and narrowness of understanding can solve. Educated in slavish dependence, and enervated by luxury and sloth, where shall we find men who will stand forth to assert the rights of man;—or claim the privilege of moral beings, who should have but one road to excellence? Slavery to monarchs and ministers, which the world will be long in freeing itself from, and whose deadly grasp stops the progress of the human mind, is not yet abolished.

Let not men then in the pride of power, use the same arguments that tyrannic kings and venal ministers have used, and fallaciously assert that woman ought to be subjected because she has always been so.—But, when man, governed by reasonable laws, enjoys his natural freedom, let him despise woman, if she do not share it with him; and, till that glorious period arrives, in descanting[2] on the folly of the sex, let him not overlook his own.

Women, it is true, obtaining power by unjust means, by practising or fostering vice, evidently lose the rank which reason would assign them, and they become either abject slaves or capricious tyrants. They lose all simplicity, all dignity of mind, in acquiring power, and act as men are observed to act when they have been exalted by the same means.

It is time to effect a revolution in female manners—time to restore to them their lost dignity—and make them, as a part of the human species, labour by reforming themselves to reform the world.

---

1 Error.

2 Holding forth, talking at length.

2. From William Godwin, *Enquiry Concerning Political Justice, and Its Influence on Morals and Happiness*, 2 vols., rev. 3rd ed. (1793; London: G.G. and J. Robinson, 1798), 2.507–10

[William Godwin's *Enquiry Concerning Political Justice* marks a watershed in the history of left-leaning philosophy and is even sometimes characterized as anarchist in its sensibilities. That description probably goes too far—the *Enquiry* does, after all, defend private property—but in this excerpt from its Appendix titled "Cooperation, Cohabition and Marriage," published in the 1798 edition, we find that Godwin's views about marriage are certainly quite radical for their time. Indeed, Godwin's views against marriage were much stronger than those of his wife, Mary Wollstonecraft (see Appendix E1, above), who seemed still to believe in it as an institution. None of this, however, stopped Godwin from being appalled by his daughter's relationship with Shelley, a relationship that began when the latter was still married to Harriet Westbrook.]

[M]arriage, as now understood, is a monopoly, and the worst of monopolies. So long as two human beings are forbidden, by positive institution, to follow the dictates of their own mind, prejudice will be alive and vigorous. So long as I seek, by despotic and artificial means, to maintain my possession of a woman, I am guilty of the most odious selfishness. Over this imaginary prize, men watch with perpetual jealousy; and one man finds his desire, and his capacity to circumvent, as much excited, as the other is excited, to traverse his projects, and frustrate his hopes. As long as this state of society continues, philanthropy[1] will be crossed and checked in a thousand ways, and the still augmenting stream of abuse will continue to flow.

The abolition of the present system of marriage, appears to involve no evils. We are apt to represent that abolition to ourselves, as the harbinger of brutal lust and depravity. But it really happens, in this, as in other cases, that the positive laws which are made to restrain our vices, irritate[2] and multiply them. Not to say, that the same sentiments of justice and happiness, which, in a state of equality, would destroy our relish for expensive gratifications, might be expected to decrease our inordinate appetites of every kind, and to lead us universally to prefer the pleasures of intellect to the pleasures of sense.[3]

It is a question of some moment, whether the intercourse of the sexes, in a reasonable state of society, would be promiscuous, or whether each man would select for himself a partner, to whom he will adhere, as long as that adherence shall continue to be the choice of both parties. Probability seems to be greatly in favour of the latter. Perhaps this side of the alternative is most favourable to population.[4] Perhaps it would suggest itself in preference, to the man who would wish to maintain the several propensities of his frame, in the order due

1 Love for other people, fellow-feeling.

2 Arouse, exacerbate.

3 I.e., of the body.

4 I.e., to the growth of the human population through sexual reproduction.

to their relative importance, and to prevent a merely sensual appetite from engrossing excessive attention. It is scarcely to be imagined, that this commerce,[1] in any state of society, will be stripped of its adjuncts,[2] and that men will as willingly hold it, with a woman whose personal and mental qualities they disapprove, as with one of a different description. But it is the nature of the human mind, to persist, for a certain length of time, in its opinion or choice. The parties therefore having acted upon selection, are not likely to forget this selection when the interview is over. Friendship, if by friendship we understand that affection for an individual which is measured singly by what we know of his worth, is one of the most exquisite gratifications, perhaps one of the most improving exercises, of a rational mind. Friendship therefore may be expected to come in aid of the sexual intercourse, to refine its grossness, and increase its delight. All these arguments are calculated to determine our judgement in favour of marriage as a salutary and respectable institution, but not of that species of marriage in which there is no room for repentance and to which liberty and hope are equally strangers.

Admitting these principles therefore as the basis of the sexual commerce, what opinion ought we to form respecting infidelity to this attachment? Certainly no ties ought to be imposed upon either party, preventing them from quitting the attachment, whenever their judgement directs them to quit it. With respect to such infidelities as are compatible with an intention to adhere to it, the point of principal importance is a determination to have recourse to no species of disguise. In ordinary cases, and where the periods of absence are of no long duration, it would seem that any inconstancy would reflect some portion of discredit on the person that practised it. It would argue that the person's propensities were not under that kind of subordination which virtue and self-government appear to prescribe. But inconstancy, like any other temporary dereliction, would not be found incompatible with a character of uncommon excellence.[3] What, at present, renders it, in many instances, peculiarly loathsome, is its being practised in a clandestine manner. It leads to a train of falsehood and a concerted hypocrisy, than which there is scarcely anything that more eminently depraves and degrades the human mind.

3. From James Lawrence, *The Empire of the Nairs: Or, The Rights of Women. An Utopian Romance*, 4 vols. (London: T. Hookham, Jun. and E.T. Hookham, 1811), 1.i–ii, viii–xi, xliii

[In 1812, Shelley wrote a letter to Lawrence (1773–1840) to announce that *The Empire of Nairs*, "which I read this Spring, succeeded in making me a perfect convert to its doctrines."[4] The novel imagines a matriarchal society, located in India, where women are heads of state and marriage does not exist. Many of Lawrence's ideas find their way into Shelley's footnotes to *Queen Mab*,

1 Social relationship.

2 Inessentials.

3 In other words, a person can be unfaithful without having a bad moral character.

4 *The Letters of Percy Bysshe Shelley*, I.323.

his poem of 1813, but they are also the foundation of *Laon and Cythna*. Several scholars have noted Cythna's resemblance to one of the warrior queens of the Nairs, but more crucial are her and Laon's frequent descriptions of marriage as a form of tyranny. Much of their vocabulary seems borrowed from Lawrence's preface (excerpted here) to his novel, in particular the identity it insists on positing between sexual inequality and slavery. Contemporary readers will be struck, and even disturbed, by Lawrence's claim that the social oppression of women in European society is as bad as, if not worse than, the enslavement of African populations; the idea was common enough in this period, though it is certainly no less problematic for being so.]

But wedlock is not only a cruel, but a partial yoke. Marriage is a prison that confines both man and wife; but, as, in a jail, one prisoner may exercise over an other the functions of a turnkey,[1] so the husband is the most favored of the two: but would they not be happy in making their escape together? Can the authority of a turnkey reconcile any prisoner to his detention?

A lover extols his mistress into a deity, and exults in paying her divine honors. What taste in every ornament of her dress; what expression in every feature of her countenance! Her mien is the mien of Venus, her air has the majesty of Juno, the wit of Minerva[2] graces her conversation; her image embellishes the solitary walk, her smile gilds the midnight dream, her presence is heaven. No courtier is so humble or submissive as he; she is the sovereign of his soul, his idol. At length the spell works its desired effect; her head cannot support the fragrance of the incense that burns at her feet; she pities her adorer, she marries him—her empire ceases, the goddess sinks into a mortal, the queen is treated as a slave: alas! poor wife!

[...]

Marriage seems ordained exclusively for the comfort of the man, that of the woman being disregarded. She must follow all his counsels without having any veto on his determinations; she must change her abode to suit his convenience; must break all the friendships of her youth, to flatter his caprice; and bear his absence, whenever he be pleased to quit her. If a man has sworn eternal fidelity to a woman, with what justice can he enter the army or navy without her permission? Or is he justified in undertaking a long voyage, and leaving her perhaps in the bloom of youth, to shiver in a bed of widowhood? Must she act the part of Penelope,[3] while her Ulysses is squandering his treasures on an oriental dancing girl, or receiving the Circean cup from the hands of a mulatto toast?[4] A husband would be surprised, on his return from his morning walk, to

1 Prison guard.

2 Venus, Juno, and Minerva are the Roman goddesses, respectively, of beauty and sexuality, marriage and childbirth, and war and wisdom.

3 In Homer's *Odyssey*, Penelope remains faithful to her husband Odysseus during his 20-year absence; he does not return the favor.

4 Slang word for a woman who is popular socially and/or sexually.

find that his other half had posted away to a ball at Bath, though he himself would not scruple to quit her to attend a meeting at New-Market.[1]

It may be said, that no political body, no literary society, no convivial meeting can be properly conducted without a president, and that marriage could not exist unless one of the parties were invested with superior authority: but first let it be proved if it be necessary or just that it should exist at all. Its abolition would be the abolition of the servitude of the one, nay, would increase the liberty and happiness of both sexes, and, far from being detrimental to population, would promote it.

[...]

O ye, who boast of your benevolent feelings, whose humanity urges you to unshackle the captive African, or to unfurl on Sierra-Leona[2] the white banner of liberty, why should ye fly so far from the polished world in quest of objects of pity? Rather rescue your sisters and manumit[3] your wives from an oppressive yoke, and promote a system which merits the attention of the politician, because favorable to population; which claims the approbation of the aristocrat, because it would ensure to the nobility a birth incontestably genuine; and demands the support of the philanthropist, because it would augment the happiness and liberty of mankind.

1 I.e., at the horse races.

2 The West African country of Sierra Leone was a major hub of the slave trade.

3 Free, release.

Appendix F: Romantic Orientalism

1. From Charles Louis de Secondat, Baron de Montesquieu, *Persian Letters*, trans. T. Flloyd, 2 vols., 4th ed. (1721; London: J. and R. Tonson, 1762), 1.71–76; 2.183, 194–96

[*Persian Letters* is an epistolary novel that uses letters to tell the story of Usbek and Rica, two Persian noblemen traveling in France, and the women they have left behind in Isfahan, a province in modern-day Iran. Among those women is Usbek's wife Roxana, who chafes under the repressive guardianship of Usbek's eunuchs, and who is conducting a secret affair with a man she loves. Over the course of the novel, it becomes clear that Roxana is fomenting unrest among the other wives, and the novel ends with her, much like Cythna, leading a rebellion that begins in the harem. This strand of the narrative runs alongside Usbek and Rica's observations about eighteenth-century Paris, where life seems sometimes dramatically different from and sometimes uncannily similar to life in Isfahan. Popular from the moment of its publication, *Persian Letters* is a classic text of the Enlightenment. It exemplifies at once its resistance to authoritarianism, its fascination with the East and especially with the private world of the harem, and its use of non-Western culture as a point of critical comparison with European norms and values.]

Letter XXVI. Usbek to Roxana, at the Seraglio at Ispahan

How happy art thou, Roxana, to be in the delightful country of Persia, and not in these poisoned climes,[1] where neither virtue nor modesty are known! How happy art thou! Thou livest in my seraglio, as in the abode of innocence, secure from the attempts of all mankind; you, with pleasure, experience a happy inability to go astray; never did man pollute you with his lascivious looks; during the freedom of festivities even your father-in-law never saw your fine mouth; you never neglected to cover it with a holy veil. Happy Roxana! whenever you have gone into the country, you have always had eunuchs to march before, to punish with death the temerity of those who did not fly from your sight. Even I myself, to whom heaven gave you to make me happy, how much trouble have I had to render myself master of that treasure,[2] which with so much constancy you defended! How distressing to me, during the first days of our marriage, not to see you! And how impatient when I had beheld you! Yet you would not satisfy it; on the contrary you increased it, by the obstinate refusals of your bashful alarms; you did not distinguish me from all other men, from whom you are always concealed. Do you recollect the day I lost you among your slaves, who betrayed me, and hid you from my searches? Do you remember another time, when finding your tears insufficient, you engaged the

1 I.e., France.

2 I.e., Roxana's virginity.

authority of your mother, to stop the eagerness of my love? Do you remember, when every other resource failed you, those you found in your own courage? You took a dagger, and threatened to sacrifice a husband, who loved you, if he persisted in requiring of you what you prized more than your husband himself. Two months passed in the struggle between love and modesty. You carried your modest scruples too far; you did not even submit after you were conquered. You defended to the last moment a dying virginity; you regarded me as an enemy who had done you a wrong, not as a husband who had loved you; you [were] above three months before you could look at me without a blush; your bashful looks seemed to reproach me with the advantage I had taken. I did not enjoy even a quiet possession; you deprived me of all those charms and graces that you could; and without having obtained the least favours, I was ravished with the greatest. If your education had been in this country, here, you would not have been so troublesome. The women here have lost all modesty; they present themselves before the men with their faces uncovered, as though they would demand of them their defeat; they watch for their looks; they see them in their mosques, their public walks, and even by themselves; the service of eunuchs is unknown to them. In the room of that noble simplicity, and that amiable modesty which reigns amongst you, a brutal impudence prevails, to which it is impossible to be accustomed. Yes, if thou wert here, Roxana, you would be enraged at the wretched shamefulness to which your sex is degenerated; you would fly these polluted places, and sigh for that sweet retreat, where you find innocence, and yourself secure, and where no dangers terrify you: in a word, where you can love me without fear of ever losing that love for me which is my due. When you heighten your beautiful complexion with the finest colours; when you perfume your whole body with the most precious essences, when you deck yourself with the richest dresses, when you endeavour to distinguish yourself from your companions by your graceful motions in dancing, and when, by the sweetness of your voice, you pleasingly dispute with them charms, affability, and gaiety, I cannot imagine you have any other object to please but myself; and when I see your modest blush, that your eyes seek mine, that you insinuate yourself into my heart by your soft alluring speeches, I cannot, Roxana, suspect[1] your love....

Letter CLXI. Roxana to Usbek, at Paris

It is true, I have imposed upon thee, I have suborned[2] thy eunuchs; I have made sport of thy jealousy; and I have found means to make thy frightful seraglio an abode of bliss and delight. I am upon the point of death; poison will soon put an end to my life; for why should I live, when the only man who rendered life desirable, is no more? I die: but my shade will be well attended. I have just sent before me the sacrilegious guards, who have shed the most precious blood in the world. How couldst thou think me weak enough to consider myself as born only to adore thy caprice? that whilst you allowed yourself the

1 Doubt.

2 Bribed.

full indulgence of all your desires, you had a right to thwart mine in every respect? No, though I have lived in a state of servitude, I contrived means to be always free: I reformed your laws by the laws of nature; and my mind has always continued in a state of independency. Thou oughtest even to thank me for the sacrifice which I have made thee; for having descended so low as to counterfeit a passion for you; for having basely concealed within my breast, what I should have published to thee; in fine,[1] for having profaned virtue, by suffering my bearing with your humours to be called by that name. You were surprised at never observing in me the transports of love: had you known me well, you would have discovered in me all the violence of hatred. But you have long enjoyed the happy deception of thinking yourself possessed of such a heart as mine: we were both satisfied; you thought me deceived, whilst I deceived you. You must doubtless be surprized at my addressing you in such a st[y]le as this. Is it possible then, that after having overwhelmed thee with my affliction, I should still have it in my power to make thee admire my resolution? But all this is over now, the poison wastes me away, my strength forsakes me, the pen drops from my hand; I find even my hatred grow weaker: I die.

2. From Constantin-Francois Chasseboeuf, Comte de Volney, *The Ruins: or a Survey of the Revolutions of Empires*, trans. James Marshall, 2nd ed. (1791; London: J. Johnson, 1795), 83–85

[One of the most important works of political philosophy written in the eighteenth century, Volney's *Ruins* is now seldom read except by scholars and specialists. Having spent some time traveling in Egypt and Syria, Volney had come to see both European and non-Western political and religious ideologies as fundamentally aligned, insofar as they all seem to produce social inequality and mass suffering while allocating wealth and power to a privileged few. While gazing upon the ruins of Palmyra, an ancient city in present-day Syria, the book's narrator encounters a spirit who grants him a vision of humanity's past, present, and future. The spirit is careful to emphasize that all great empires eventually fall, driven to self-destruction by their own rapacity. In this excerpt from Chapter 12, "Lessons Taught by Ancient, Repeated in Modern Times," the spirit accuses religious leaders of misrepresenting the true nature of God, who certainly cannot want the people of the world to kill each other in His name.]

["]What madness is this which strikes my ear? What blind and fatal insanity possesses the human mind? Sacrilegious prayers, return to the earth from whence you came! Ye concave heavens, repel these murderous vows, these impious thanksgivings! Is it thus, O man, you worship the Divinity? And do you think that he, whom you call Father of all, can receive with complacence the homage of free-booters[2] and murderers? Ye conquerors, with what sentiments does he behold your arms reeking with blood that he has created? Ye

1 Ultimately.

2 Plunderers.

conquered, what hope can you place in useless moans? Is he a man that he should change, or the son of man that he should repent? Is he governed like you by vengeance and compassion, by rage and by weariness! Base idea, how much unworthy of the Being of Beings! Hear these men, and you would imagine that God is a Being capricious and mutable; that now he loves, and now he hates; that he chastises one, and indulges another; that hatred is engendered and nourished in his bosom; that he spreads snares for men, and delights in the fatal effects of imprudence; that he permits ill, and punishes it; that he foresees guilt, and acquiesces; that he is to be bought with gifts like a partial judge; that he reverses his edicts like an undiscerning despot; that he gives and revokes his favours because it is his will, and is to be appeased only by servility like a savage tyrant. I now completely understand what is the deceit of mankind, who have pretended that God made man in his own image, and who have really made God in theirs; who have ascribed to him their weakness, their errors, and their vices; and in the conclusion, surprised at the contradictory nature of their own assertions, have attempted to cloke it with hypocritical humility, and the pretended impotence of human reason, calling the delirium of their own understandings the sacred mysteries of heaven."

3. From Robert Southey, *Thalaba the Destroyer*, 2 vols., 2nd ed. (1801; London: Longman, Hurst, Rees, and Orme, 1809), I.109–17, Book III, lines 295–353

[Although it cannot be said to be an especially accurate representation of the faith of its eponymous Muslim hero, *Thalaba the Destroyer* is unusual in presenting a positive, even idyllic view of life in the Middle East to its Anglophone audience. The poem tells of a young orphan's quest to avenge his murdered family, and of his love for his adoptive sister, Oneiza, with whom he is united finally in death. Scholars have noted the poem's eccentric amalgam of Islamic tradition, Babylonian myth, and Christian allegory, a mix of influences and elements that shows just how malleable the orientalism of Shelley's age was. Southey's account of the developing love between Thalaba and Oneiza, as they appear in the Third Book of *Thalaba* below, bears obvious similarities to the story of Laon and Cythna. There are similarities here, too, with the scenes in Mary Shelley's *Frankenstein* (1818) featuring the relationship between Felix De Lacey and Safie, who is consistently referred to as "the Arabian."]

'Tis the cool evening hour:
The Tamarind[1] from the dew
Sheaths its young fruit, yet green.
Before their Tent the mat is spread,
The old man's aweful[2] voice
Intones the holy Book.
What if beneath no lamp-illumin'd dome,

1 A densely foliated tree that produces an edible, pod-like fruit.

2 Reverent.

Its marble walls bedeck'd with flourish'd truth,
Azure and gold adornment? sinks the word
With deeper influence from the Imam's voice,
Where in the day of congregation, crowds
Perform the duty-task?
Their Father is their Priest,
The Stars of Heaven their point of prayer,
And the blue Firmament
The glorious Temple, where they feel
The present Deity!

Yet through the purple glow of eve
Shines dimly the white moon.
The slacken'd bow, the quiver, the long lance,
Rest on the pillar of the Tent.
Knitting light palm-leaves for her brother's brow,
The dark-eyed damsel sits;
The Old Man tranquilly
Up his curl'd pipe inhales
The tranquillizing herb.[1]
So listen they the reed of Thalaba,
While his skill'd fingers modulate
The low, sweet, soothing, melancholy tones,
Or if he strung the pearls of Poesy,
Singing with agitated face
And eloquent arms, and sobs that reach the heart,
A tale of love and woe;
Then, if the brightening Moon, that lit his face
In darkness favoured her[s],
Oh! even with such a look, as, fables say,
The mother Ostrich fixes on her egg,
Till that intense affection
Kindle its light of life,[2]
Even in such deep and breathless tenderness
Oneiza's soul is centered on the youth,
So motionless, with such an ardent gaze,..
Save when from her full eyes
Quickly she wipes away the gushing tears
That dim his image there.

She call'd him Brother! was it sister-love
Which made the silver rings
Round her smooth ankles and her tawny arms,
Shine daily brighten'd? for a brother's eye
Were her long fingers tinged,

---

1 Tobacco or hashish.

2 Legend has it that ostriches stare at their eggs to make them hatch.

As when she trimm'd the lamp,
And thro' the veins and delicate skin
The light shone rosy? that the darkened lids
Gave yet a softer lustre to her eye?
That with such pride she trick'd
Her glossy tresses, and on holy-day
Wreath'd the red flower-crown round their jetty[1] waves?
How happily the years
Of Thalaba went by!

4. From Sydney Owenson (Lady Morgan), *The Missionary*, 3 vols. (London: J.J. Stockdale, 1811), 3.174–82

["It is really a divine thing," wrote Shelley about *The Missionary*. "Since I have read this book I have read no other—but I have thought strangely."[2] While Owenson's tempestuous novel of forbidden love between a Portuguese monk and a Hindu priestess may not seem like an obvious choice for capturing the poet's imagination, Shelley had a strong sentimental streak as well as a fondness for Gothic tropes and overwrought, even lurid narratives. Moreover, Owenson's very public criticism of the British occupation of Ireland puts her work in political sympathy with Shelley's, and both authors tend to invest the figure of the couple with progressive social power. If Cythna's horseback rescue of Laon in Canto Sixth puts Cythna in Richard Hurd's literary line of female warriors, her decision to join Laon on the pyre in Canto Twelfth was likely inspired by this scene from Volume 3, Chapter 4 of *The Missionary*, in which Luxima attempts to join her lover Hilarion as he is about to be executed by representatives of the Spanish Inquisition. Although Luxima is saved, her attempt at sati or self-immolation provokes a minor uprising against the Spanish presence in Kashmir, where the novel is set.]

In this aweful interval, while the presiding officers of death were preparing to bind their victim to the stake, a form scarcely human, darting with the velocity of lightning through the multitude, reached the foot of the pile, and stood before it, in a grand and aspiring attitude; the deep red flame of the slowly kindling fire shone through a transparent drapery which flowed in loose folds from the bosom of the seeming vision, and tinged with golden hues, those long dishevelled tresses, which streamed like the rays of a meteor on the air;—thus bright and aerial as it stood, it looked like a spirit sent from Heaven in the aweful moment of dissolution to cheer and to convey to the regions of the blessed, the soul which would soon arise, pure from the ordeal of earthly suffering.

The sudden appearance of the singular phantom struck the imagination of the credulous and awed multitude with superstitious wonder.—Even the ministers of death stood for a moment, suspended in the execution of their dread-

1 Jet-black.

2 *The Letters of Percy Bysshe Shelley*, I.107.

ful office. The Christians fixed their eyes upon the *cross*, which glittered on a bosom whose beauty scarcely seemed of mortal mould,[1] and deemed themselves the witnesses of a miracle, wrought for the salvation of a persecuted martyr, whose innocence was asserted by the firmness and fortitude with which he met a dreadful death.

The Hindoos gazed upon the sacred impress of *Brahma*, marked on the brow of his consecrated offspring; and beheld the fancied *herald* of the tenth *Avatar*,[2] announcing vengeance to the enemies of their religion. The condemned victim, still confined in the grasp of the officers of the bowstring, with eyes starting from their sockets, saw only the *unfortunate* he had made—the creature he adored—his disciple!—his mistress!—the Pagan priestess—the Christian Neophyte—his still lovely, though much changed Luxima. A cry of despair escaped from his bursting heart; and in the madness of the moment, he uttered aloud her name. Luxima, whose eyes and hands had been hitherto raised to Heaven, while she murmured the *Gayatra*, pronounced by the Indian women before their voluntary immolation,[3] now looked wildly round her, and, catching a glimpse of the Missionary's figure, through the waving of the flames, behind which he struggled in the hands of his guards, she shrieked, and in a voice scarcely human, exclaimed, "My beloved, I come!—*Brahma* receive and eternally unite our spirits!"—She sprang upon the pile: the fire, which had only kindled in that point where she stood, caught the light drapery of her robe—a dreadful death assailed her—the multitude shouted in horrid frenzy—the Missionary rushed forward—no force opposed to it, could resist the energy of madness, which nerved his powerful arm—he snatched the victim from a fate he sought not himself to avoid—he held her to his heart the flames of her robe were extinguished in his close embrace;—he looked round him with a dignified and triumphant air—the officers of the Inquisition, called on by their superiors, who now descended from the platforms, sprang forward to seize him:—for a moment, the timid multitude were *still* as the pause of a brooding storm.—Luxima clung round the neck of her deliverer—the Missionary, with a supernatural strength, warded off the efforts of those who would have torn her from him—the hand of fanaticism, impatient for its victim, aimed a dagger at his heart; its point was received in the bosom of the Indian,—she shrieked, and called upon "Brahma!"—Brahma! Brahma! was re-echoed on every side. A sudden impulse was given to feelings long suppressed: the timid spirits of the Hindoos rallied to an event which touched their hearts, and roused them from their lethargy of despair;—the sufferings, the oppression they had so long endured, seemed now epitomized before their eyes, in the person of their celebrated and distinguished Prophetess—they believed it was their god who addressed them from her lips—they rushed forward with a hideous cry, to rescue his priestess and to avenge the long slighted cause of their religion, and

1 Template, shape.

2 In Hinduism, the appearance or manifestation of a deity on earth.

3 Owenson associates the chanting of the Gāyatrī mantra with the controversial practice of sati, in which a widow suicides by self-immolation on the funeral pyre of her deceased husband.

their freedom;—they fell with fury on the Christians, they rushed upon the cowardly guards of the Inquisition, who let fall their arms, and fled in dismay.

5. From Lord Byron, *The Giaour, a Fragment of a Turkish Tale*, 11th ed. (1813; London: John Murray, 1814), 3–8, lines 103–67

[Byron's relationship to orientalism is famously complicated. Unlike Shelley, Byron traveled widely outside of Western Europe, visiting Albania, Smyrna, Istanbul, and, of course, his beloved Greece. Although he died in 1824 fighting in the Greek War of Independence against the Ottoman Empire, Byron mostly resists negative characterizations of the Turks or of Islamic culture generally. *The Giaour*, for example, begins with a rousing appeal to Greece to free itself from Ottoman rule, but the rest of the poem ironizes this call to arms by portraying ethnic and religious conflict as destructive to all who participate in it: after murdering his Muslim enemy in cold blood, the Giaour (or "infidel") of the title is cursed to become a sort of vampire, unable to die. In this excerpt, his terrible immortality seems at first to celebrate but ultimately to lament the prospect of intergenerational violence. Although *Laon and Cythna* makes only a few direct references to Greece—Laon implies that he was born or at least grew up in Argolis, on the eastern part of the Peloponnese peninsula, and it is in Argolis that he begins his political activism—the historical association of Greece with democracy is invoked in Shelley's poem much in the same way as it is in Byron's: as a counterpoint to both Ottoman and British imperialism.]

Clime of the unforgotten brave!—
Whose land from plain to mountain-cave
Was Freedom's home or Glory's grave—
Shrine of the mighty! can it be,
That this is all remains of thee?
Approach thou craven crouching slave—
Say, is not this Thermopylae?[1]
These waters blue that round you lave
Oh servile offspring of the free—
Pronounce what sea, what shore is this?
The gulf, the rock of Salamis![2]
These scenes—their story not unknown—
Arise, and make again your own;
Snatch from the ashes of your sires
The embers of their former fires,
And he who in the strife expires

1 Byron refers to a famous episode in the Greco-Persian Wars (492–449 BCE) known as the Battle of Thermopylae (480 BCE), in which a vastly outnumbered Greek force held back the army of Xerxes, King of Persia, for several days before they finally fell.

2 Another reference to the Greco-Persian conflict, this one to the Battle of Salamis (480 BCE), in which the Greeks decisively defeated the Persian navy.

Will add to theirs a name of fear,
That Tyranny shall quake to hear,
And leave his sons a hope, a fame,
They too will rather die than shame:
For Freedom's battle once begun,
Bequeathed by bleeding Sire to Son,
Though baffled oft is ever won.
Bear witness, Greece, thy living page,
Attest it many a deathless age!
While kings in dusty darkness hid,
Have left a nameless pyramid,
Thy heroes—though the general doom
Hath swept the column from their tomb,
A mightier monument command,
The mountains of their native land!
There points thy Muse to stranger's eye,
The graves of those that cannot die!
'Twere long to tell, and sad to trace,
Each step from splendour to disgrace;
Enough—no foreign foe could quell
Thy soul, till from itself it fell,
Yes! Self-abasement pav'd the way
To villain-bonds and despot-sway.

What can he tell who treads thy shore?
  No legend of thine olden time,
No theme on which the muse might soar,
High as thine own in days of yore,
  When man was worthy of thy clime.
The hearts within thy valleys bred,
The fiery souls that might have led
  Thy sons to deeds sublime;
Now crawl from cradle to the grave,
Slaves—nay, the bondsmen[1] of a slave,[2]
  And callous,[3] save to crime;
Stain'd with each evil that pollutes
Mankind, where least above the brutes;
Without even savage virtue blest,

---

1 Indentured servants; persons working (often in difficult or extreme conditions) to pay off a debt.

2 [Byron's note:] Athens is the property of the Kislar Aga, (the slave of the seraglio and guardian of the women), who appoints the Waywode.—A pandar and eunuch—these are not polite yet true appellations—now *governs* the *governer* of Athens. [The Kizlar Agha was the head eunuch of the Imperial Harem (located in Istanbul) of the Ottoman Sultans; a waywode is a term used to describe a low-level official, including the governor of a town or province. Cf. p. 89, II.xxxvi.321.]

3 Hardened, indifferent.

Without one free or valiant breast.
Still to the neighbouring ports they waft
Proverbial wiles, and ancient craft;
In this the subtle Greek is found,
For this, and this alone, renown'd.
In vain might Liberty invoke
The spirit to its bondage broke,
Or raise the neck that courts the yoke:
No more her sorrows I bewail,
Yet this will be a mournful tale,
And they who listen may believe,
Who heard it first had cause to grieve.

6. From Thomas Love Peacock, *Ahrimanes* (c. 1815). First published in 1909, reprinted here from *The Halliford Edition of the Works of Thomas Love Peacock*, ed. H.F.B. Brettsmith and C.E. Jones (New York: AMS P, 1967), 7.265–76, lines 1–270

[The first canto of Peacock's *Ahrimanes* is here printed in its entirety, so that the reader can see just how striking the similarities are between Peacock's poem and Canto First of *Laon and Cythna*. Once Peacock (1785–1866) discarded his draft, which he shared with Shelley, he appears not to have minded that his friend lifted so many of its elements—from its Spenserian stanzas to its Zoroastrian symbolism—wholesale, especially since both writers clearly had in mind Volney's *The Ruins* (Appendix F2), which also features a prophetic spirit lecturing its protagonist on the evils of the modern world. Most noteworthy, however, is Peacock's invocation of Necessity, here (as in *Laon and Cythna*), a name for the inexorable and ultimately progressive movement of human history.]

I.

In silver eddies glittering to the moon
Araxes[1] rolls his many-sounding tide.
Fair as the dreams of hope, and past as soon,
But in succession infinite supplied,
The rapid waters musically glide.
Now, where the cliff's phantastic[2] shadow laves,
Silent and dark, they roll their volumed pride.
Now, by embowering woods and solemn caves,
Around some jutting rock the struggling torrent raves.

1 The Aras river, also known as the Araxes, runs through Turkey, Armenia, Azerbaijan, and Iran.

2 Strange, seemingly magical.

II.

Darassah stands beside the lonely shore,
Intently gazing on the imaged beam,
As one whose steps each lonely haunt explore
Of nymph or naiad,[1]—grove, or rock, or stream—
Nature his guide, his object, and his theme.
Ah no—Darassah's eyes these forms survey
As phantoms of a half-remembered dream:
His eyes are on the water's glittering play:
Their mental sense is closed—his thoughts are far away.

III.

But central in the flood of liquid light,
A sudden spot its widening orb revealed,
Jet black among the mirrored beams of night,
Jet black, and round as Celtic warrior's shield,
A sable circle in a silver field.
With sense recalled and motionless surprise,
Deeming some fearful mystery there concealed,
He marked that shadowy orb's expanding size,
Till slowly from its breast a form began to rise—

IV.

A female form: and even as marble pale
Her cheeks: her eyes unearthly fire illumed:
Far o'er her shoulders streamed a sable veil,
Where flowers of living flame inwoven bloomed;
No mortal robe might bear them unconsumed:
A crown her temples bound: on such ne'er gazed
Eyes that had seen primeval kings entombed:
Twelve points it bore; on every point upraised
A star—a heavenly star—with dazzling radiance blazed.

V.

Lovely she was—not loveliness that might
In mortal heart enkindle light desire—
But such as decked the form of youthful Night,
When, on the bosom of her anarch sire,[2]
With gentler passion she did first inspire

---

1 A water nymph or spirit.

2 I.e., Chaos, the lawless (or "anarch") parent of Night, also known as Nyx.

The gloomy soul of Erebus severe;[1]
Ere from her breast, on wings of golden fire,
Primordial love sprang o'er the infant sphere,
And bade young Time[2] arise and lead the vernal year.

VI.

Her right hand held a wand, whose potent sway
Her liquid path, the buoyant waves, obeyed.
Still as she moved, the moon-beams died away,
And shade around her fell—a circling shade—
That gave no outline of the wondrous maid.
Her form—soft gliding as the summer gale—
In that portentous darkness shone arrayed,
Shone by her starry crown, her fiery veil,
And those refulgent[3] eyes that made their radiance pale.

VII.

"Why—simple dweller of the Araxian isle"—
Thus, as she pressed the shore, the genius[4] said—
"Seek'st thou this spot, to muse and mourn the while,
Beside this river's ever-murmuring bed,
When gentle sleep has her dominion spread
On every living thing around, but thee?
The silent stars, that twinkle o'er thy head,
Shed rest and peace on hill, and flower, and tree;
All but the eternal stream, that flows melodiously."

VIII.

Solemn her voice, as music's vesper[5] peal
From distant choir to cloistered echo borne,
Where the deep notes through pillared twilight steal,
Breathing tranquillity to souls that mourn.
The awe-struck youth replied: "Of one so lorn[6]
Canst thou, empyreal[7] spirit, deign require

---

1 Peacock refers to Nyx's union with the primordial god Erebus, who was associated with darkness or shadow.
2 Chronos, Greek deity who personifies time.
3 Shining brightly.
4 Spirit.
5 Evening, or evening prayer service.
6 Forlorn, forsaken.
7 Heavenly, unearthly.

The secret woes by which his soul is torn?
Sure from the fountain of eternal fire
Thy wondrous birth began, great Mithra's[1] self thy sire.

IX.

"Through many an age amid these island-bowers
The simple fathers of our race have dwelt:
To them spontaneous Nature fruits and flowers,
By toil unsought, with partial bounty dealt:
At Oromazes'[2] sylvan shrine they knelt:
And morn and eve did choral suppliance flow
From hearts that love and mingled reverence felt,
To him who gave them every bliss to know
That simple hearts can wish, or heavenly love bestow.

X.

"But years passed on, and strange perversion ran
Among the dwellers of the peaceful isle:
And one, more daring than the rest, began
To fell the grove, and point the massy pile;
And raised the circling fence with evil wile,
And to his brethren said: These bounds are mine:
And did with living victims first defile
The verdant turf of Oromazes' shrine;
Sad offering sure, and strange, to mercy's source divine.

XI.

"And ill example evil followers drew;
Till common good and common right were made
The fraudful tenure of a powerful few:
The many murmured, trembled, and obeyed.
Then peace and freedom fled the sylvan shade,
And care arose, and toil, unknown before:
And some the hollowed alder's trunk essayed,
And left, with tearful eyes, their natal shore.
Swift down the stream they went, and they returned no more.

---

1 Mithra is a Zoroastrian deity, associated with promises, oaths, and contracts.

2 I.e., Ahura Mazda, Zoroastrianism's primary deity, whose name is derived from the Avestan words for light (ahura) and wisdom (mazda).

XII.

"And I too, oft, beyond that barrier rock,
That hides from view the river's onward way—
Where, eddying round its base with ceaseless shock,
The waves, that flash, and disappear for aye,[1]
Their parting murmurs to my ear convey—
In fancy turn my meditative gaze,
And trace, encircled by their powerful sway,
Some blooming isle where love unfettered strays,
And peace and freedom dwell as here in earlier days.

XIII.

"But one there is for whom my tears are shed;
A maid of wealthier lot and prouder line:
With her my happy infant hours I led;
And sweet our mutual task, at morn to twine
The votive[2] wreath round Oromazes' shrine.—
She mourns, a captive in her father's home—
Alone I rove, to murmur and repine—
Alone, where sparkling waves symphonious[3] foam,
I breathe my secret pangs to heaven's empyreal dome.—"

XIV.

"Leave tears to slaves"—the genius answering said,—
"Adventurous deed the noble mind beseems.[4]
Oh shame to manhood! thus, with listless tread,
In tears and sighs and inconclusive dreams
To waste thy hours by groves and murmuring streams.
I bring thee power for weakness, joy for woe,
And certain bliss for hope's fallacious schemes,
Unless thou lightly thy own weal[5] forego,
And scorn the splendid lot thy bounteous fates bestow.

XV.

"This gifted ring shall every barrier break:
The maid thou lovest thy wandering steps shall share:
When night returns, with her this isle forsake,

1 Forever.
2 Made as an offering.
3 In harmony.
4 Befits.
5 Well-being, personal interest.

From this thy favored haunt: my guardian care
To waft ye hence, the vessel shall prepare.
The monarch of the world[1] hath chosen thee
High trust, and power, and dignity to bear.
I come, obedient to his high decree,
To set from error's spell thy captive senses free.

XVI.

"Deem'st thou, when blood of living victims flows,
'Mid incense smoke, in denser volumes curled,
That Oromazes there a glance bestows,
A glance of joy, to see the death-blows hurled?
No—far remote, in orient clouds enfurled,
Nor prayer nor sacrificial rite he heeds.
His reign is past: his rival rules the world.
From Ahrimanes[2] now all power proceeds:
For him the altar burns: for him the victim bleeds.

XVII.

"Parent of being, mistress of the spheres,
Supreme Necessity o'er all doth reign:
She guides the course of the revolving years,
With power no prayers can change, no force restrain;
Binding all nature in her golden chain,
Whose infinite connection links afar
The smallest atom of the sandy plain
And the last ray of heaven's remotest star,
That round the verge of space wheels its refulgent car.

XVIII.

"She to two gods, sole agents of her will,
By turns has given her delegated sway:
Her sovereign laws obedient they fufill:
Inferior powers their high behests obey.
First Oromazes—lord of peace and day—
Dominion held o'er nature and mankind.
Now Ahrimanes rules, and holds his way
In storms: for such his task by her assigned,
To shake the world with war, and rouse the powers of mind.

---

1 I.e., Oromazes.

2 I.e., Angra Mainyu or Ahriman, the "destructive spirit" of Zoroastrian mythology.

XIX.

"She first on chaos poured the streams of light
And bade from that mysterious union rise
Primordial love: the heavenly lion's might
Bore him rejoicing through the new-born skies.
Then glowed the infant world with countless dyes
Of fruits and flowers; and virgin nature smiled,
Emerging first from ancient night's disguise
And elemental discord, vast and wild,
Which primogenial[1] love had charmed and reconciled.

XX.

"Then man arose: to him the world was given,
Unknowing then disease, or storm, or dearth:[2]
The eternal balance, in the central heaven,
Marked the free tenure[3] of his equal birth,
And equal right to all the bounteous earth
Of fruit or flower, his pristine food, might yield.
Nor private roof he knew, nor blazing hearth,
Nor marked with barrier-lines the fruitful field,
Nor learned in martial strife the uprooted oak to wield.

XXI.

"Then Oromazes reigned.—Profoundly calm
His empire, as the lake's unruffled breast,
When evening twilight melts in dews of balm,
And rocks and woods in calm reflection rest,
As if for aye indelibly imprest[4]
Were those fair forms, in waveless light arrayed.—
No sigh, no wish, the peaceful heart confest;
Save when the youth, beneath the myrtle shade,
Wooed to his fond embrace the easy-yielding maid.

XXII.

"No pillared fanes[5] to Oromazes rose;
For him no priest the destined victim led.
The choral hymn, in swelling sound that flows,

---

1 First-born.

2 Famine.

3 Period, length of time, scope.

4 Impressed, printed on.

5 Temples.

Where round the marble altar streaming red
The slow procession moves with solemn tread,
His empire owned not:—but his bounty grew,
By prayer or hymn nor sought nor merited:
No altar but the peaceful heart he knew—
His only temple-vault, the heaven's ethereal blue.[1]

XXIII.

"Such was the infant world, and such the reign
Of cloudless sunshine and oblivious[2] joy;
Till rose the scorpion in the empyreal plain,[3]
In fated hour, their empire to destroy,
And with unwonted[4] cares the course alloy[5]
Of mortal being and terrestrial time;
That man might all his god-like powers employ
The toilsome steep of wealth and fame to climb,
To rugged labor trained and glory's thirst sublime.[6]

XXIV.

"To Ahrimanes thus devolved the power,
Which still he holds through all the realms of space.
He bade the sea to swell—the storm to lower—
And taught mankind the pliant bow to brace,
And point the shaft, and urge the sounding chace,[7]
And force from veins of flint the seeds of fire;
Till, as more daring thought found gradual place,
He bade the mind to nobler prey aspire,
Of war, and martial fame kindling the high desire.

XXV.

"For him on earth unnumbered temples rise,
And altars burn, and bleeding victims die:
Albeit the sons of men his name disguise

---

1 Cf. 2 Corinthians 6:16: "And what agreement hath the temple of God with idols? for ye are the temple of the living God; as God hath said, I will dwell in them, and walk in them; and I will be their God, and they shall be my people."

2 Innocent.

3 I.e., until the constellation Scorpio, or in Zoroastrian cosmology Gazdum, rose in the sky.

4 Unaccustomed, new.

5 Mix, corrupt.

6 Immense, unending.

7 Chase, hunt.

In other names, that choice or chance supply,
To him alone their incense soars on high.
The god of armies—the avenging god—
Seevah[1] or Allah—Jove or Mars[2]—they cry:
'Tis Ahrimanes still that wields the rod;
To him all nature bends, and trembles at his nod.

XXVI.

"Yea, even on Oromazes' self they call,
But Ahrimanes hears their secret prayer.
Not in the name that from the lips may fall,
But in the thought the heart's recesses bear,
The sons of earth the power they serve declare.
Wherever priests awake the battle strain,
And bid the torch of persecution glare,
And curses ring along the vaulted fane—
Call on what god they may—their god Ahrimane.

XXVII.

"Favor to few, to many wealth he shews:[3]
None with impunity his power may brave.
Two classes only of mankind he knows,
The lord and serf—the tyrant and the slave.
Some hermit-sage, where lonely torrents rave,
May muse and dream of Oromazes still:
Despised he lives, and finds a nameless grave.
The chiefs and monarchs of the world fulfil
Great Ahrimane's behests—the creatures of his will.

XXVIII.

"Say—hadst thou rather grovel with the crowd,
The wretched thing and tool of lordly might,
Or, where the battle-clarion brays aloud,
Blaze forth conspicuous in the fields of fight,
And bind thy brow with victory's chaplet[4] bright,
And be the king of men?—Thy choice is free.—
Receive this ring.—Observe the coming night.—
The monarch of the world hath chosen thee
To spread his name on earth, in power and majesty.—"

---

1 The Hindu god Shiva.

2 In Roman mythology, Jove is the king of the gods, and Mars is the god of war.

3 Cf. Alexander Pope, *The Rape of the Lock* (1712/14): "Favors to none, to all she smiles extends," in *The Major Works*, ed. Pat Rogers (Oxford: Oxford UP, 2006), 2.10.

4 Garland.

XXIX.

She said, and gave the ring. The youth received
The glittering spell, in awe and mute amaze;[1]
Standing like one almost of sense bereaved,
That fixes on the vacant air his gaze,
Where 'wildered[2] fancy's troubled eye surveys
Dim-flitting forms, obscure and undefined,
That doubtful thoughts and shadowy feelings raise,
Leaving no settled image on the mind:
Like cloud-built rocks and towers, dissolved ere half-combined.

XXX.

Nor stayed she longer parle;[3] but round her form
A sable vapor, thickly-mantling, drew
Its volumed folds, dark as the summer's storm.
It wrapped her round, and in an instant flew,
Scattered like mist, though not a zephyr blew,
And left no vestige that she there had been.
The river rolled in light. The moonbeams threw
Their purest radiance on the lonely scene;
And hill, and grove, and rock, slept in the ray serene.

---

1 Amazement.

2 Bewildered, disoriented.

3 I.e., she said no more.

Appendix G: Mary Shelley's "Note on The Revolt of Islam*"*

1. From Mary Wollstonecraft Shelley, "Note on *The Revolt of Islam*," *The Poetical Works of Percy Bysshe Shelley*, 4 vols. (London: Edward Moxon, 1839), 1.374–78

[After her husband's death, Mary Shelley devoted herself to the task of editing both his prose and his poetical works. Her introductions to the volumes she compiled often contain personal anecdotes that both shed light on the circumstances under which a particular text was written and offer potential interpretations of their contents. In this account of the composition of *Laon and Cythna*—which she refers to as *The Revolt of Islam*, the name given to the poem's second incarnation—Mary Shelley offers the intriguing suggestion that the poem grew, at least in part, out of Shelley's grief over the deaths of Fanny Imlay (Mary's half-sister) and of his first wife Harriet Westbrook. She also suggests that *Laon and Cythna* was inspired by Byron's more experimental work of 1816, though it is clear from her tone that she considered Shelley infinitely more skilled than Byron when it came to abstract, philosophical speculation.]

Shelley possessed two remarkable qualities of intellect—a brilliant imagination, and a logical exactness of reason. His inclinations led him (he fancied) almost alike to poetry and metaphysical discussions. I say "he fancied," because I believe the former to have been paramount, and that it would have gained the mastery even had he struggled against it. However, he said that he deliberated at one time whether he should dedicate himself to poetry or metaphysics, and resolving on the former, he educated himself for it, discarding in a great measure his philosophical pursuits, and engaging himself in the study of the poets of Greece, Italy, and England. To these may be added a constant perusal of portions of the Old Testament—the Psalms, the Book of Job, the Prophet Isaiah, and others, the sublime poetry of which filled him with delight.

As a poet, his intellect and compositions were powerfully influenced by exterior circumstances, and especially by his place of abode. He was very fond of travelling, and ill-health increased this restlessness. The sufferings occasioned by a cold English winter made him pine, especially when our colder spring arrived, for a more genial climate. In 1816 he again visited Switzerland, and rented a house on the banks of the Lake of Geneva; and many a day, in cloud or sunshine, was passed alone in his boat—sailing as the wind listed, or weltering[1] on the calm waters. The majestic aspect of nature ministered such thoughts as he afterwards enwove in verse. His lines on the Bridge of the Arve, and his Hymn to Intellectual Beauty, were written at this time. Perhaps during this summer his genius was checked by association with another poet, whose nature was utterly dissimilar to his own, yet who, in the poem he wrote at that

1 Rolling.

time, gave tokens that he shared for a period the more abstract and etherealised inspiration of Shelley.[1] The saddest events[2] awaited his return to England; but such was his fear to wound the feelings of others that he never expressed the anguish he felt, and seldom gave vent to the indignation roused by the persecutions he underwent; while the course of deep unexpressed passion, and the sense of injury, engendered the desire to embody themselves in forms defecated[3] of all the weakness and evil which cling to real life.

He chose therefore for his hero a youth nourished in dreams of liberty, some of whose actions are in direct opposition to the opinions of the world; but who is animated throughout by an ardent love of virtue, and a resolution to confer the boons of political and intellectual freedom on his fellow-creatures. He created for this youth a woman such as he delighted to imagine—full of enthusiasm for the same objects; and they both, with will unvanquished, and the deepest sense of the justice of their cause, met adversity and death. There exists in this poem a memorial of a friend of his youth.[4] The character of the old man who liberates Laon from his tower prison, and tends on him in sickness, is founded on that of Doctor Lind, who, when Shelley was at Eton, had often stood by to befriend and support him, and whose name he never mentioned without love and veneration.[5]

During the year 1817, we were established at Marlow, in Buckinghamshire. Shelley's choice of abode was fixed chiefly by this town being at no great distance from London, and its neighbourhood to the Thames. The poem was written in his boat, as it floated under the beech groves of Bisham, or during wanderings in the neighbouring country, which is distinguished for peculiar beauty. The chalk hills break into cliffs that overhang the Thames, or form valleys clothed with beech; the wilder portion of the country is rendered beautiful by exuberant vegetation; and the cultivated part is peculiarly fertile. With all this wealth of nature which, either in the form of gentlemen's parks or soil dedicated to agriculture, flourishes around, Marlow was inhabited (I hope it is altered now) by a very poor population. The women are lace-makers, and lose their health by sedentary labour, for which they were very ill paid. The poor-laws[6] ground to the dust not only the paupers, but those who had risen just above that state, and were obliged to pay poor-rates. The changes produced by peace following a long war, and a bad harvest, brought with them the most heart-rending evils to the poor. Shelley afforded what alleviation he could. In the winter, while bringing out his poem, he had a severe attack of ophthalmia,[7] caught while visiting the poor cottages. I mention these things,—for this

---

1 The poet is Lord Byron; the "tokens" might be any of the less strongly narrative, grimmer work Byron produced during the summer of 1816, including "Darkness," "Prometheus," and "The Dream."

2 I.e., the suicides of Mary Shelley's half-sister Fanny Imlay and of Shelley's first wife, Harriet Westbrook Shelley.

3 Evacuated, emptied.

4 See p. 84, note 1.

5 See p. 102, note 1.

6 See p. 233, note 3.

7 Inflammation of the eye.

minute and active sympathy with his fellow-creatures gives a thousandfold interest to his speculations, and stamps with reality his pleadings for the human race.

The poem, bold in its opinions and uncompromising in their expression, met with many censurers, not only among those who allow of no virtue but such as supports the cause they espouse, but even among those whose opinions were similar to his own. I extract a portion of a letter written in answer to one of these friends. It best details the impulses of Shelley's mind, and his motives: it was written with entire unreserve; and is therefore a precious monument of his own opinion of his powers, of the purity of his designs, and the ardour with which he clung, in adversity and through the valley of the shadow of death,[1] to views from which he believed the permanent happiness of mankind must eventually spring. [Mary Shelley concludes her note with a modified version of her husband's letter to William Godwin reprinted in Appendix B3 above.]

1 Cf. Psalm 23: "Yea, though I walk through the valley of the shadow of death, I will fear no evil: for thou art with me."

Works Cited and Select Bibliography

Recent Editions of Shelley's Works

The Bodleian Shelley Manuscripts: A Facsimile Edition, with Full Transcriptions and Scholarly Apparatus. Ed. Donald H. Reiman et al. 23 vols. Vols. 1–22: New York and London: Garland, 1986–97. Vol. 23: New York: Routledge, 2002.

The Complete Poetical Works of Percy Bysshe Shelley. Ed. Neville Rogers. 2 vols. Oxford: Clarendon, 1972 and 1975.

The Complete Poetry of Percy Bysshe Shelley. 3 vols to date. Ed. Donald Reiman and Neil Fraistat (Vols. I and II) and Reiman, Fraistat, Nora Crook, et al. (Vol. III). Baltimore: Johns Hopkins UP, 2000, 2004, and 2012.

The Complete Works of Percy Bysshe Shelley. Ed. Roger Ingpen and Walter E. Peck. 10 vols. New York: Gordian, 1965.

The Letters of Percy Bysshe Shelley. Ed. Frederick L. Jones. 2 vols. Oxford: Clarendon, 1964.

Percy Bysshe Shelley: The Major Works. Ed. Zachary Leader and Michael O'Neill. Oxford: Oxford UP, 2003.

The Poems of Shelley. Ed. Geoffrey Matthews and Kelvin Everest. 2 of 3 vols to date. London: Longman, 1989 and 2000.

The Prose Works of Percy Bysshe Shelley. Ed. E.B. Murray. Oxford: Clarendon, 1992. 1 vol. published.

Shelley's Poetry and Prose. Ed. Donald H. Reiman and Neil Fraistat. 2nd ed. New York: W.W. Norton, 2002.

Historical Editions of Primary Texts

Bacon, Francis. "Of Goodness, and Goodness of Nature." *The Works of Francis Bacon, Volume the First, Containing Essays Moral, Economic, and Political*. London: M. Jones, 1815. 52–56.

Burke, Edmund. *Reflections on the Revolution in France, and on the Proceedings in Certain Societies in London Relative to That Event. In a Letter Intended to Have Been Sent to a Gentleman in Paris*. 1st ed. London: J. Dodsley, 1790.

Byron, George Gordon, Lord. Canto II. *Childe Harold's Pilgrimage, a Romaunt: And Other Poems*. 5th ed. London: John Murray, 1812.

——. *The Giaour, a Fragment of a Turkish Tale*. 11th ed. London: John Murray, 1814.

[Coleridge, John Taylor.] "Shelley's Revolt of Islam." *Quarterly Review* 21.42 (1819): 460–71.

Darwin, Erasmus. *The Botanic Garden, Part II. Containing The Loves of the Plants. A Poem. With Philosophical Notes*. London: J. Johnson, 1791.

Drummond, William. *Academical Questions*. London: Cadell and Davies, 1805.

Godwin, William. *Enquiry Concerning Political Justice, and Its Influence on Morals and Happiness*. 2 vols. Rev. 3rd ed. London: G.G. and J. Robinson, 1798.

——. *Mandeville: A Tale of the Seventeenth Century in England*. 3 vols. Longman, Hurst, Rees, Orme and Brown, 1817.

Holcroft, Thomas. *Anna St. Ives*. 7 vols. London: Shepperson and Reynolds, 1792.

Hunt, Leigh. "Literary Notices, No. 39." *The Examiner* 527 (1818): 75.

——. "Literary Notices, No. 41." *The Examiner* 531 (1818): 139–41.

——. "*The Quarterly Review* and the *Revolt of Islam*." *The Examiner* 615 (1819): 652–53.

——. *The Story of Rimini, a Poem*. London: J. Murray, 1816.

Hurd, Richard. *Letters on Chivalry and Romance*. London: A. Millar, 1762.

Lambe, William. *Reports on the Effects of a Peculiar Regimen on Scirrhous Tumours and Cancerous Ulcers*. London: J. Mawman, 1809.

Lawrence, James. *The Empire of the Nairs: or, The Rights of Women. An Utopian Romance*. 4 vols. London: T. Hookham, Jun. and E.T. Hookham, 1811.

[Lockhart, John Gibson.] "Observations on the Revolt of Islam." *Blackwood's Edinburgh Magazine* 4.22 (1819): 475–82.

——. "On the Cockney School of Poetry No. I." *Blackwood's Edinburgh Magazine* 2 (1817): 38–41.

[Malthus, Thomas Robert.] *Essay on the Principle of Population, As It Affects the Future Improvement of Society. With Remarks on the Speculations of Mr. Godwin, M. Condorcet, and Other Writers*. London: J. Johnson, 1798.

Montesquieu, Charles Louis de Secondat, Baron de. *Persian Letters*. Trans. T. Flloyd. 2 vols. 4th ed. London: J. and R. Tonson, 1762. Originally published in French, 1721.

Moore, Thomas. *Lalla Rookh, an Oriental Romance*. London: Longman, Hurst, Rees, Orme and Brown, 1817.

Owenson, Sydney (Lady Morgan). *The Missionary*. 3 vols. London: J.J. Stockdale, 1811.

Paine, Thomas. *Rights of Man: Part the Second: Combining Principle and Practice*. London: J.S. Jordan, 1792.

Rousseau, Jean-Jacques. *Émile, ou, de l'Éducation*, 4 vols. Amsterdam: Jean Néaulme, 1762.

Shelley, Percy Bysshe. *Laon and Cythna; Or, the Revolution of the Golden City: A Vision of the Nineteenth Century*. London: Sherwood, Neely, & Jones; C. and J. Ollier, 1817.

——. "On Love." [Ed. Mary Wollstonecraft Shelley.] *The Keepsake for 1829*. London: Hurst, Chance, & Co., 1828. 47–49.

——. *The Revolt of Islam*. London: C. and J. Ollier, 1818.

——. *A Vindication of Natural Diet*. London: J. Callow, 1813.

Southey, Robert. *Thalaba the Destroyer*. 2 vols. 2nd ed. London: Longman, Hurst, Rees, and Orme, 1809.

Sterne, Laurence. *A Sentimental Journey through France and Italy*. London: T. Becket and P.A. DeHondt, 1768.

Tasso, Torquato. *La Gerusalemme Liberata*. 2 vols. 1581. Venice: Vitarelli, 1811.

Volney, Constantin-François de Chasseboeuf, Comte de. *The Ruins, or a Survey of the Revolutions of Empires*. Trans. James Marshall. 2nd ed. London: J. Johnson, 1795. Originally published in French, 1791.

Voltaire (François-Marie Arouet). *Letters Concerning the English Nation*. London: C. Davis and A. Lyon, 1733.

Williams, Helen Maria. *Letters from France: Containing Many New Anecdotes Relative to the Revolution, and the Present State of French Manners*. London: G.G.J. and J. Robinson, 1792.

——. *Letters Written in France in the Summer 1790, to a Friend in England*. London: T. Cadell, 1790.

Wollstonecraft, Mary. *A Vindication of the Rights of Woman: with Strictures on Political and Moral Subjects*. 2nd ed. London: J. Johnson, 1792.

——. *The Vindications: The Rights of Men and the Rights of Woman*. Ed. D.L. Macdonald and Kathleen Scherf. Peterborough, ON: Broadview P, 1997.

Modern Editions of Primary Texts

Aeschylus. *Persians, Seven Against Thebes, Suppliants, Prometheus Bound*. Trans. Alan H. Sommerstein. Cambridge, MA: Harvard UP, 2009.

Alighieri, Dante. *The Inferno*. Trans. Allen Mandelbaum. New York: Bantam, 1982.

Apuleius. *Metamorphoses, Books 7–11*. Trans. J. Arthur Hanson. Cambridge, MA: Harvard UP, 1989.

Blake, William. *The Complete Poetry and Prose of William Blake*. Ed. David V. Erdman. New York: Anchor Books, 1997.

Byron, George Gordon, Lord. *Byron's Letters and Journals*. 12 vols. Ed. Leslie A. Marchand. Cambridge, MA: Harvard UP, 1973–81.

——. *The Complete Poetical Works*. 7 vols. Ed. Jerome J. McGann. Oxford: Clarendon, 1980–92.

Coleridge, Samuel Taylor. *Poetical Works I: Poems (Reading Text)*. Ed. J.C.C. Mays. Princeton, NJ: Princeton UP, 2001.

——, and William Wordsworth. *Lyrical Ballads: 1798 and 1800*. Ed. Michael Gamer and Dahlia Porter. Peterborough, ON: Broadview P, 2008.

Empson, William. *Seven Types of Ambiguity*. New York: New Directions, 1966.

Herodotus. *The History*. Trans. David Grene. Chicago: U of Chicago P, 1988.

Hesiod. *Works and Days; Theogony; The Shield of Herakles*. Trans. Richmond Lattimore. Ann Arbor: U of Michigan P, 1991.

Homer. *The Iliad of Homer*. Trans. Richmond Lattimore. Chicago: U of Chicago P, 2011.

——. *The Odyssey of Homer*. Trans. Richmond Lattimore. New York: Harper Perennial, 2007.

Keats, John. *The Letters of John Keats: Volume 1, 1814–1818*. Ed. Hyder Edward Rollins. Cambridge, MA: Harvard UP, 1958.

Locke, John. *Essay Concerning Human Understanding*. Ed. Peter H. Nidditch. Oxford: Oxford UP, 1979.

Lucretius. *De Rerum Natura.* Trans. W.H.D. Rouse, rev. Martin Ferguson Smith. Cambridge, MA: Harvard UP, 1992.

Milton, John. *Paradise Lost*. Ed. Gordon Teskey. New York: W.W. Norton, 2004.

Ovid. *The Art of Love and Other Poems.* Trans. J.H. Mozley, rev. G.P. Goold. Cambridge, MA: Harvard UP, 1979.

——. *Metamorphoses.* Trans. Frank Justus Miller, rev. G.P. Goold. 2 Vols. Cambridge, MA: Harvard UP, 1984.

Peacock, Thomas Love. *Ahrimanes. The Halliford Edition of the Works of Thomas Love Peacock*. Ed. H.F.B. Brettsmith and C.E. Jones. 10 vols. 1909. New York: AMS P, 1967. 7.265–76.

——. *Memoirs of Shelley*. Ed. Humbert Wolfe. 2 vols. London: J.M. Dent & Sons, 1933.

Pindar. *The Odes of Pindar.* Trans. Anthony Verity. Oxford: Oxford UP, 2008.

Plato. *Symposium*. Ed. and trans. Alexander Nehamas and Paul Woodruff. Indianapolis: Hackett, 1989.

——. *Timaeus.* Trans. Donald J. Zeyl. Indianapolis: Hackett, 1989.

Shelley, Mary Wollstonecraft. *The Journals of Mary Shelley, 1814–1844.* Ed. Paula R. Feldman and Diana Scott-Kilvert. 2 vols. Oxford: Clarendon, 1987.

——. *The Letters of Mary Wollstonecraft Shelley*. Ed. Betty T. Bennett. 3 vols. Baltimore: Johns Hopkins UP, 1980–88.

Shelley, Percy Bysshe. *A Philosophical View of Reform*. Ed. T.W. Rolleston. London: Oxford UP, 1920.

——. *Zastrozzi and St. Irvyne*. Ed. Stephen C. Behrendt. Peterborough, ON: Broadview P, 2002.

Spenser, Edmund. *The Faerie Queene*. Ed. A.C. Hamilton, Hiroshi Yamashita, and Toshiyuki Suzuki. London and New York: Longman, 2001.

Thucydides. *History of the Peloponnesian War.* Trans. Rex Warner. New York: Penguin, 1972.

Virgil. *Eclogues, Georgics, Aeneid I–VI.* Trans. H. Rushton Fairclough. Cambridge, MA: Harvard UP, 1986.

——. *Aeneid, VII–XII, Appendix Vergiliana.* Trans. H. Rushton Fairclough, rev. G.P. Goold. Cambridge, MA: Harvard UP, 2001.

Wordsworth, William. *The Prelude: 1799, 1805, 1850*. Ed. Jonathan Wordsworth, M.H. Abrams, and Stephen Gill. New York: W.W. Norton, 1979.

Secondary Reading

Aravamudan, Srinivas. *Enlightenment Orientalism: Resisting the Rise of the Novel*. Chicago: U of Chicago P, 2012.

Bewell, Alan. "Percy Bysshe Shelley and Revolutionary Climatology." *Romanticism and Colonial Disease*. Baltimore: Johns Hopkins UP, 1999. 205–41.

Bieri, James. *Percy Bysshe Shelley: A Biography*. Baltimore: Johns Hopkins UP, 2008.

Bonca, Teddi Chichester. *Shelley's Mirrors of Love: Narcissism, Sacrifice, and Sorority*. Albany, NY: SUNY P, 1999.

Butler, Marilyn. *Romantics, Rebels, and Reactionaries: English Literature and Its Background, 1760–1830*. Oxford: Oxford UP, 1981.

Cameron, Keith Neil. "A Major Source of *The Revolt of Islam*." *PMLA* 56.1 (1941): 175–206.

Chandler, James. *England in 1819: The Politics of Literary Culture and the Case of Romantic Historicism*. Chicago: U of Chicago P, 1998.

Cohen-Vrignaud, Gerard. *Radical Orientalism: Rights, Reform, and Romanticism*. Cambridge: Cambridge UP, 2015.

Crook, Nora, and Stephen Allen. "The Marlow Expurgation." *The Times Literary Supplement* 5734 (2013): 14.

Curran, Stuart. *Shelley's Annus Mirabilis: The Maturing of an Epic Vision*. Los Angeles: Huntingdon Library P, 1975.

De Man, Paul. "Shelley Disfigured." *Deconstruction and Criticism*. Ed. Harold Bloom. London: Continuum, 1979. 32–61.

Duff, David. *Romance and Revolution: Shelley and the Politics of a Genre*. Cambridge: Cambridge UP, 1994.

Duffy, Cian. *Shelley and the Revolutionary Sublime*. Cambridge: Cambridge UP, 2005.

Foot, Paul. *Red Shelley*. London: Sidgwick & Jackson, 1980.

——. *Shelley's Revolutionary Year*. London: Redwords, 1990.

Garcia, Humberto. *Islam and the English Enlightenment, 1670–1840*. Baltimore: Johns Hopkins UP, 2012.

Gladden, Samuel L. *Shelley's Textual Seductions: Plotting Utopia in the Erotic and Political Works*. London: Routledge, 2002.

Goslee, Nancy Moore. *Shelley's Visual Imagination*. Cambridge: Cambridge UP, 2011.

Graham, Walter. "Shelley and *The Empire of the Nairs*." *PMLA* 40.4 (1925): 881–91.

Hogle, Jerrold E. *Shelley's Process: Radical Transference and the Development of His Major Works*. Oxford: Oxford UP, 1989.

Holmes, Richard. *Shelley: The Pursuit*. London: Weidenfeld and Nicolson, 1974.

Jacobs, Carol. *Uncontainable Romanticism: Shelley, Brontë, Kleist*. Baltimore: Johns Hopkins UP, 1989.

Jager, Colin. *Unquiet Things: Secularism in the Romantic Age*. Philadelphia: U of Pennsylvania P, 2014.

Jones, F.L. "The Revision of Laon and Cythna." *Journal of English and Germanic Philology* 32 (1933): 366–72.

Keach, William. *Arbitrary Power: Romanticism, Language, Politics*. Princeton, NJ: Princeton UP, 2004.

——. *Shelley's Style*. London: Routledge & Kegan Paul, 1985.

Kelley, Theresa. *Reinventing Allegory*. Cambridge: Cambridge UP, 1997.

Kelly, Gary. *The English Jacobin Novel, 1780–1805*. Oxford: Clarendon, 1976.

Kucich, Greg. *Keats, Shelley, and Romantic Spenserianism*. University Park: Pennsylvania State UP, 1991.
Landes, Joan B. *Women and the Public Sphere in the Age of the French Revolution*. Ithaca, NY: Cornell UP, 1988.
Leask, Nigel. *British Romantic Writers and the East: Anxieties of Empire*. Cambridge: Cambridge UP, 1992.
Makdisi, Saree. *Romantic Imperialism: Universal Empire and the Culture of Modernity*. Cambridge: Cambridge UP, 1998.
——. *William Blake and the Impossible History of the 1790s*. Chicago: U of Chicago P, 2003.
McLane, Maureen. *Romanticism and the Human Sciences: Poetry, Population, and the Discourse of the Species*. Cambridge: Cambridge UP, 2000. 109–58.
McNeice, Gerald. *Shelley and the Revolutionary Idea*. Cambridge, MA: Harvard UP, 1971.
Mellor, Anne K. *Romanticism and Gender*. London and New York: Routledge, 1993.
Morton, Timothy, ed. *The Cambridge Companion to Shelley*. Cambridge: Cambridge UP, 2006.
——. *Shelley and the Revolution in Taste: The Body and the Natural World*. Cambridge: Cambridge UP, 1994.
O'Neill, Michael, and Anthony Howe, with the assistance of Madeleine Callaghan. *The Oxford Handbook of Percy Bysshe Shelley*. Oxford: Oxford UP, 2013.
Priestman, Martin. *Romantic Atheism: Poetry and Freethought, 1780–1830*. Cambridge: Cambridge UP, 1999.
Reiman, Donald H. "Shelley as Agrarian Reactionary." *Romantic Texts and Contexts*. Columbia: U of Missouri P, 1987. 260–74.
Robinson, Charles E. *Shelley and Byron: The Eagle and the Snake Wreathed in Flight*. Baltimore: Johns Hopkins UP, 1976.
Said, Edward. *Orientalism*. New York: Vintage, 1979.
St. Clair, William. *The Godwins and the Shelleys: A Biography of a Family*. Baltimore: Johns Hopkins UP, 1991.
Stuart, Tristram. "Shelley and the Return to Nature." *The Bloodless Revolution: A Cultural History of Vegetarianism from 1600 to Modern Times*. New York: W.W. Norton, 2006. 372–98.
Viswanathan, Gauri. *Outside the Fold: Conversion, Modernity, and Belief*. Princeton, NJ: Princeton UP, 1998.
Webb, Timothy. *The Violet in the Crucible: Shelley and Translation*. Oxford: Oxford UP, 1977.

From the Publisher

A name never says it all, but the word "Broadview" expresses a good deal of the philosophy behind our company. We are open to a broad range of academic approaches and political viewpoints. We pay attention to the broad impact book publishing and book printing has in the wider world; we began using recycled stock more than a decade ago, and for some years now we have used 100% recycled paper for most titles. Our publishing program is internationally oriented and broad-ranging. Our individual titles often appeal to a broad readership too; many are of interest as much to general readers as to academics and students.

Founded in 1985, Broadview remains a fully independent company owned by its shareholders—not an imprint or subsidiary of a larger multinational.

For the most accurate information on our books (including information on pricing, editions, and formats) please visit our website at www.broadviewpress.com. Our print books and ebooks are also available for sale on our site.

On the Broadview website we also offer several goods that are not books—among them the Broadview coffee mug, the Broadview beer stein (inscribed with a line from Geoffrey Chaucer's *Canterbury Tales*), the Broadview fridge magnets (your choice of philosophical or literary), and a range of T-shirts (made from combinations of hemp, bamboo, and/or high-quality pima cotton, with no child labor, sweatshop labor, or environmental degradation involved in their manufacture).

All those goods are available through the "merchandise" section of the Broadview website. When you buy Broadview goods you can support other goods too.

broadview press
www.broadviewpress.com

The interior of this book is printed on 100% recycled paper.